Eat!

The
QUICK-LOOK
COOKBOOK

GABRIELA SCOLIK + TEAM / INFOGRAPHICS: NO.PARKING

weldon**owen**

cook without heat

cook

roast

stew

fry and deep-fry

grill

bake

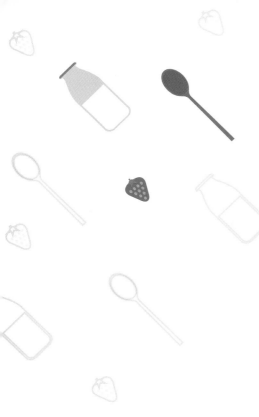

preserve

401 make refrigerator pickles	415 make apricot jam
402 preserve mushrooms	416 make raspberry jam
403 preserve tomatoes	417 make mixed berry jam
404 make barbecue sauce	418 make blackberry jelly
405 prepare tomato ketchup	419 make red currant jelly
406 make english pickles	420 make grape jelly
407 make fruit chutney	421 make lemon jelly
408 make apricot chutney	422 make orange marmalade
409 make peach chutney	423 preserve apple purée
410 make plum chutney	424 make apple compote
411 make mango chutney	425 make pear compote
412 salt-preserve lemons	426 make cherry compote
413 make lemon curd	427 make plum compote
414 make strawberry jam	

drink

428 serve and pair champagne	435 remove cork bits from wine	452 mix a negroni
429 serve and pair pinot grigio	436 evaluate wine	453 enjoy a long island iced tea
430 serve and pair chardonnay	437 say "beer" in different languages	454 mix a blue blazer
431 serve and pair pinot noir	438 rim a glass with sugar or salt	455 find a hangover remedy
432 serve and pair merlot	439 mix a classic martini	456 brew a restorative tea
433 serve and pair cabernet sauvignon	440 shake up some martini variations	457 brew tea fit for a queen
434 open a bottle of wine	441 enjoy a cuba libre	458 make russian tea in a samovar
	442 serve a perfect piña colada	459 serve thai iced tea
	443 mix a strawberry margarita	460 shake up a greek frappé
	444 serve a manhattan	461 make a new orleans iced coffee
	445 mix a mojito	462 froth up a turkish coffee
	446 enjoy a caipirinha	463 pull a perfect espresso
	447 serve a white russian	464 pour a latte leaf
	448 mix a tequila sunrise	465 enjoy an irish coffee
	449 serve a tom collins	466 blend a fruit smoothie
	450 serve a cape cod	467 mix a vegetable smoothie
	451 enjoy a sidecar	468 make a fruity soda pop float

Bon Appétit!

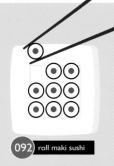

092 roll maki sushi

Do you yearn to craft a perfect pie? Fry up some traditional tempura? Mix a classic cocktail (#439)? Look no further! In EAT! THE QUICK-LOOK COOKBOOK, a team of food mavens and graphic artists have come together to create hundreds of fully illustrated step-by-step recipes as your guide to creating a world of flavor. Whether you're a seasoned chef looking to expand your kitchen repertoire or a newly minted foodie who's perplexed by pomegranates (see item #054) this is the book you need. Sit down, pour yourself a glass of something refreshing (maybe #446), and start your culinary journey. Use this book the next time you're looking to impress a dinner party (#454's a crowd-pleaser!), roll up some sushi (#092), or make amazing profiteroles (#392)—or for when you invite the Queen over for tea (#457).

439 mix a classic martini

In these pages you will discover hundreds of new dishes and old favorites, as well as hints on stocking your kitchen, understanding nutrition and food safety, caring for kitchen tools—and getting those annoying cork bits out of your wine (#435). Recipes draw from a wide range of global cuisines including such delicacies as pot-au-feu (#175), green Thai curry (#204), and beer-can chicken (#326, because we're classy like that).

Have a great time as you cook, eat, and drink your way through these pages. Bon appétit! Buon appetito! Itadakimasu! Eet smakelijk! Guten Appetit! (#038)

435 remove cork bits from wine

038 say "bon appétit" in other languages

EAT! THE QUICK-LOOK COOKBOOK is divided into 12 handy chapters, organized by cooking technique. If you can grill it, fry it, bake it, or roast it, you'll probably find it here.

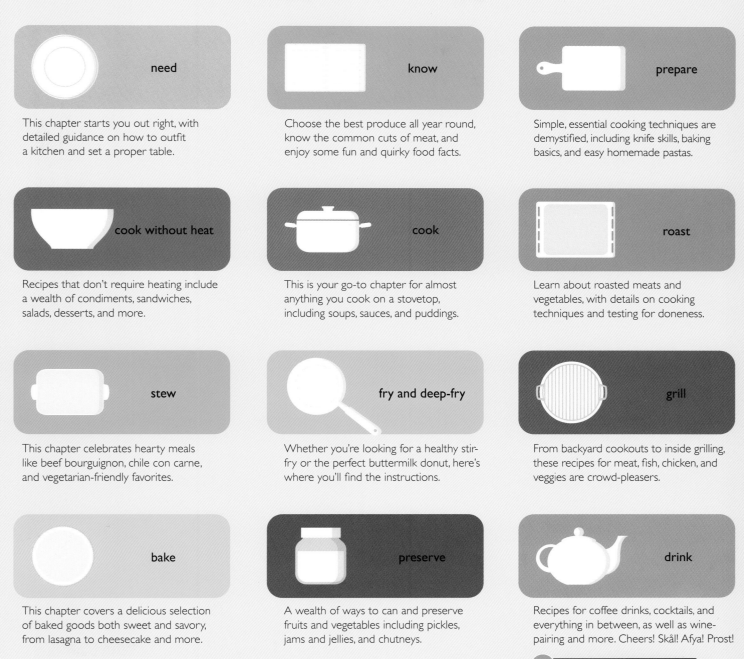

need

This chapter starts you out right, with detailed guidance on how to outfit a kitchen and set a proper table.

know

Choose the best produce all year round, know the common cuts of meat, and enjoy some fun and quirky food facts.

prepare

Simple, essential cooking techniques are demystified, including knife skills, baking basics, and easy homemade pastas.

cook without heat

Recipes that don't require heating include a wealth of condiments, sandwiches, salads, desserts, and more.

cook

This is your go-to chapter for almost anything you cook on a stovetop, including soups, sauces, and puddings.

roast

Learn about roasted meats and vegetables, with details on cooking techniques and testing for doneness.

stew

This chapter celebrates hearty meals like beef bourguignon, chile con carne, and vegetarian-friendly favorites.

fry and deep-fry

Whether you're looking for a healthy stir-fry or the perfect buttermilk donut, here's where you'll find the instructions.

grill

From backyard cookouts to inside grilling, these recipes for meat, fish, chicken, and veggies are crowd-pleasers.

bake

This chapter covers a delicious selection of baked goods both sweet and savory, from lasagna to cheesecake and more.

preserve

A wealth of ways to can and preserve fruits and vegetables including pickles, jams and jellies, and chutneys.

drink

Recipes for coffee drinks, cocktails, and everything in between, as well as wine-pairing and more. Cheers! Skål! Afya! Prost!

The recipes in **EAT! THE QUICK-LOOK COOKBOOK** are presented graphically. All recipes have a number—so you can find them easily. Should you be looking for a particular recipe or keyword, you can find it in the index at the back of the book which is sorted alphabetically.

LIST OF INGREDIENTS On the cutting board you find the list of ingredients, how much you need and how to prepare them (e.g. 1 onion, finely chopped). The list of ingredients is at the same time your shopping list. The measurements are for **4 people**. The dotted lines mark the different working steps.

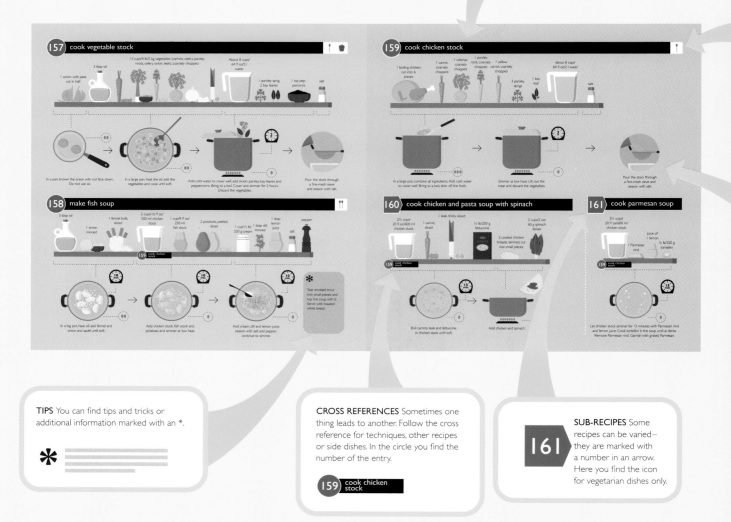

TIPS You can find tips and tricks or additional information marked with an *.

✳

CROSS REFERENCES Sometimes one thing leads to another. Follow the cross reference for techniques, other recipes or side dishes. In the circle you find the number of the entry.

159 cook chicken stock

161 **SUB-RECIPES** Some recipes can be varied— they are marked with a number in an arrow. Here you find the icon for vegetarian dishes only.

ICON GUIDE:

Wooden spoons stand for
the level of difficulty:

easy

medium

difficult

vegetarian

Quick recipes that are ready to eat
in less than 30 minutes.

How many 8 fl oz/250 ml jars you'll
need to can or preserve this item.

ZOOMS Close-up
views show
important details.

SYMBOL GUIDE Many symbols point to important aspects of a recipe, including cooking time, heat or temperature. Here are the symbols you will find throughout the book:

 The kitchen timer shows the cooking, cooling or resting time.

 How hot? Cook at low, medium or high temperature—that applies to electric, gas or induction stoves.

The wooden spoon means that the dish must be stirred constantly.

 Shows the temperature of the oven or the deep-frying oil. If you have a convection oven deduct 50°F/20°C from the indicated heat.

 Let chill in the refrigerator or freezer.

 Shows the cooking temperature in the center of the meat. Always measure at the thickest point (not close to the bone). Attention: never touch the bottom of the cooking pot with the thermometer. Purchasing a cooking thermometer is worth it!

USEFUL TIPS

- Always read the recipe closely before you start.

- Gather all kitchen equipment you need before starting (including oven gloves and a dish towel).

- Prepare the ingredients as shown in the recipe. With good preparation (mise en place) cooking will be easier!

- Given temperatures are approximate values, every oven is different—you might need to adjust the temperature to your oven. The same applies to the cooking time—here we also used approximate values.

- If the peel of citrus fruits is used, always buy untreated organic produce and wash it before usage.

- If you are taking ingredients from the refrigerator let stand at room temperature before using them. That especially applies to meat and eggs.

- Never add beaten egg whites to the batter all at once. Always add it in small portions.

- Instead of using an immersion blender, you can also use an electric blender. Be careful with hot soups!

- If ingredients have to be whisked for a long time, you can use a handheld electric mixer or a stand mixer with beaters instead of an egg whisk.

- If you are using a double boiler be careful with the temperature; some mixtures will form lumps if they get too hot.

- Cold pressed oils, also called virgin oils, shouldn't be heated to high temperatures. Use them for salads and other cold dishes. Refined oils can be heated to high temperatures. Use them for cooking.

- If a sauce contains lumps, pour it through a sieve.

- Don't hesitate to add liquids like stock or water to a dish if you feel it is necessary.

- To test whether a cake is done, stick a skewer in its middle and pull it back out. The cake is done when the skewer comes out clean.

- Recipes are there to be changed. Vary the ingredients according to taste and availability of ingredients.

need

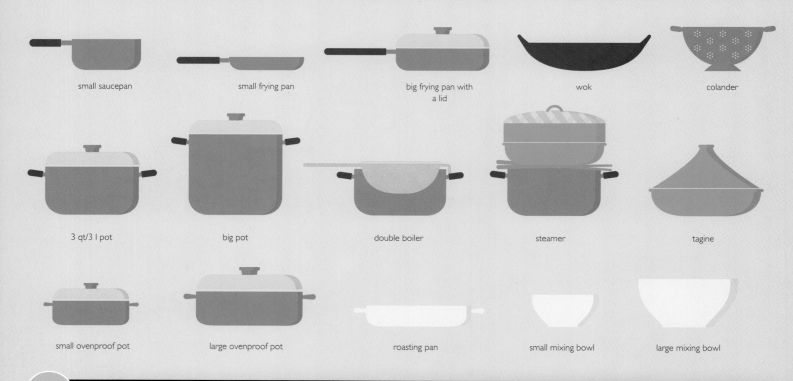

small saucepan

small frying pan

big frying pan with a lid

wok

colander

3 qt/3 l pot

big pot

double boiler

steamer

tagine

small ovenproof pot

large ovenproof pot

roasting pan

small mixing bowl

large mixing bowl

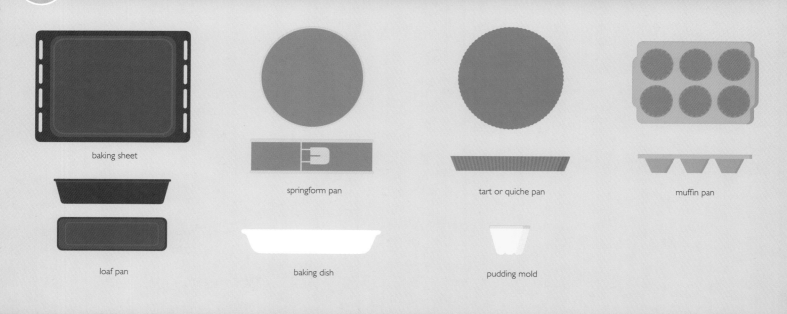

baking sheet

springform pan

tart or quiche pan

muffin pan

loaf pan

baking dish

pudding mold

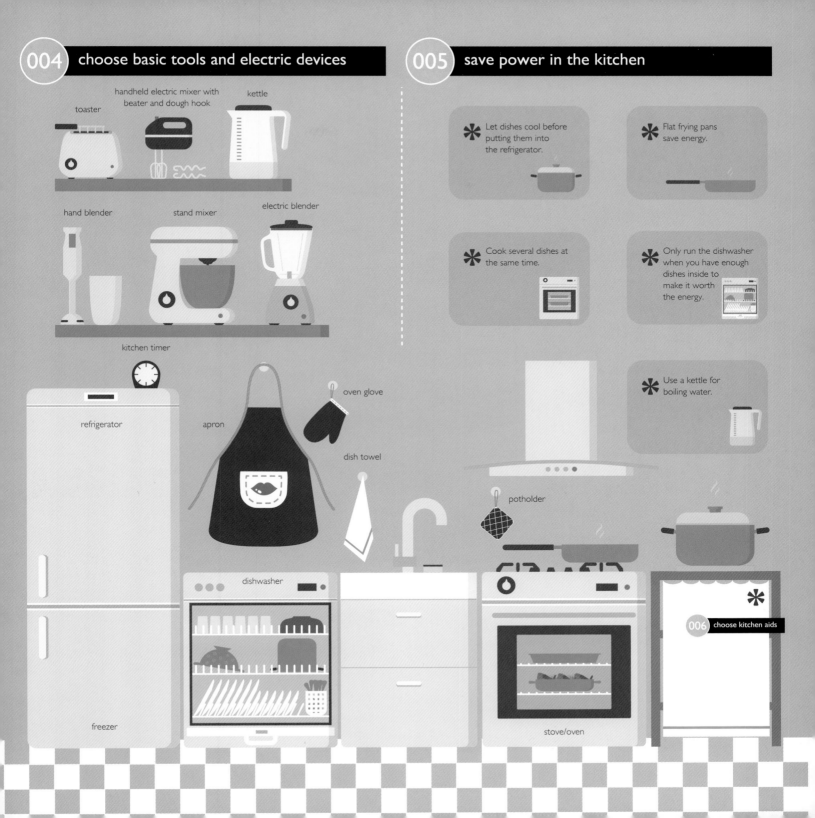

004 choose basic tools and electric devices

toaster

handheld electric mixer with beater and dough hook

kettle

hand blender

stand mixer

electric blender

kitchen timer

refrigerator

apron

oven glove

dish towel

dishwasher

freezer

005 save power in the kitchen

✳ Let dishes cool before putting them into the refrigerator.

✳ Flat frying pans save energy.

✳ Cook several dishes at the same time.

✳ Only run the dishwasher when you have enough dishes inside to make it worth the energy.

✳ Use a kettle for boiling water.

potholder

stove/oven

✳ 006 choose kitchen aids

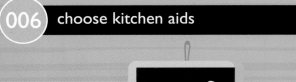

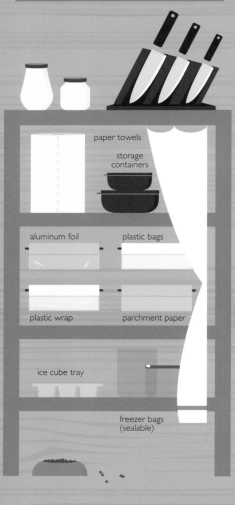

paper towels

storage containers

aluminum foil

plastic bags

plastic wrap

parchment paper

ice cube tray

freezer bags (sealable)

spatula

can opener

kitchen scissors

whisk

brush

nutcracker

ladle

dough scraper

funnel

skimmer

pastry bag

flour sifter

tea strainer

vegetable peeler

fine-mesh sieve

pastry cutter

potato ricer

kitchen scale

measuring cup

grater

wooden spoon

corkscrew   cooking thermometer

cutting board

meat tenderizer

rolling pin

mortar and pestle

cheese knife

zester

paring knife

butter knife

cleaver

chef's knife

all-purpose knife

carving knife and fork

filleting knife

bread knife

sharpening steel

knife and fork

soup spoon

fish knife and fork

chopsticks

cake server, dessert cutlery

ice cream spoon

tea spoon

coffee spoon

sauce ladle

carving set

salad servers

baby bottle

4 extra teats

bottle warmer for baby food

grater for fruit

baby spoon

bib

children's plate

children's cutlery

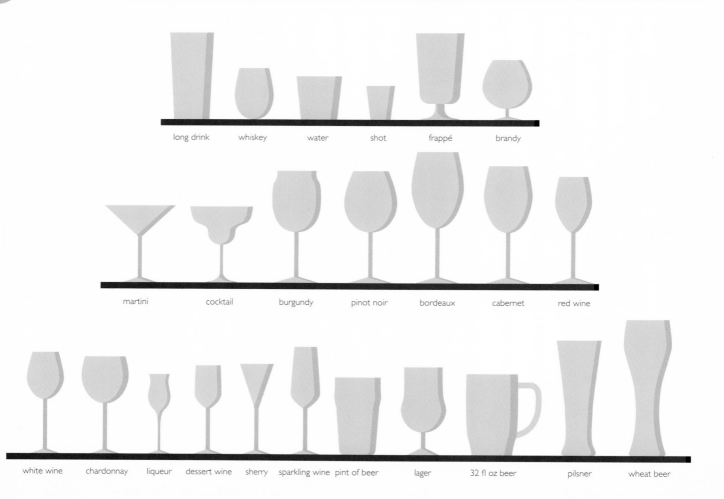

long drink   whiskey   water   shot   frappé   brandy

martini   cocktail   burgundy   pinot noir   bordeaux   cabernet   red wine

white wine   chardonnay   liqueur   dessert wine   sherry   sparkling wine   pint of beer   lager   32 fl oz beer   pilsner   wheat beer

012 set the perfect table

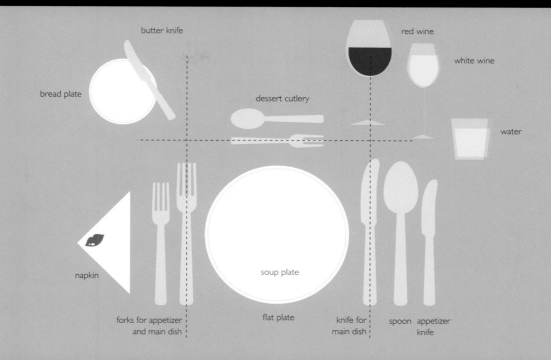

butter knife

red wine

white wine

bread plate

dessert cutlery

water

napkin

soup plate

forks for appetizer
and main dish

flat plate

knife for
main dish

spoon appetizer
knife

013 choose basic crockery for the table

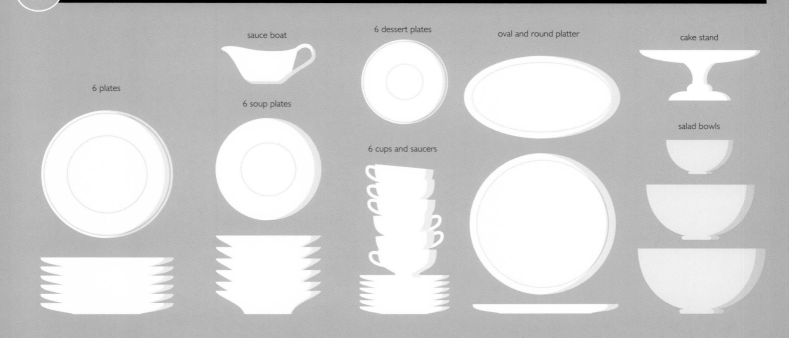

sauce boat

6 dessert plates

oval and round platter

cake stand

6 plates

6 soup plates

salad bowls

6 cups and saucers

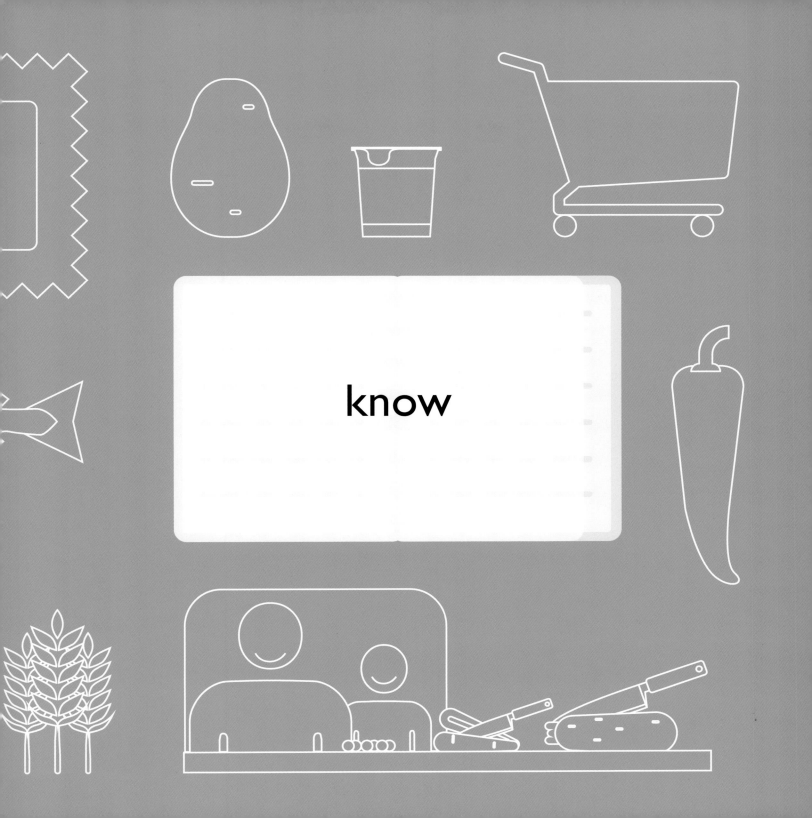

know

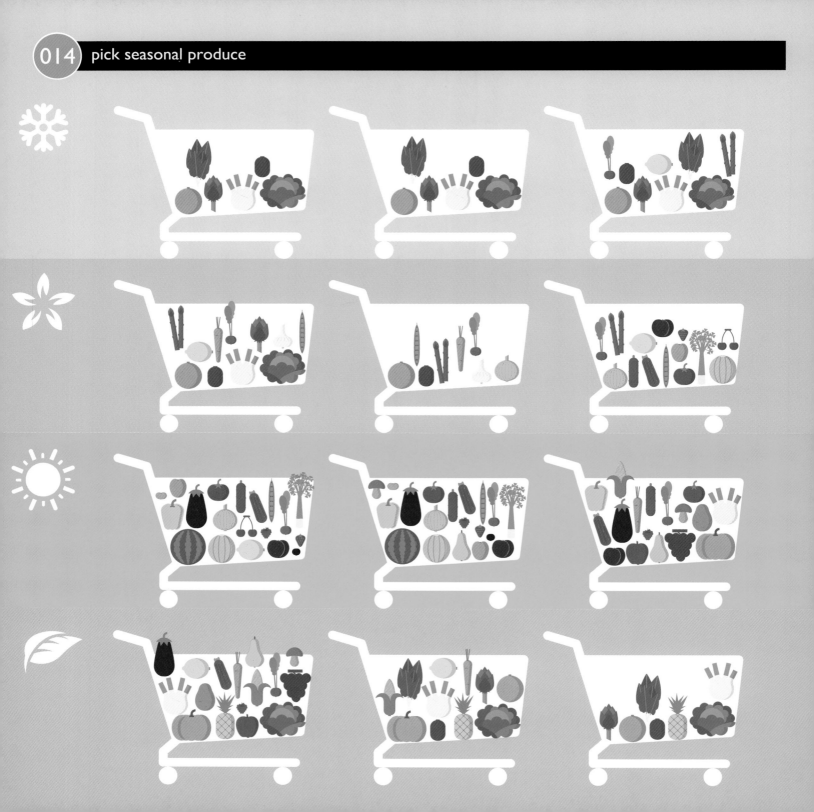

46°F
(8°C)

41°F
(5°C)

36°F
(2°C)

50°F
(10°C)

0°F
(−18°C)

50°F
(10°C)

46°F
(8°C)

50°F
(10°C)

in calories…

1 grape 2	1 cup of coffee 2
1 tsp black pepper 5	1 cucumber 10
1 tsp sugar 15	1 apricot 15
1 marshmallow 25	1 carrot 30

non-fat milk 33 (3 fl oz/100 ml)

1 plum 35

1 slice of bacon 36

low fat milk 43 (3 fl oz/100 ml)

1 cookie 50

1 vodka shot 50

1 tbsp jelly 54

1 gin and tonic 56

1 slice of salami 58

1 tbsp vinaigrette 60

1 slice of wholewheat bread 67

1 slice of white bread 68

1 vegetarian burger 73

1 apple 80

3 tbsp cream 80

1 egg 82

orange juice 88 (7 fl oz/200 ml)

1 tbsp peanut butter 94

1 fried egg 99

1 banana 100

1 piece of fruitcake 112

non-fat yogurt 115 (6½ oz/ 200 g)

white wine 116 (5 fl oz/150 ml)

red wine 120 (5 fl oz/ 150 ml)

1 tbsp olive oil 121

1 chicken drumstick 130

1 potato 145

5 sushi 160

1 martini 184

ice cream 200 (3½ oz/100 g)

1 pint of guinness 210

chips 250 (1½ oz/50 g)

minestrone 260 (8 fl oz/250 ml)

1 sandwich 270

1 piece of cheesecake 321

emmenthal 360 (3½ oz/100 g)

1 avocado 380

large french fries 400

almonds 545 (3½ oz/100 g)

1 large burger 560

30 minutes of...

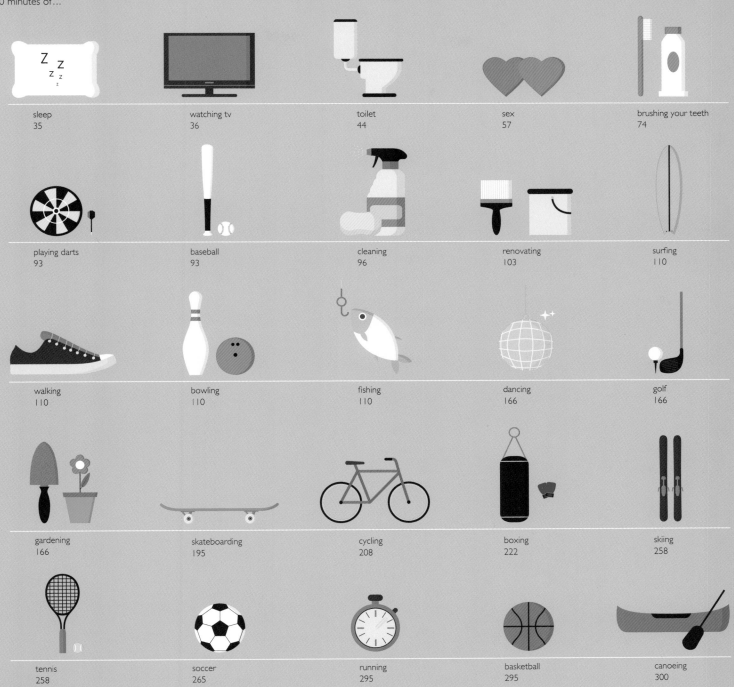

sleep
35

watching tv
36

toilet
44

sex
57

brushing your teeth
74

playing darts
93

baseball
93

cleaning
96

renovating
103

surfing
110

walking
110

bowling
110

fishing
110

dancing
166

golf
166

gardening
166

skateboarding
195

cycling
208

boxing
222

skiing
258

tennis
258

soccer
265

running
295

basketball
295

canoeing
300

consume food throughout the world

The numbers show the annual food consumption of a fully grown adult in kilograms. Source: FAO

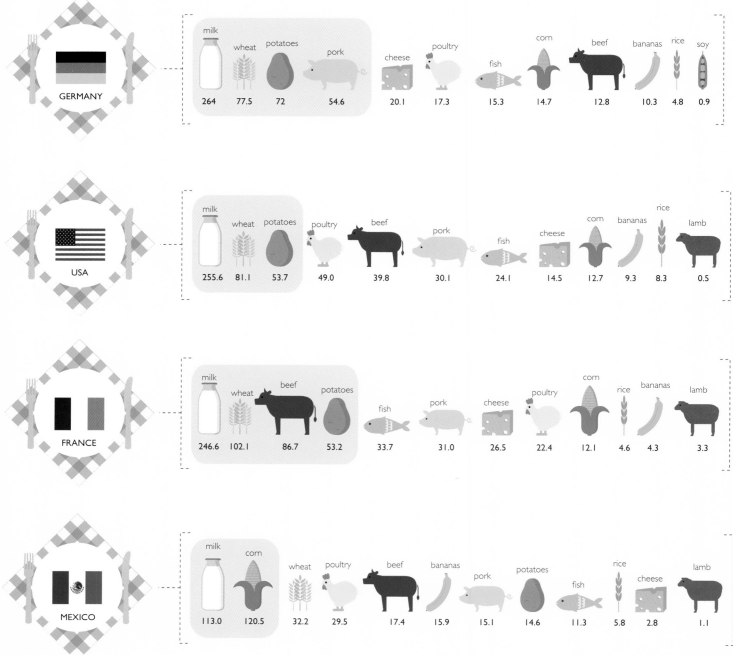

GERMANY

milk	wheat	potatoes	pork	cheese	poultry	fish	corn	beef	bananas	rice	soy
264	77.5	72	54.6	20.1	17.3	15.3	14.7	12.8	10.3	4.8	0.9

USA

milk	wheat	potatoes	poultry	beef	pork	fish	cheese	corn	bananas	rice	lamb
255.6	81.1	53.7	49.0	39.8	30.1	24.1	14.5	12.7	9.3	8.3	0.5

FRANCE

milk	wheat	beef	potatoes	fish	pork	cheese	poultry	corn	rice	bananas	lamb
246.6	102.1	86.7	53.2	33.7	31.0	26.5	22.4	12.1	4.6	4.3	3.3

MEXICO

milk	corn	wheat	poultry	beef	bananas	pork	potatoes	fish	rice	cheese	lamb
113.0	120.5	32.2	29.5	17.4	15.9	15.1	14.6	11.3	5.8	2.8	1.1

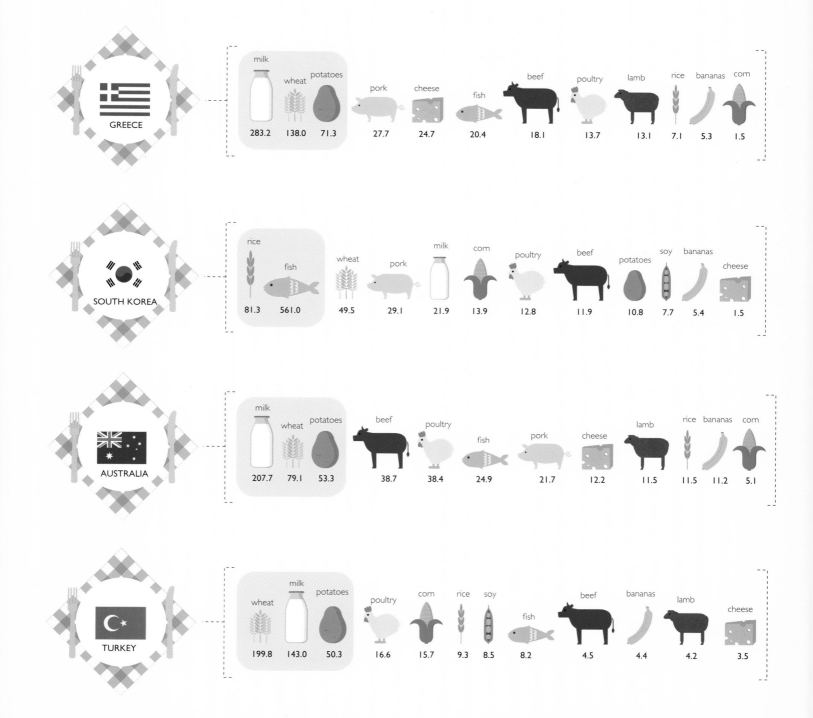

GREECE

milk 283.2 · wheat 138.0 · potatoes 71.3 · pork 27.7 · cheese 24.7 · fish 20.4 · beef 18.1 · poultry 13.7 · lamb 13.1 · rice 7.1 · bananas 5.3 · corn 1.5

SOUTH KOREA

rice 81.3 · fish 561.0 · wheat 49.5 · pork 29.1 · milk 21.9 · corn 13.9 · poultry 12.8 · beef 11.9 · potatoes 10.8 · soy 7.7 · bananas 5.4 · cheese 1.5

AUSTRALIA

milk 207.7 · wheat 79.1 · potatoes 53.3 · beef 38.7 · poultry 38.4 · fish 24.9 · pork 21.7 · cheese 12.2 · lamb 11.5 · rice 11.5 · bananas 11.2 · corn 5.1

TURKEY

wheat 199.8 · milk 143.0 · potatoes 50.3 · poultry 16.6 · corn 15.7 · rice 9.3 · soy 8.5 · fish 8.2 · beef 4.5 · bananas 4.4 · lamb 4.2 · cheese 3.5

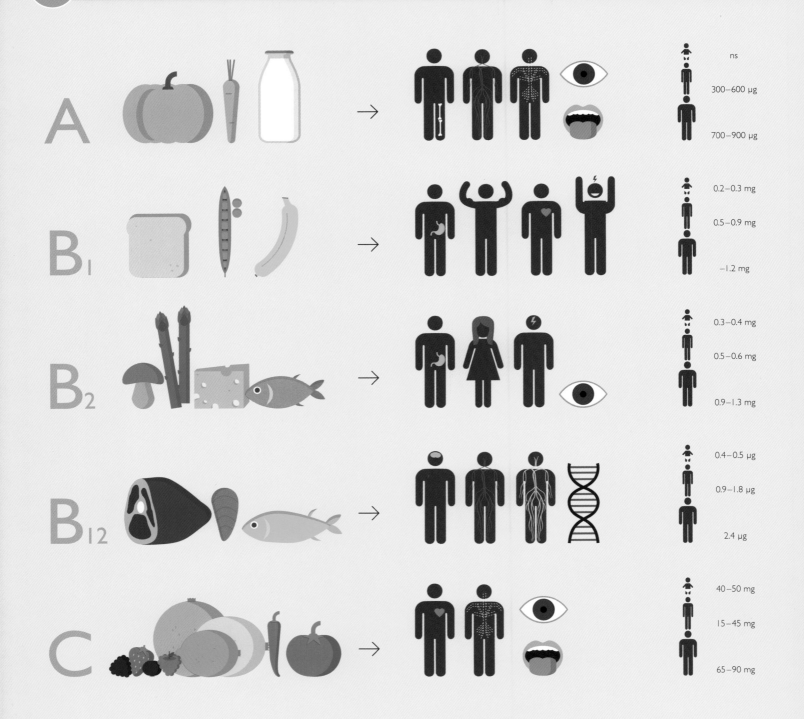

A		ns
		300–600 µg
		700–900 µg
B1		0.2–0.3 mg
		0.5–0.9 mg
		–1.2 mg
B2		0.3–0.4 mg
		0.5–0.6 mg
		0.9–1.3 mg
B12		0.4–0.5 µg
		0.9–1.8 µg
		2.4 µg
C		40–50 mg
		15–45 mg
		65–90 mg

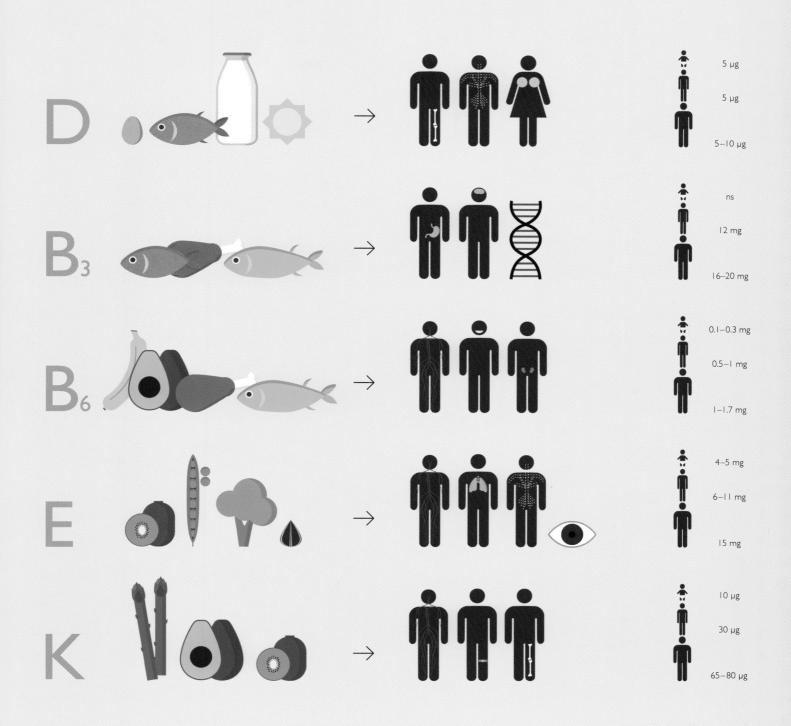

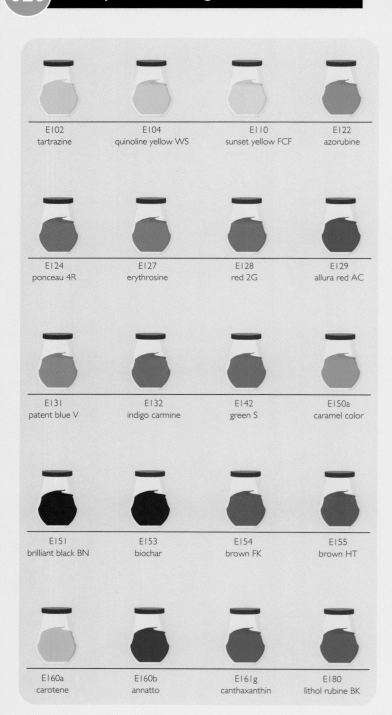

E102 tartrazine	E104 quinoline yellow WS	E110 sunset yellow FCF	E122 azorubine
E124 ponceau 4R	E127 erythrosine	E128 red 2G	E129 allura red AC
E131 patent blue V	E132 indigo carmine	E142 green S	E150a caramel color
E151 brilliant black BN	E153 biochar	E154 brown FK	E155 brown HT
E160a carotene	E160b annatto	E161g canthaxanthin	E180 lithol rubine BK

soy sauce
honey
potatoes
beans
carrots
thyme
mushrooms
onions
DUCK

rosemary
potatoes
celery
ground paprika
onions
mushrooms
GOOSE

cabbage
potatoes
mustard
lemon
rosemary
garlic
thyme
carrots
mushrooms
GAME

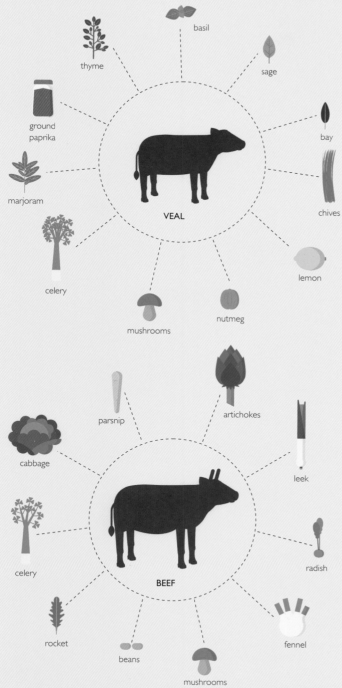

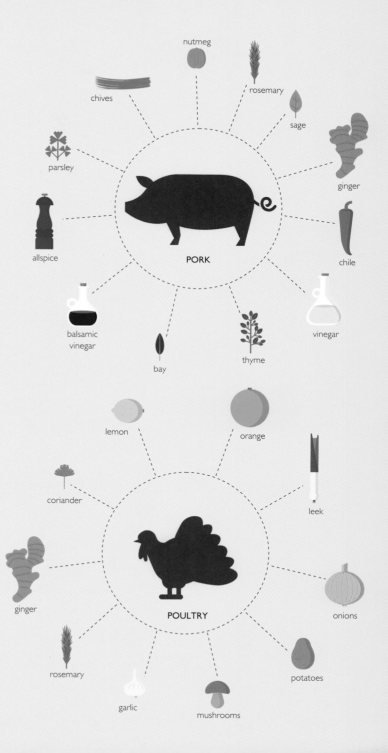

VEAL

basil · sage · thyme · bay · ground paprika · chives · marjoram · lemon · celery · nutmeg · mushrooms

PORK

nutmeg · rosemary · chives · sage · parsley · ginger · allspice · chile · balsamic vinegar · vinegar · bay · thyme

BEEF

parsnip · artichokes · cabbage · leek · celery · radish · rocket · fennel · beans · mushrooms

POULTRY

lemon · orange · coriander · leek · ginger · onions · rosemary · potatoes · garlic · mushrooms

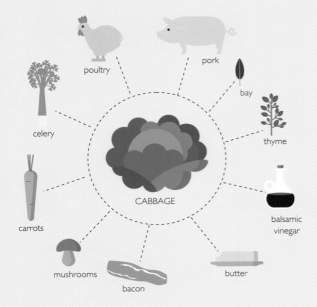

poultry

pork

bay

celery

thyme

carrots

CABBAGE

balsamic vinegar

carrots

mushrooms

butter

bacon

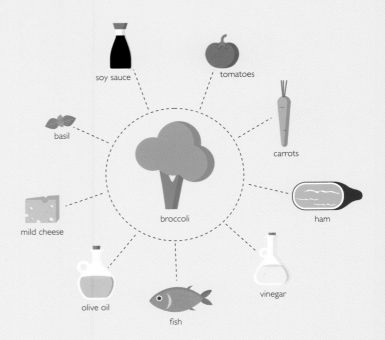

soy sauce

tomatoes

basil

carrots

mild cheese

broccoli

ham

olive oil

fish

vinegar

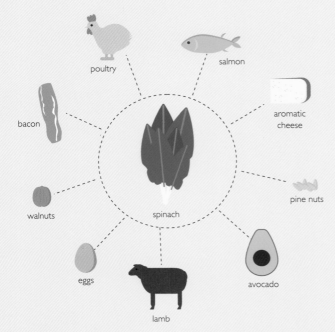

poultry

salmon

bacon

aromatic cheese

walnuts

spinach

pine nuts

eggs

lamb

avocado

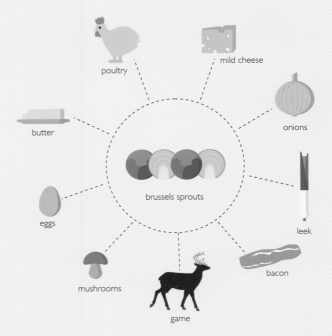

poultry

mild cheese

butter

onions

eggs

brussels sprouts

leek

mushrooms

game

bacon

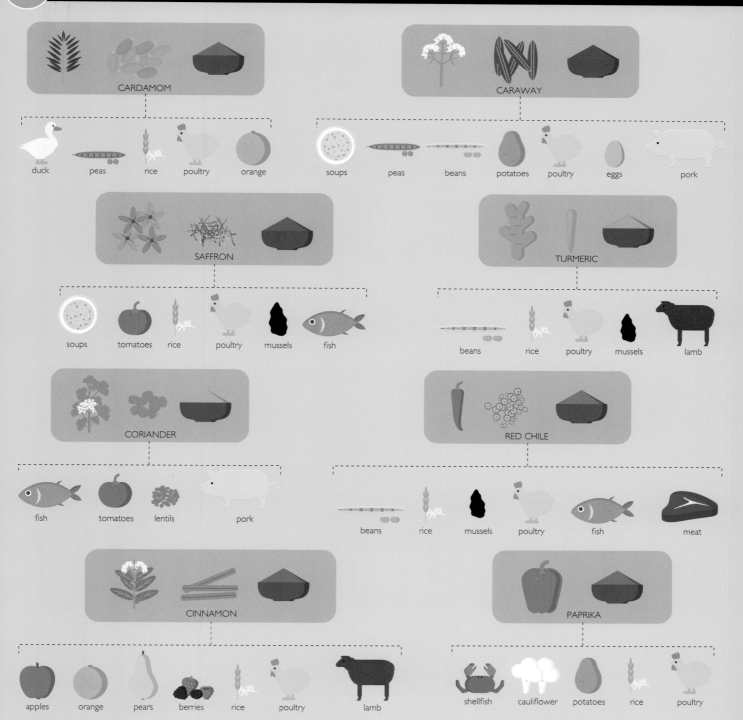

CARDAMOM

duck   peas   rice   poultry   orange

CARAWAY

soups   peas   beans   potatoes   poultry   eggs   pork

SAFFRON

soups   tomatoes   rice   poultry   mussels   fish

TURMERIC

beans   rice   poultry   mussels   lamb

CORIANDER

fish   tomatoes   lentils   pork

RED CHILE

beans   rice   mussels   poultry   fish   meat

CINNAMON

apples   orange   pears   berries   rice   poultry   lamb

PAPRIKA

shellfish   cauliflower   potatoes   rice   poultry

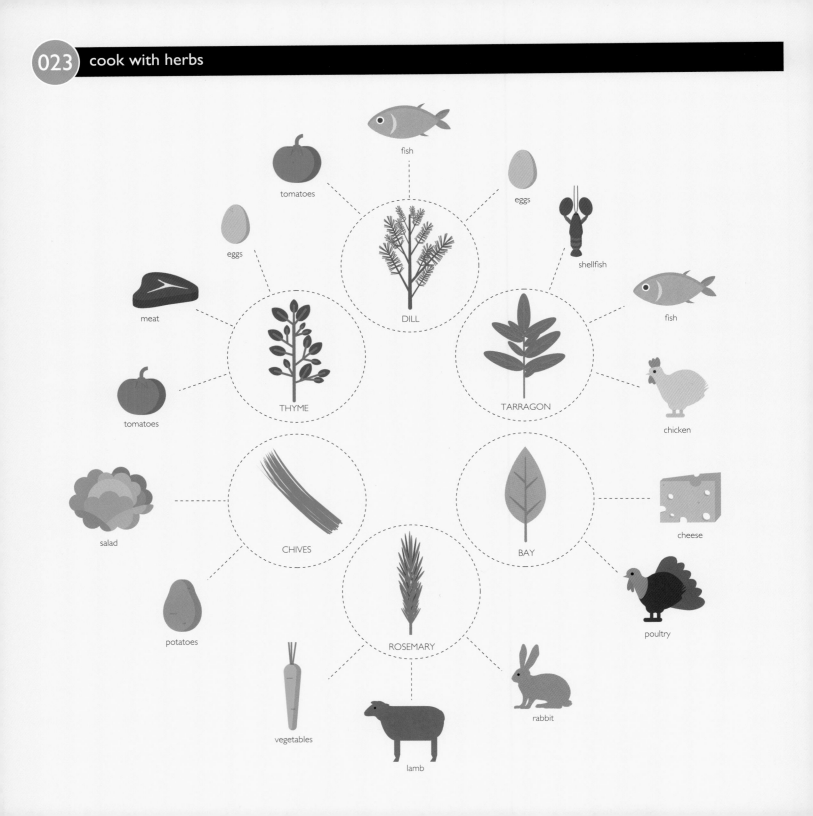

fish

tomatoes

eggs

eggs

shellfish

meat

fish

DILL

THYME

TARRAGON

tomatoes

chicken

salad

CHIVES

BAY

cheese

potatoes

ROSEMARY

poultry

vegetables

rabbit

lamb

The pungency (spicy heat) of chile peppers is measured in Scoville heat units. The number of units shows how many drops of water must be used to dilute a sample of the chile pepper so no more spiciness can be traced.

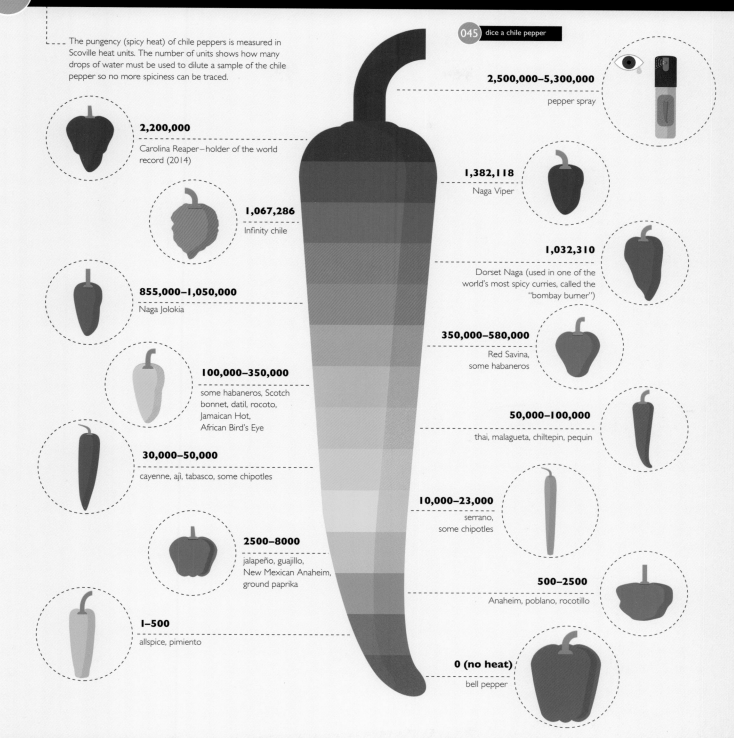

045 dice a chile pepper

2,500,000–5,300,000

pepper spray

2,200,000

Carolina Reaper–holder of the world record (2014)

1,382,118

Naga Viper

1,067,286

Infinity chile

1,032,310

Dorset Naga (used in one of the world's most spicy curries, called the "bombay burner")

855,000–1,050,000

Naga Jolokia

350,000–580,000

Red Savina, some habaneros

100,000–350,000

some habaneros, Scotch bonnet, datil, rocoto, Jamaican Hot, African Bird's Eye

50,000–100,000

thai, malagueta, chiltepin, pequin

30,000–50,000

cayenne, ají, tabasco, some chipotles

10,000–23,000

serrano, some chipotles

2500–8000

jalapeño, guajillo, New Mexican Anaheim, ground paprika

500–2500

Anaheim, poblano, rocotillo

1–500

allspice, pimiento

0 (no heat)

bell pepper

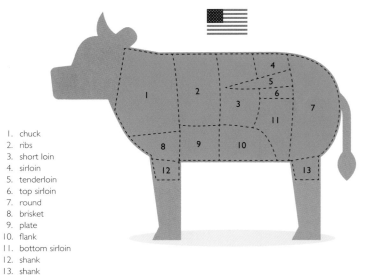

1. chuck
2. ribs
3. short loin
4. sirloin
5. tenderloin
6. top sirloin
7. round
8. brisket
9. plate
10. flank
11. bottom sirloin
12. shank
13. shank

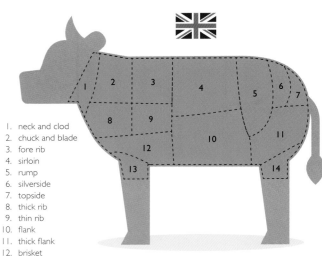

1. neck and clod
2. chuck and blade
3. fore rib
4. sirloin
5. rump
6. silverside
7. topside
8. thick rib
9. thin rib
10. flank
11. thick flank
12. brisket
13. shin
14. leg

1. joue
2. collier
3. basses-côtes
4. entrecôte
5. faux fillet
6. aloyau fillet
7. romsteck
8. culotte
9. gros bout de poitrine
10. bôite à moelle
11. plates-côtes
12. bavette d'aloyau
13. tranche grasse
14. gîte à la noix
15. gîte de devant
16. poitrine
17. flanchet
18. gîte de derrière

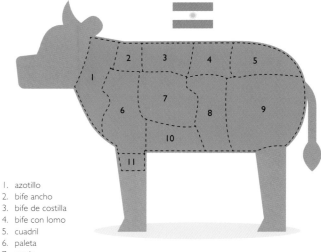

1. azotillo
2. bife ancho
3. bife de costilla
4. bife con lomo
5. cuadril
6. paleta
7. asado
8. vacío
9. nalga
10. matambre
11. osso buco

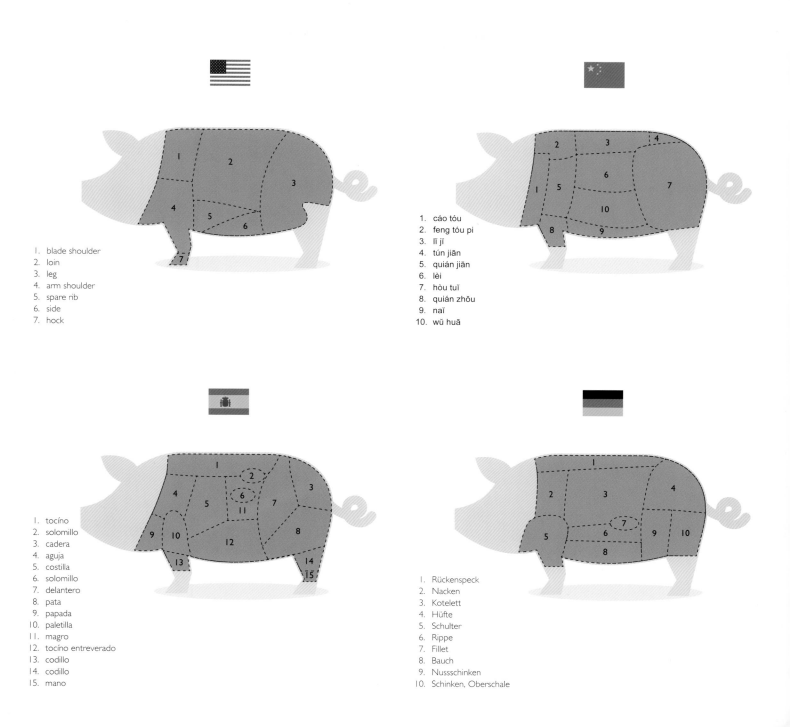

1. blade shoulder
2. loin
3. leg
4. arm shoulder
5. spare rib
6. side
7. hock

1. cáo tóu
2. feng tóu pi
3. lǐ jǐ
4. tún jiān
5. quián jiān
6. lèi
7. hòu tuǐ
8. quián zhǒu
9. naǐ
10. wǔ huā

1. tocíno
2. solomillo
3. cadera
4. aguja
5. costilla
6. solomillo
7. delantero
8. pata
9. papada
10. paletilla
11. magro
12. tocíno entreverado
13. codillo
14. codillo
15. mano

1. Rückenspeck
2. Nacken
3. Kotelett
4. Hüfte
5. Schulter
6. Rippe
7. Fillet
8. Bauch
9. Nussschinken
10. Schinken, Oberschale

choose which fish are ok to eat

FARMED

shark catfish

salmon
(certified)

sturgeon

shrimp
(certified)

trout

striped bass

cichlid

sea bass

shrimp
(not certified)

ATLANTIC

coryphaena / mahi mahi

herring

white tuna
(certified)

swordfish

shrimp

red tuna

hake

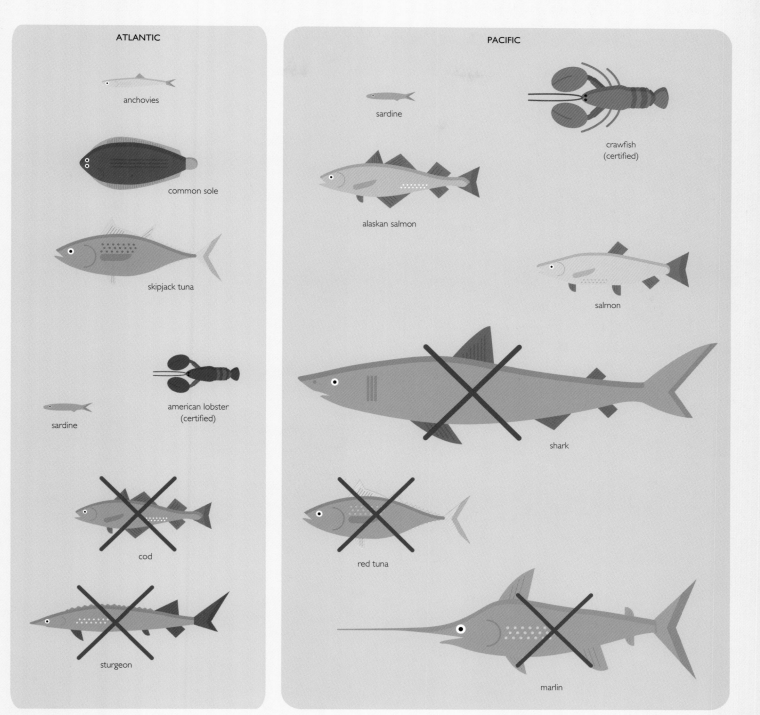

ATLANTIC

anchovies

common sole

skipjack tuna

sardine

american lobster
(certified)

cod

sturgeon

PACIFIC

sardine

crawfish
(certified)

alaskan salmon

salmon

shark

red tuna

marlin

Source: Marine Conservation Society 2014. www.mcsuk.org

145 cook pasta
152 pair pasta with sauce

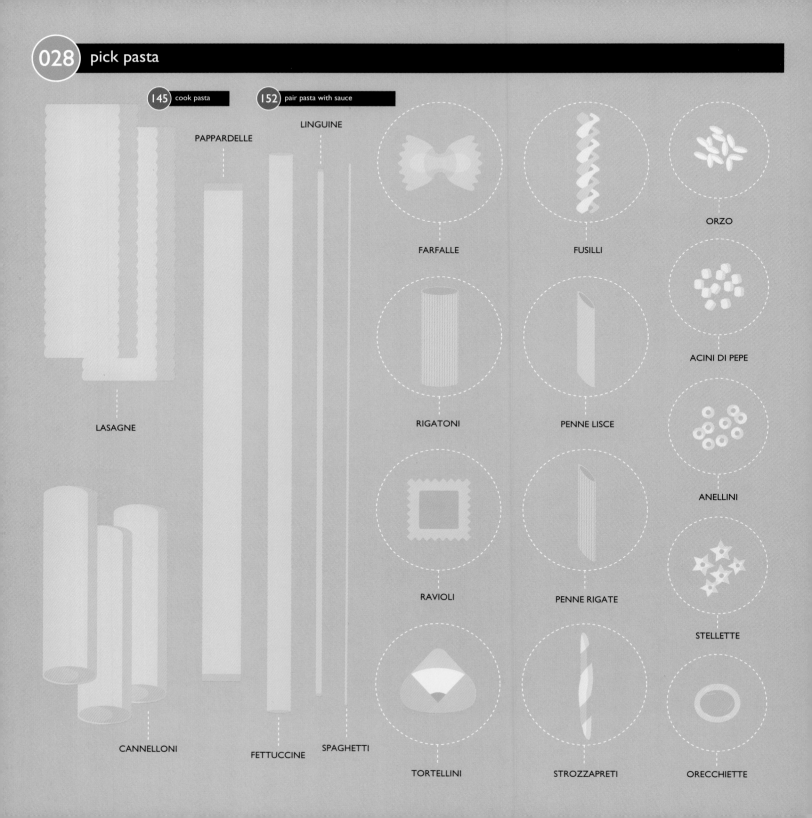

PAPPARDELLE

LINGUINE

FARFALLE

FUSILLI

ORZO

LASAGNE

RIGATONI

PENNE LISCE

ACINI DI PEPE

ANELLINI

RAVIOLI

PENNE RIGATE

STELLETTE

CANNELLONI

FETTUCCINE

SPAGHETTI

TORTELLINI

STROZZAPRETI

ORECCHIETTE

464 pour a latte leaf

LATTE MACCHIATO
- - - - - milk froth
- - - - espresso

CAFÉ AU LAIT
milk froth - - - -
espresso - - - -

CAFÉ MOCHA
milk froth - - - -
- - - - - whipped cream
- - - chocolate syrup
- - - - espresso

AMERICANO
- - - - hot water
- - - - espresso

CAFÉ BREVA
- - - whipped cream
milk - - - -
- - - - espresso

CAPPUCCINO
milk froth - - - -
- - - - espresso

463 pull a perfect espresso

ESPRESSO CON PANNA
- - - whipped cream
- - - espresso

ESPRESSO MACCHIATO
- - milk froth
- - - espresso

ESPRESSO
espresso - - -

CORRETTO
- - - brandy
- - - espresso

AFFOGATO
- - - espresso
1 scoop of ice cream - - - -

one cup of coffee
(8 fl oz/240 ml)
contains 135 mg of caffeine.

black tea
8 fl oz/240 ml =
70 mg caffeine

energy drink
8 fl oz/240 ml =
70 mg caffeine

espresso
1 fl oz/30 ml =
45 mg caffeine

green tea 8 fl oz/240 ml = 35 mg caffeine

ice tea 8 fl oz/240 ml = 15 mg caffeine

hot chocolate 8 fl oz/240 ml = 8 mg caffeine

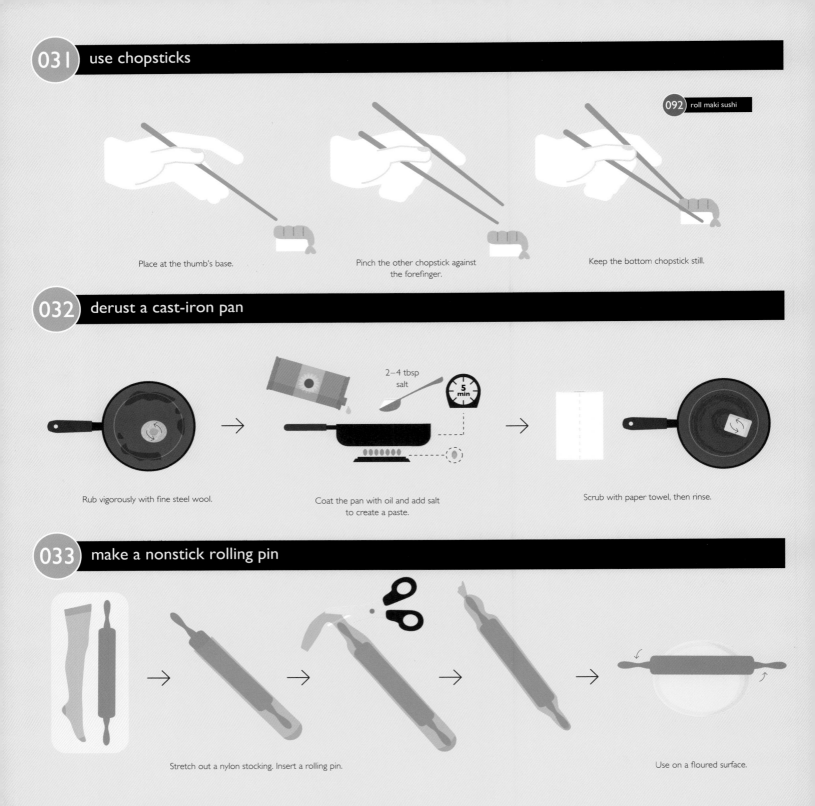

031 | use chopsticks

092 roll maki sushi

Place at the thumb's base.

Pinch the other chopstick against the forefinger.

Keep the bottom chopstick still.

032 | derust a cast-iron pan

2–4 tbsp salt

5 min

Rub vigorously with fine steel wool.

Coat the pan with oil and add salt to create a paste.

Scrub with paper towel, then rinse.

033 | make a nonstick rolling pin

Stretch out a nylon stocking. Insert a rolling pin.

Use on a floured surface.

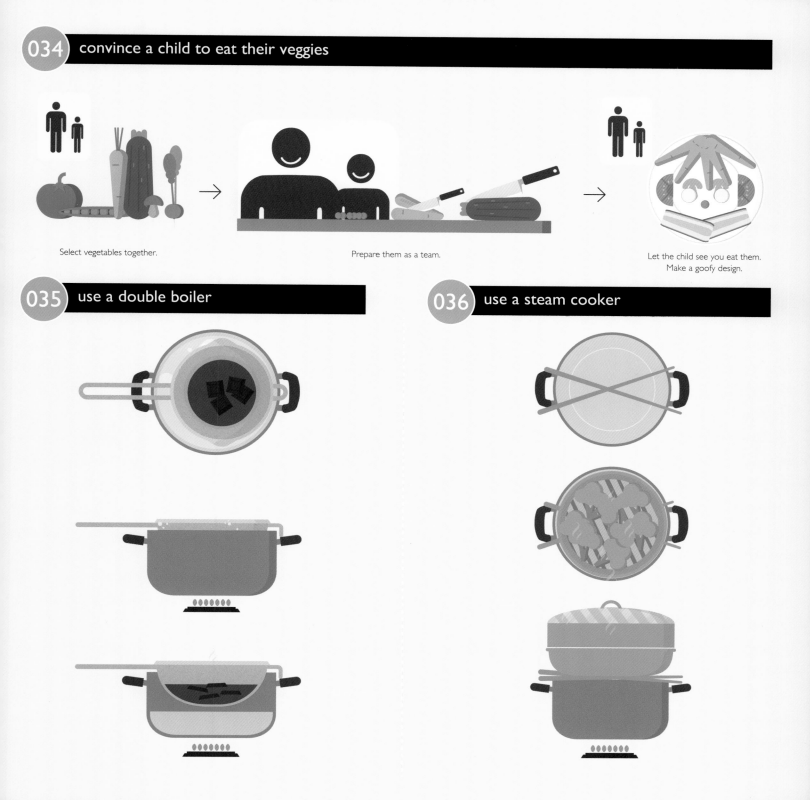

034 convince a child to eat their veggies

Select vegetables together.

Prepare them as a team.

Let the child see you eat them.
Make a goofy design.

035 use a double boiler

036 use a steam cooker

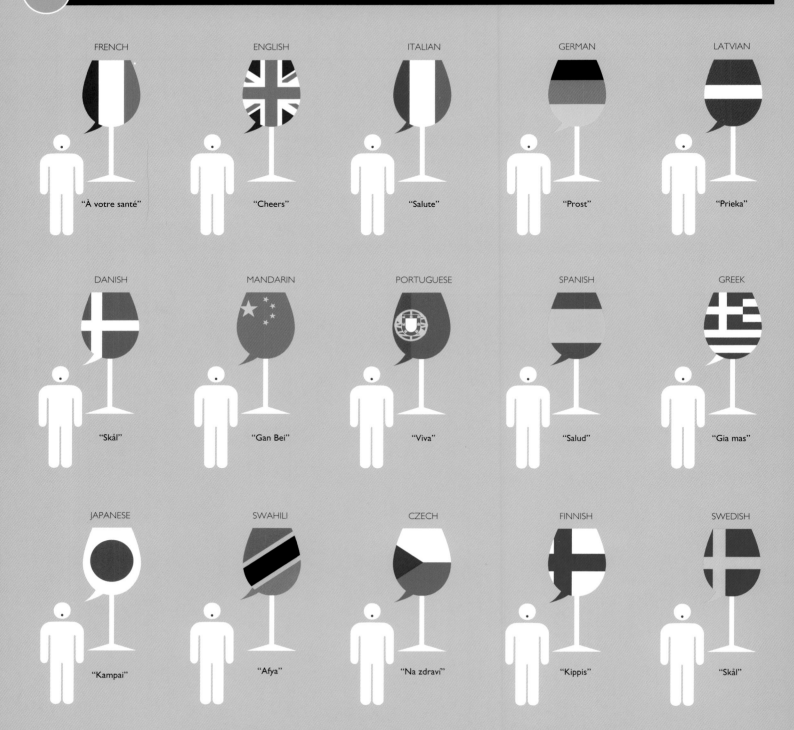

FRENCH
"À votre santé"

ENGLISH
"Cheers"

ITALIAN
"Salute"

GERMAN
"Prost"

LATVIAN
"Prieka"

DANISH
"Skål"

MANDARIN
"Gan Bei"

PORTUGUESE
"Viva"

SPANISH
"Salud"

GREEK
"Gia mas"

JAPANESE
"Kampai"

SWAHILI
"Afya"

CZECH
"Na zdraví"

FINNISH
"Kippis"

SWEDISH
"Skål"

prepare

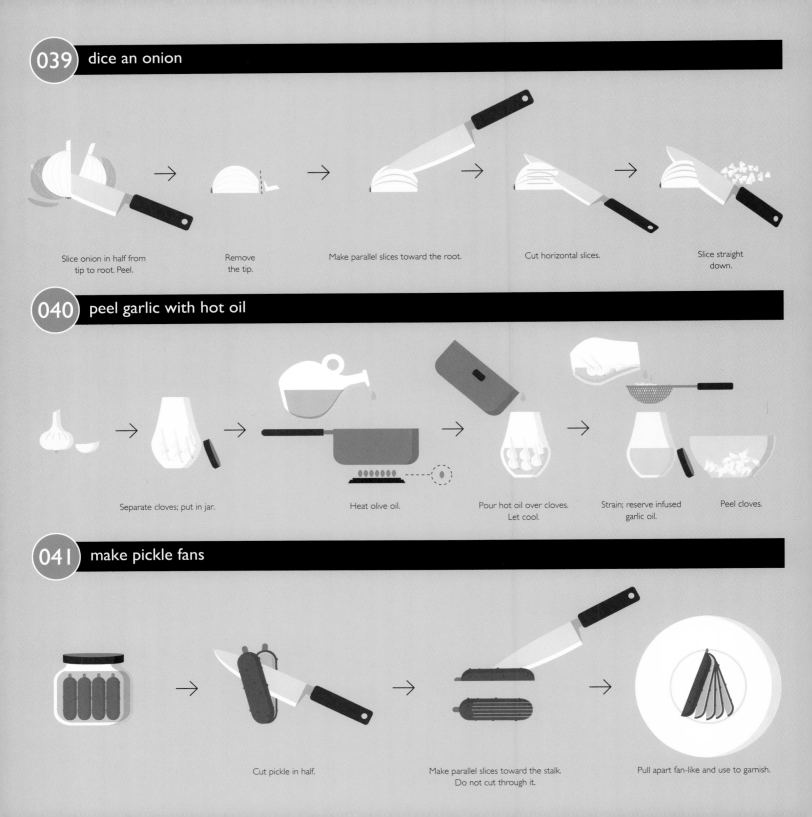

039   dice an onion

Slice onion in half from tip to root. Peel.

Remove the tip.

Make parallel slices toward the root.

Cut horizontal slices.

Slice straight down.

040   peel garlic with hot oil

Separate cloves; put in jar.

Heat olive oil.

Pour hot oil over cloves. Let cool.

Strain; reserve infused garlic oil.

Peel cloves.

041   make pickle fans

Cut pickle in half.

Make parallel slices toward the stalk. Do not cut through it.

Pull apart fan-like and use to garnish.

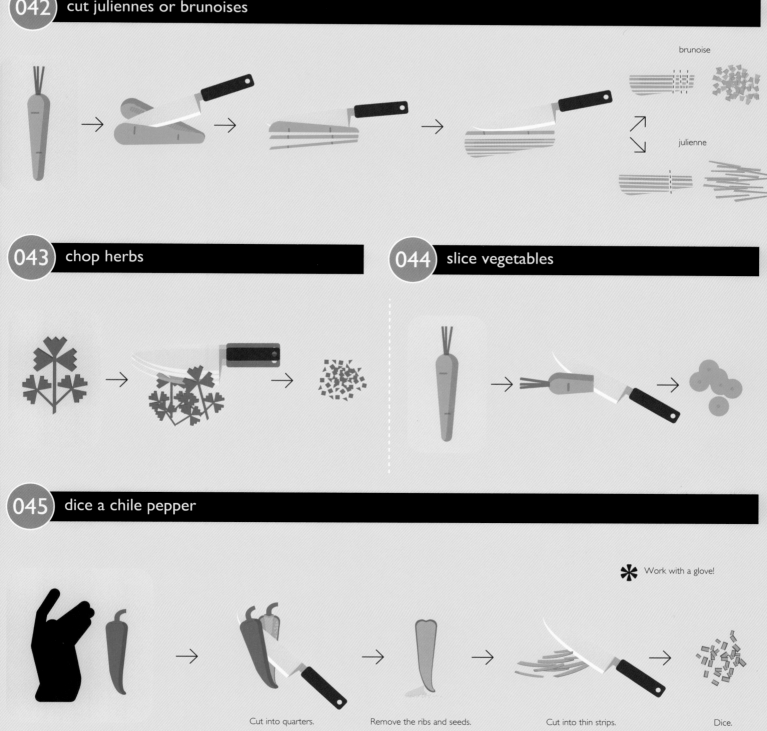

042 cut juliennes or brunoises

brunoise

julienne

043 chop herbs

044 slice vegetables

045 dice a chile pepper

✳ Work with a glove!

Cut into quarters.   Remove the ribs and seeds.   Cut into thin strips.   Dice.

Rotate, charring each side.

Steam in a plastic bag to loosen the skin.

Peel off the skin and remove the stem.

2 sprigs of parsley   2 sprigs of rosemary
2 sprigs of thyme   2 bay leaves

Tie together with a string.

Cook the bouquet garni with the other ingredients and remove before serving.

Peel ginger.

Cut into fine slices.

Cut the slices into strips and mince them.

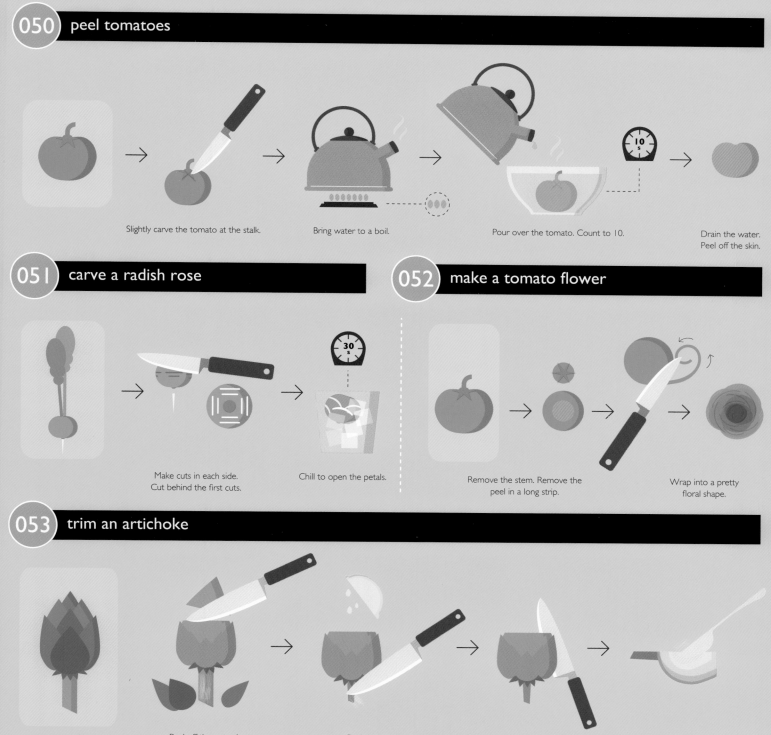

050 peel tomatoes

Slightly carve the tomato at the stalk.

Bring water to a boil.

Pour over the tomato. Count to 10.

Drain the water.
Peel off the skin.

051 carve a radish rose

Make cuts in each side.
Cut behind the first cuts.

Chill to open the petals.

052 make a tomato flower

Remove the stem. Remove the
peel in a long strip.

Wrap into a pretty
floral shape.

053 trim an artichoke

Peel off the outer leaves.
Slice off the top one-third.

Peel the stem;
rub with lemon.

Cut into quarters.

Discard the fibrous choke.

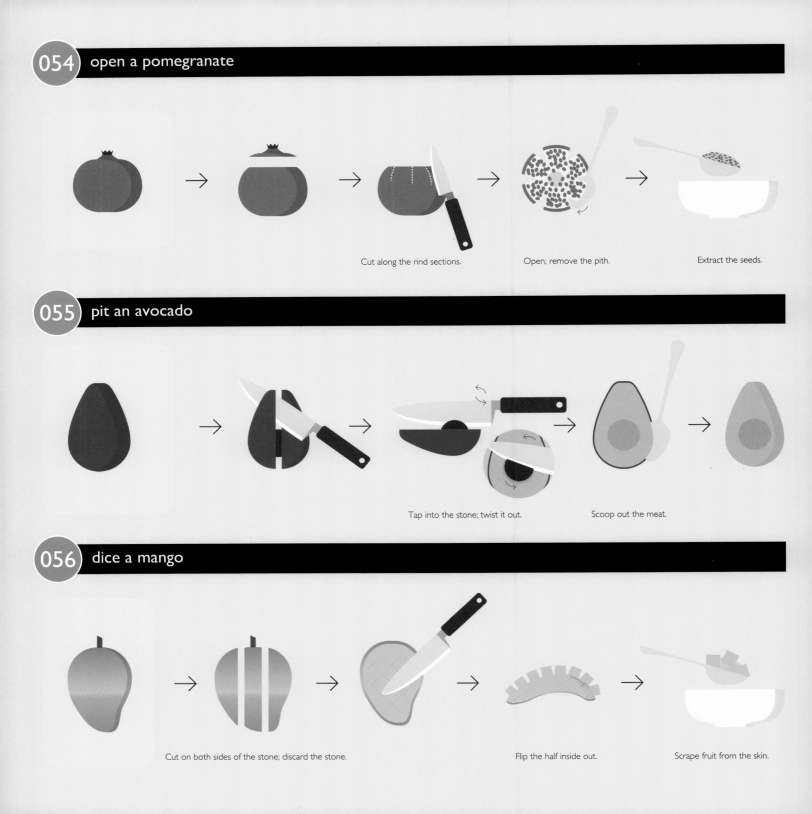

054 open a pomegranate

Cut along the rind sections.

Open; remove the pith.

Extract the seeds.

055 pit an avocado

Tap into the stone; twist it out.

Scoop out the meat.

056 dice a mango

Cut on both sides of the stone; discard the stone.

Flip the half inside out.

Scrape fruit from the skin.

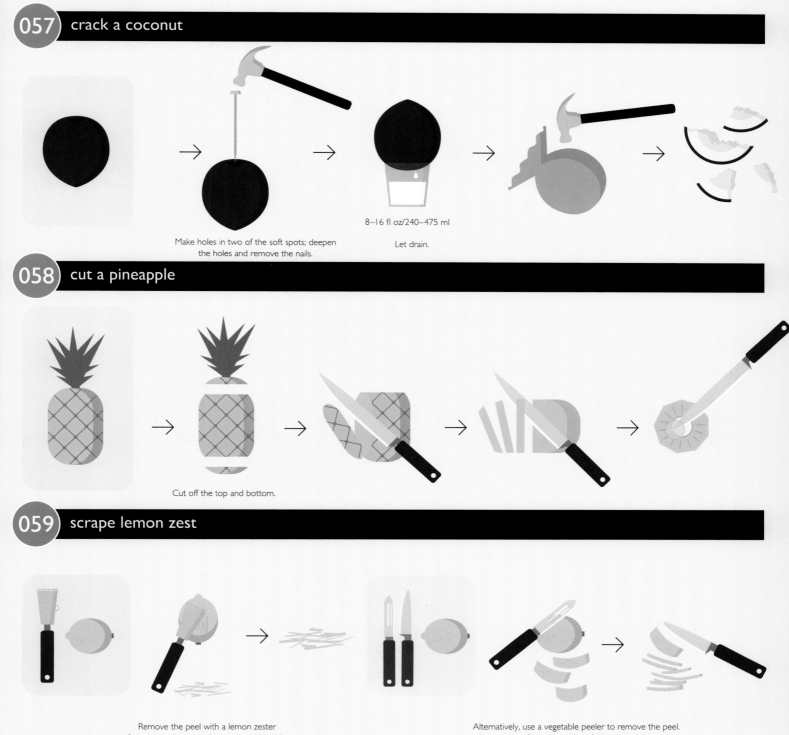

057 crack a coconut

Make holes in two of the soft spots; deepen the holes and remove the nails.

8–16 fl oz/240–475 ml

Let drain.

058 cut a pineapple

Cut off the top and bottom.

059 scrape lemon zest

Remove the peel with a lemon zester from top to bottom without the white pith.

Alternatively, use a vegetable peeler to remove the peel. Cut the peel into fine strips.

I

Cut off the lower bulb.

2

Remove the tough outer leaves.

3

Cut the stalk into fine slices.

3

Cut the lemongrass in half.

Flatten the bulb using a meat tenderizer. Cook with the other ingredients; remove before serving.

3

For skewers trim the top and root end of the lemongrass stalk and thread meat or shrimp onto the lemongrass stalks.

Twist off the head; pull off the shell.

Cut along the vein.

Pull out the intestine.

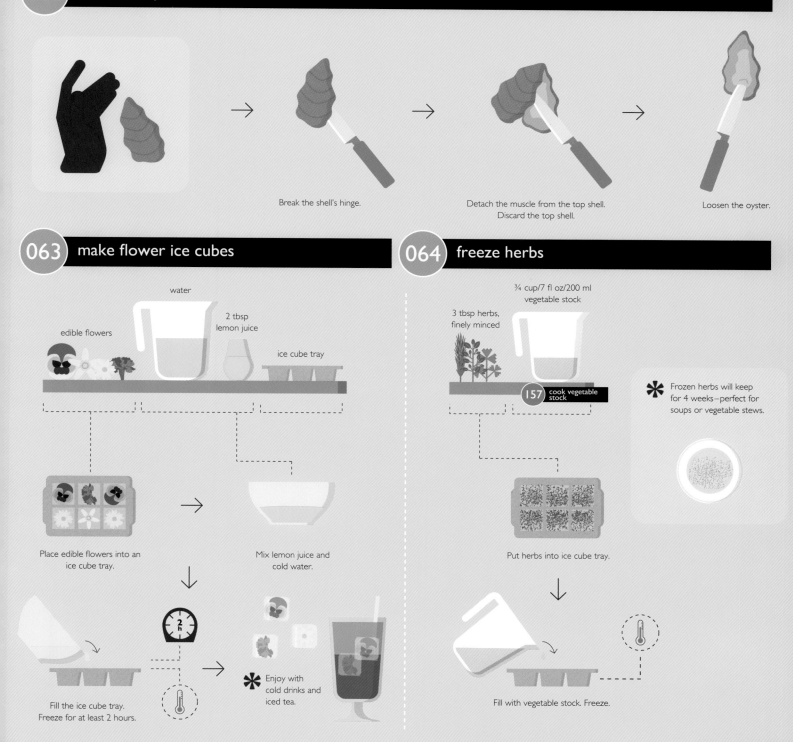

062 shuck an oyster

Break the shell's hinge.

Detach the muscle from the top shell.
Discard the top shell.

Loosen the oyster.

063 make flower ice cubes

water

2 tbsp
lemon juice

edible flowers

ice cube tray

Place edible flowers into an
ice cube tray.

Mix lemon juice and
cold water.

2 H

Fill the ice cube tray.
Freeze for at least 2 hours.

✽ Enjoy with
cold drinks and
iced tea.

064 freeze herbs

¾ cup/7 fl oz/200 ml
vegetable stock

3 tbsp herbs,
finely minced

157 cook vegetable
stock

✽ Frozen herbs will keep
for 4 weeks—perfect for
soups or vegetable stews.

Put herbs into ice cube tray.

Fill with vegetable stock. Freeze.

065 roll pasta dough

1 ¾ cups/9 oz/280 g flour

4 egg yolks

2 tbsp olive oil

Make a well in the flour. Add the egg-oil mixture.

Draw in the flour.

30 min

Roll the dough into a ball. Knead on a floured surface. Cover and let it rest.

Divide into quarters.

Flatten each into a disc.

Flip and roll again.

Check for translucence.

066 cut fettuccine

✳ When dried they keep for 1–2 days.

Spread; let dry.

067 fold tortellini

✳ Refrigerated they keep for 1 day.

Add filling; wet the edges.

Fold; firmly press down the edges.

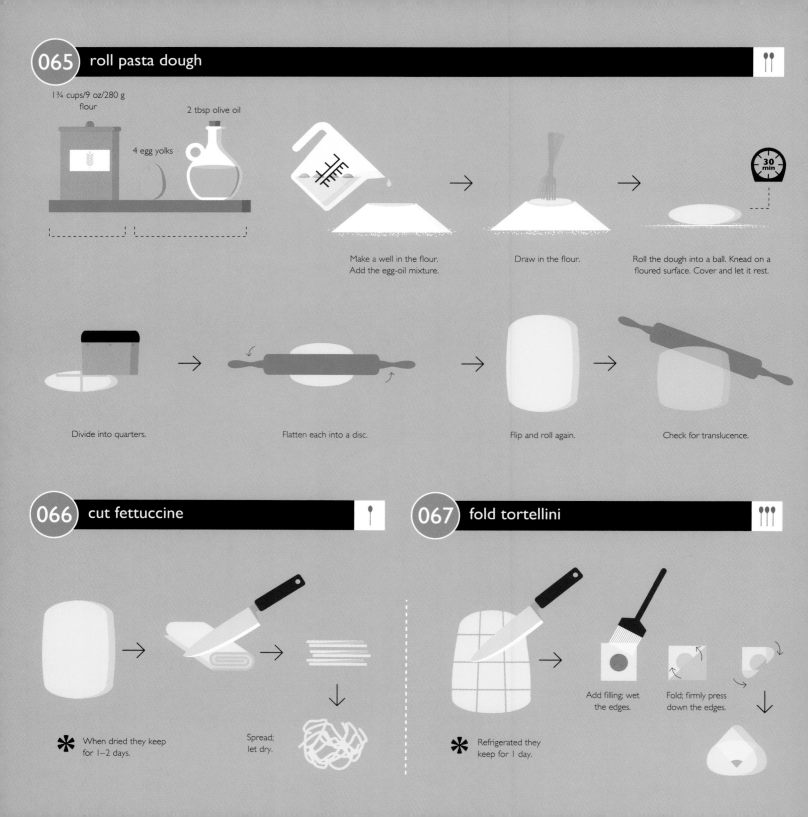

1½ cups/12 fl oz/ 375 ml milk

⅓ cup/2½ oz/ 80 g dark molasses

2 tsp salt

3 tsp dry yeast

1 egg, separated

2 cups/10 oz/315 g bread flour

2 tbsp oatmeal

2 tbsp sunflower seeds

x 4

Warm up milk and molasses, add salt.
Add the yeast; let it rest for 10 minutes.

Whisk the egg yolk.

Combine the yeast mixture,
egg yolks and flour.

Let the dough rise in a warm place
until doubled.

Add sunflower seeds and oatmeal,
knead and leave to proof again.

070 prepare pizza dough

4 cups/16 oz/500 g
all-purpose flour

3 tsp
dry yeast

2 tbsp olive oil

1¼ cups/10 fl oz/300 ml
lukewarm water

1 tsp salt

356	bake pizza	360	bake pizza with onions and olives
357	bake pizza napoletana	361	bake pizza bianca
358	bake pizza pomodoro e mozzarella	362	bake pizza quattro formaggi
359	bake pizza cardinale	363	bake focaccia

30 min

5 min

Combine all ingredients in a large bowl.
Knead the dough.

Let the dough rest.

Form 4–6 dough balls.
Roll out in a round shape.

071 make yeast dough

4 cups/16 oz/500 g
all-purpose flour

5 tsp
dry yeast

3 tbsp sugar

1 pinch of salt

¼ cup/2 oz/
65 g butter

1¾ cups/15 fl oz/450 ml
lukewarm milk

3 eggs

| 322 | make doughnuts |
| 397 | bake cinnamon rolls |

15 min

10 min

1 h

Put the flour in a bowl and make a well in the center.
Crumble in the yeast and add sugar, salt and 2 tbsp of milk.
Leave to proof.

Add the eggs and the rest of the milk.
Mix well with a handheld electric mixer.

The dough should be glossy and smooth.
Cover and leave to proof in a warm place

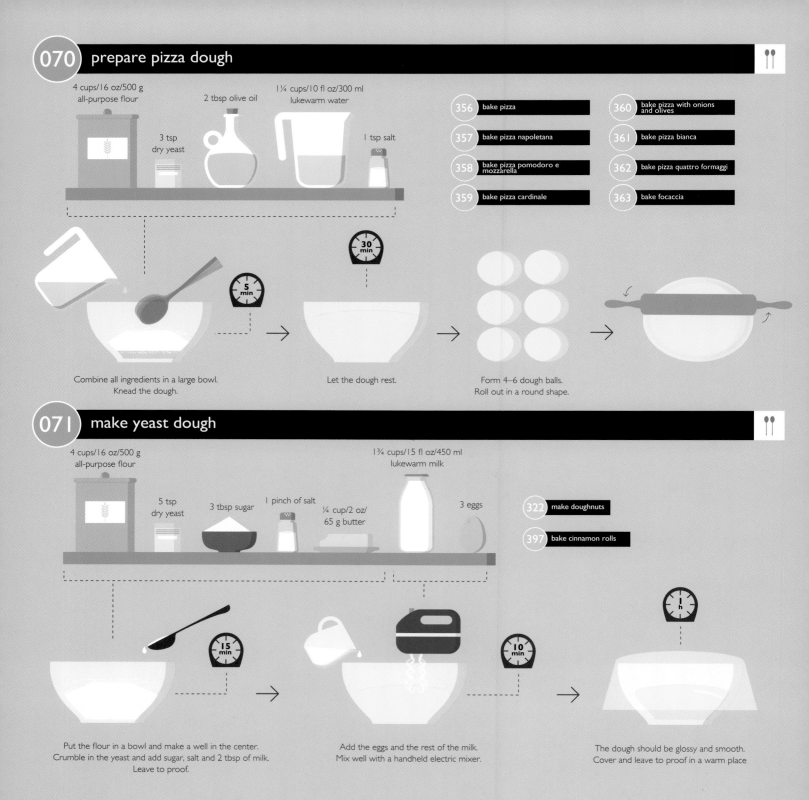

braid challah bread

Form three thick and three thin rolls with the yeast dough.

071 make yeast dough

Make a braid with the three thick pieces; then braid the three thin pieces.

1 2 3

3 2 1

Stack; brush with egg wash.

make choux pastry

½ cup/4 fl oz/120 ml water

¾ cup/3 oz/80 g cake flour

2 eggs

¼ cup/2 oz/50 g butter, diced

½ tsp salt

392 make profiteroles

15 min

Whisk the eggs.

Bring water, butter and salt to a boil; remove from the heat.

Slowly add flour. Stir well until the mixture comes off the sides of the pan.

Remove from the heat; gradually add whisked eggs. Process the paste straight away.

1¼ cups/6½ oz/200 g cake flour

½ cup/3½ oz/100 g butter, in cubes

4 tbsp water

½ tbsp salt

2 tbsp sugar

1 egg

381 make lemon tart

Put flour on a working surface and make a well in the center.

Add all other ingredients.

Knead together working from the inside to the outside until a smooth dough forms.

Cover the dough and let it rest in a chilled place.

2 cups/8 oz/250 g cake flour

1 tbsp salt

½ cup/4 oz/125 g butter, in cubes

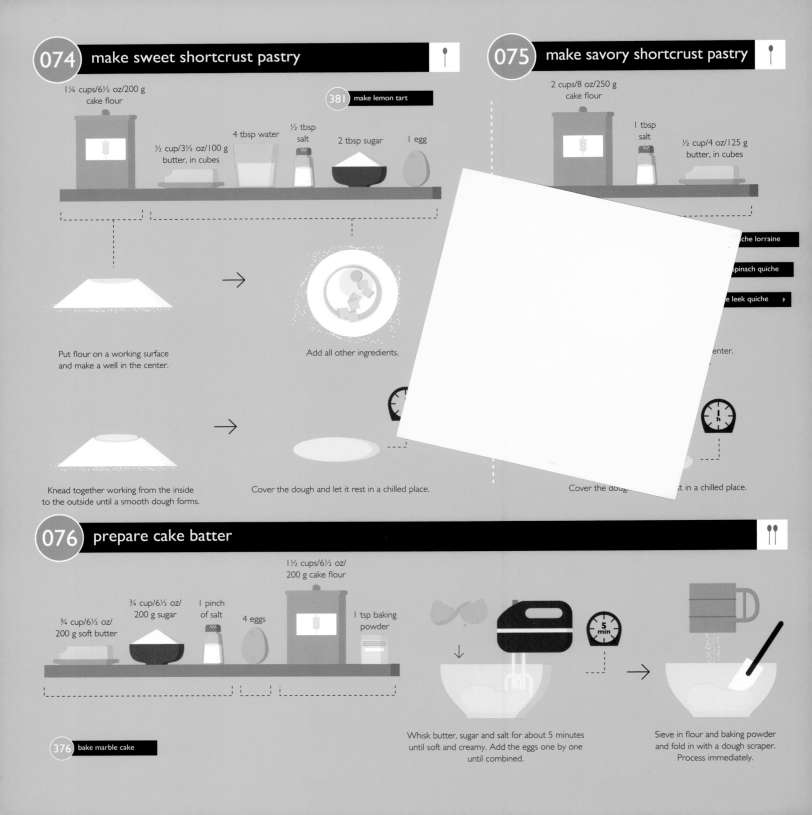

...che lorraine

...spinach quiche

...e leek quiche

...center.

Cover the dough...st in a chilled place.

¾ cup/6½ oz/200 g soft butter

¾ cup/6½ oz/200 g sugar

1 pinch of salt

4 eggs

1½ cups/6½ oz/200 g cake flour

1 tsp baking powder

376 bake marble cake

5 min

Whisk butter, sugar and salt for about 5 minutes until soft and creamy. Add the eggs one by one until combined.

Sieve in flour and baking powder and fold in with a dough scraper. Process immediately.

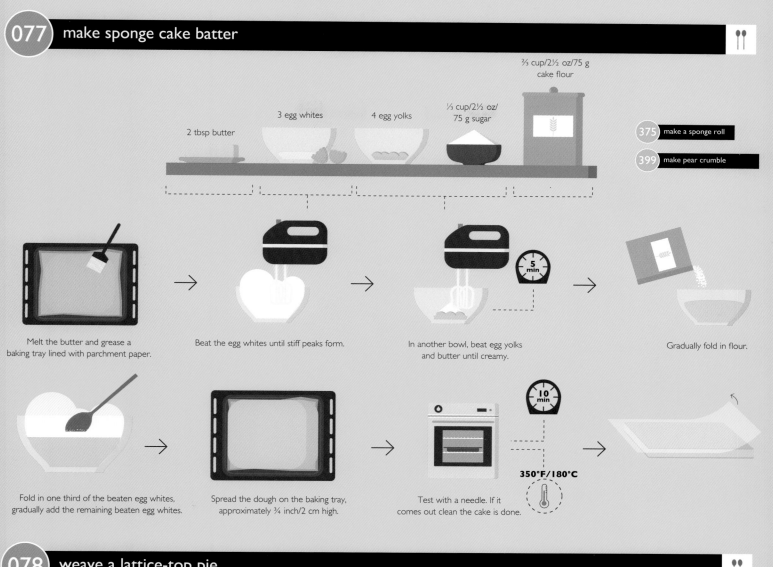

2 tbsp butter

3 egg whites

4 egg yolks

⅓ cup/2½ oz/ 75 g sugar

⅔ cup/2½ oz/75 g cake flour

375 make a sponge roll

399 make pear crumble

Melt the butter and grease a baking tray lined with parchment paper.

Beat the egg whites until stiff peaks form.

In another bowl, beat egg yolks and butter until creamy.

Gradually fold in flour.

Fold in one third of the beaten egg whites, gradually add the remaining beaten egg whites.

Spread the dough on the baking tray, approximately ¾ inch/2 cm high.

Test with a needle. If it comes out clean the cake is done.

350°F/180°C

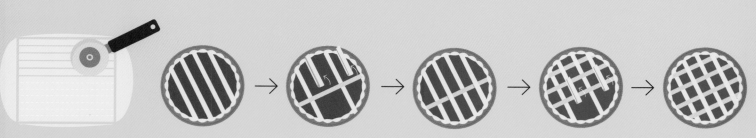

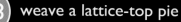

Continue until covered.

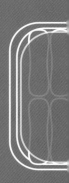
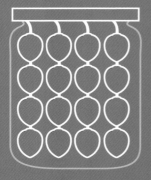
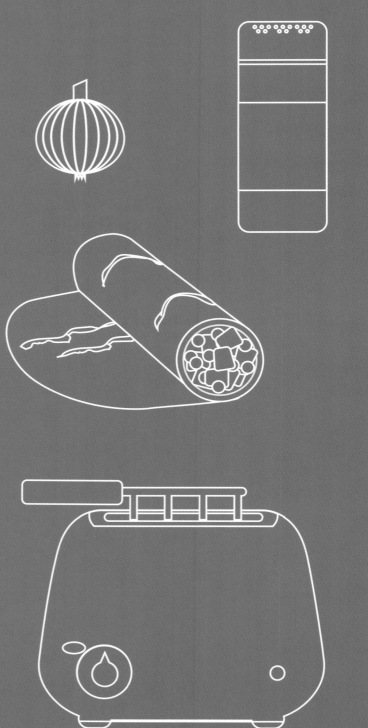

cook without heat

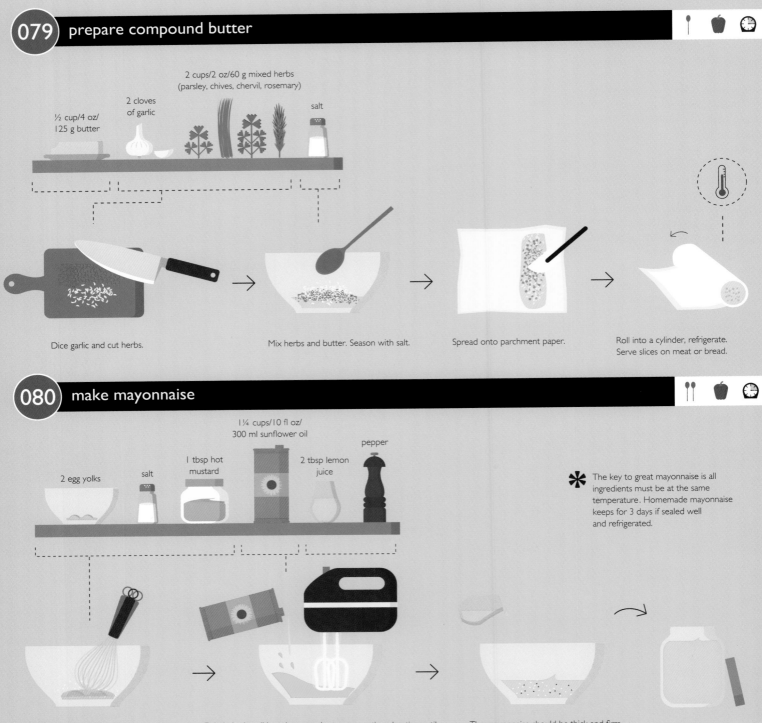

½ cup/4 oz/ 125 g butter

2 cloves of garlic

2 cups/2 oz/60 g mixed herbs
(parsley, chives, chervil, rosemary)

salt

Dice garlic and cut herbs.

Mix herbs and butter. Season with salt.

Spread onto parchment paper.

Roll into a cylinder, refrigerate.
Serve slices on meat or bread.

2 egg yolks

salt

1 tbsp hot mustard

1¼ cups/10 fl oz/ 300 ml sunflower oil

2 tbsp lemon juice

pepper

* The key to great mayonnaise is all ingredients must be at the same temperature. Homemade mayonnaise keeps for 3 days if sealed well and refrigerated.

Whisk egg yolks, salt and mustard.

Drizzle in the oil in a slow, steady stream; continue beating until creamy. All the oil must be absorbed before you add any more.

The mayonnaise should be thick and firm. Season with lemon juice, salt and pepper.

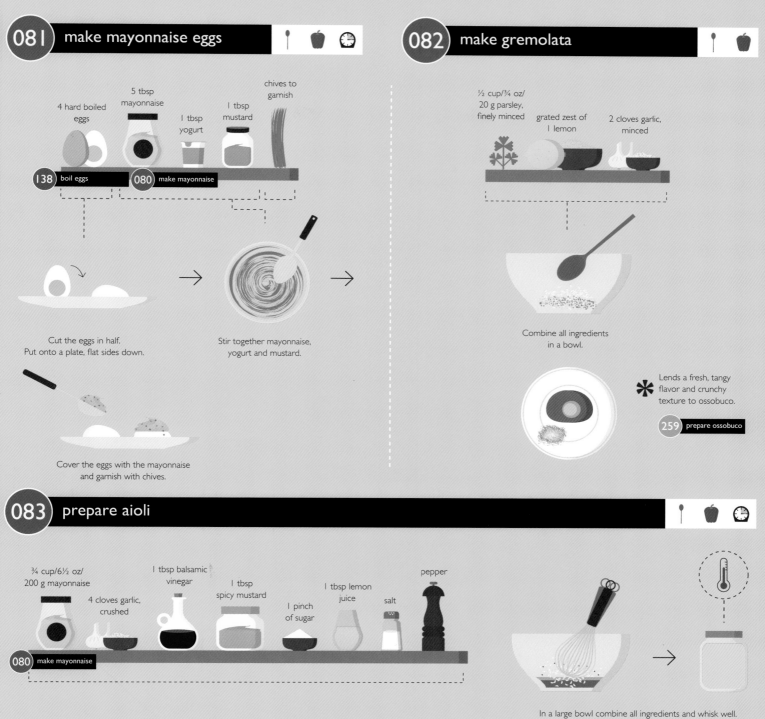

081 make mayonnaise eggs

4 hard boiled eggs

5 tbsp mayonnaise

1 tbsp yogurt

1 tbsp mustard

chives to garnish

138 boil eggs

080 make mayonnaise

Cut the eggs in half.
Put onto a plate, flat sides down.

Stir together mayonnaise,
yogurt and mustard.

Cover the eggs with the mayonnaise
and garnish with chives.

082 make gremolata

½ cup/¾ oz/
20 g parsley,
finely minced

grated zest of
1 lemon

2 cloves garlic,
minced

Combine all ingredients
in a bowl.

Lends a fresh, tangy
flavor and crunchy
texture to ossobuco.

259 prepare ossobuco

083 prepare aioli

¾ cup/6½ oz/
200 g mayonnaise

4 cloves garlic,
crushed

1 tbsp balsamic
vinegar

1 tbsp
spicy mustard

1 pinch
of sugar

1 tbsp lemon
juice

salt

pepper

080 make mayonnaise

In a large bowl combine all ingredients and whisk well.
Cover and refrigerate overnight.

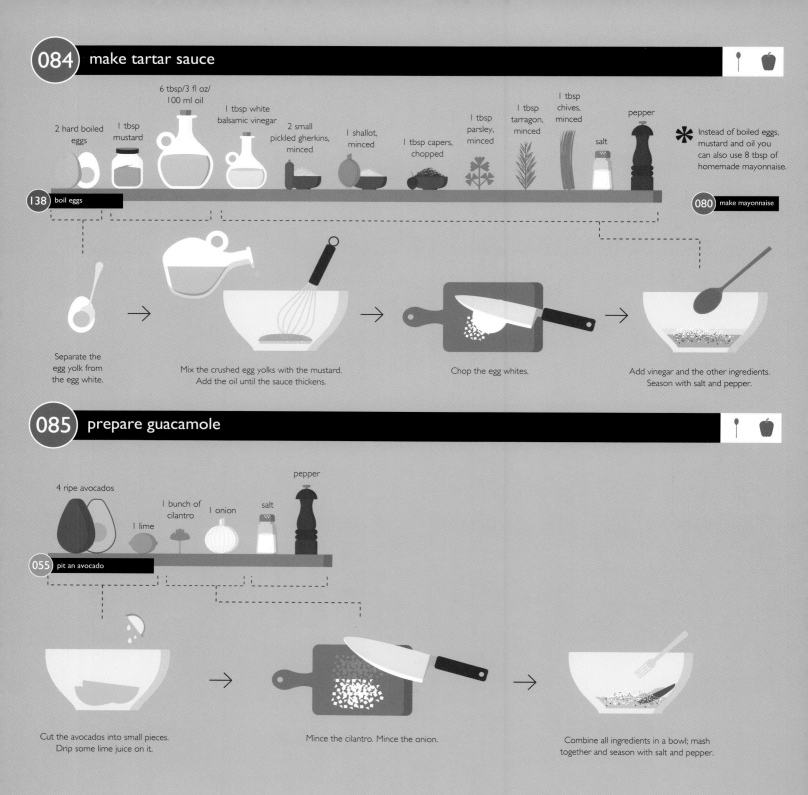

084 make tartar sauce

2 hard boiled eggs

1 tbsp mustard

6 tbsp/3 fl oz/ 100 ml oil

1 tbsp white balsamic vinegar

2 small pickled gherkins, minced

1 shallot, minced

1 tbsp capers, chopped

1 tbsp parsley, minced

1 tbsp tarragon, minced

1 tbsp chives, minced

salt

pepper

✱ Instead of boiled eggs, mustard and oil you can also use 8 tbsp of homemade mayonnaise.

138 boil eggs

080 make mayonnaise

Separate the egg yolk from the egg white.

Mix the crushed egg yolks with the mustard. Add the oil until the sauce thickens.

Chop the egg whites.

Add vinegar and the other ingredients. Season with salt and pepper.

085 prepare guacamole

4 ripe avocados

1 lime

1 bunch of cilantro

1 onion

salt

pepper

055 pit an avocado

Cut the avocados into small pieces. Drip some lime juice on it.

Mince the cilantro. Mince the onion.

Combine all ingredients in a bowl; mash together and season with salt and pepper.

make tzatziki

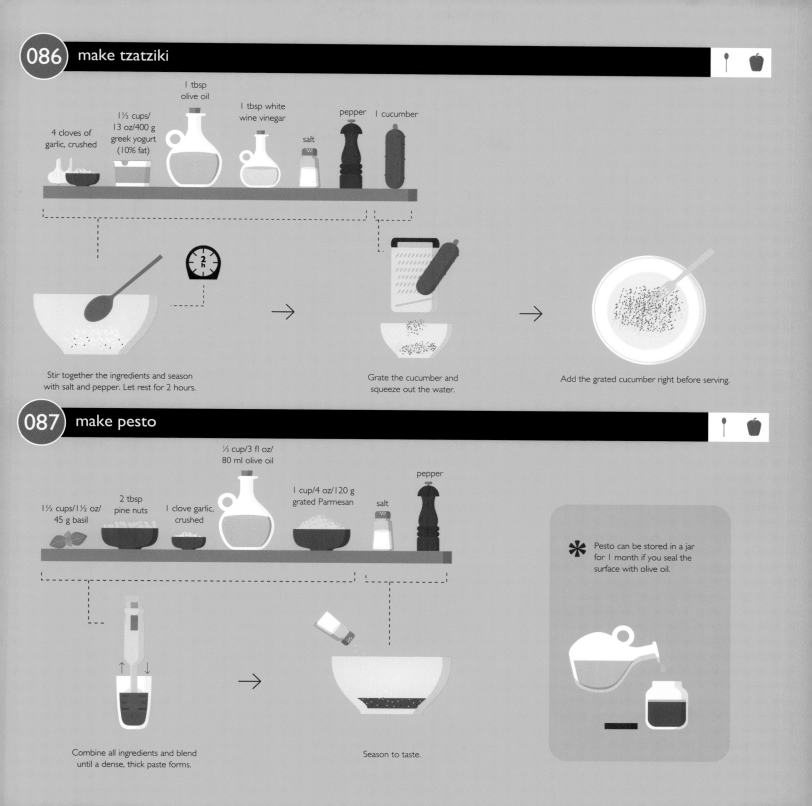

4 cloves of garlic, crushed

1 ½ cups/ 13 oz/400 g greek yogurt (10% fat)

1 tbsp olive oil

1 tbsp white wine vinegar

salt

pepper

1 cucumber

Stir together the ingredients and season with salt and pepper. Let rest for 2 hours.

Grate the cucumber and squeeze out the water.

Add the grated cucumber right before serving.

make pesto

1 ½ cups/1 ½ oz/ 45 g basil

2 tbsp pine nuts

1 clove garlic, crushed

⅓ cup/3 fl oz/ 80 ml olive oil

1 cup/4 oz/120 g grated Parmesan

salt

pepper

Combine all ingredients and blend until a dense, thick paste forms.

Season to taste.

✳ Pesto can be stored in a jar for 1 month if you seal the surface with olive oil.

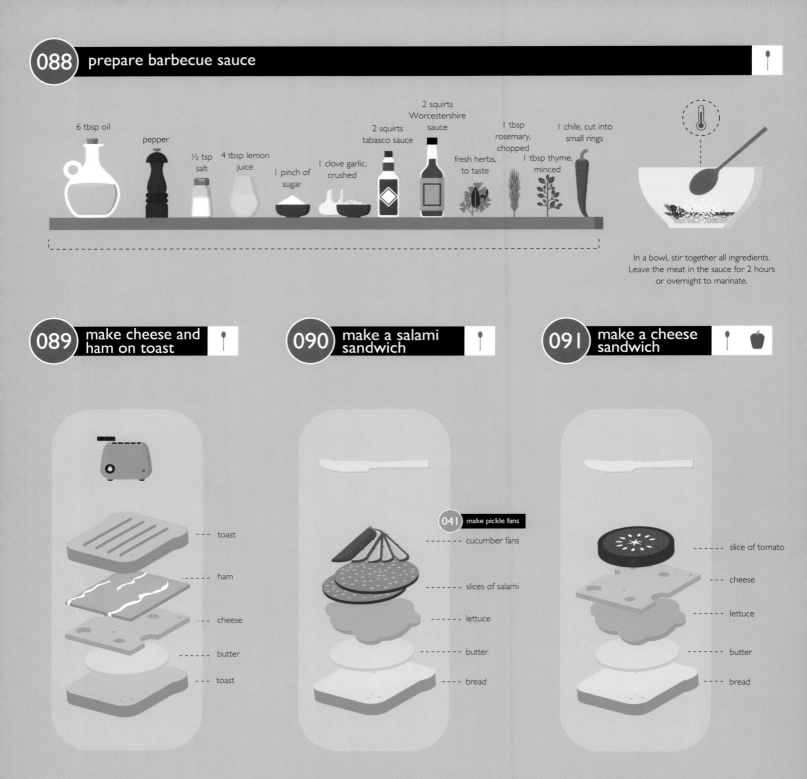

088 prepare barbecue sauce

6 tbsp oil

pepper

½ tsp salt

4 tbsp lemon juice

1 pinch of sugar

1 clove garlic, crushed

2 squirts tabasco sauce

2 squirts Worcestershire sauce

fresh herbs, to taste

1 tbsp rosemary, chopped

1 tbsp thyme, minced

1 chile, cut into small rings

In a bowl, stir together all ingredients. Leave the meat in the sauce for 2 hours or overnight to marinate.

089 make cheese and ham on toast

toast

ham

cheese

butter

toast

090 make a salami sandwich

041 make pickle fans

cucumber fans

slices of salami

lettuce

butter

bread

091 make a cheese sandwich

slice of tomato

cheese

lettuce

butter

bread

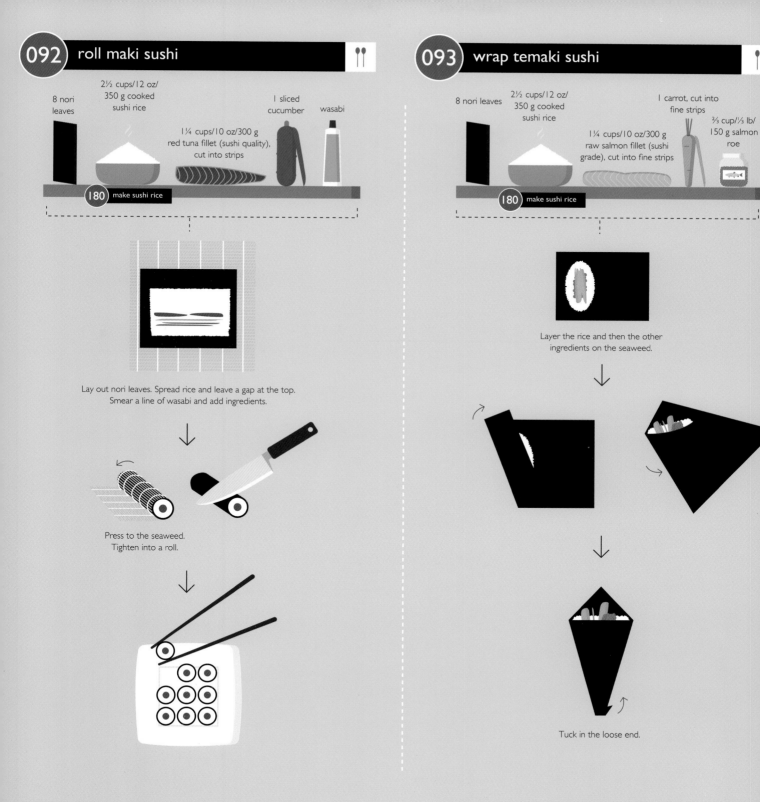

092 roll maki sushi

8 nori leaves

2½ cups/12 oz/ 350 g cooked sushi rice

1¼ cups/10 oz/300 g red tuna fillet (sushi quality), cut into strips

1 sliced cucumber

wasabi

180 make sushi rice

Lay out nori leaves. Spread rice and leave a gap at the top. Smear a line of wasabi and add ingredients.

Press to the seaweed.
Tighten into a roll.

093 wrap temaki sushi

8 nori leaves

2½ cups/12 oz/ 350 g cooked sushi rice

1¼ cups/10 oz/300 g raw salmon fillet (sushi grade), cut into fine strips

1 carrot, cut into fine strips

⅔ cup/⅓ lb/ 150 g salmon roe

180 make sushi rice

Layer the rice and then the other ingredients on the seaweed.

Tuck in the loose end.

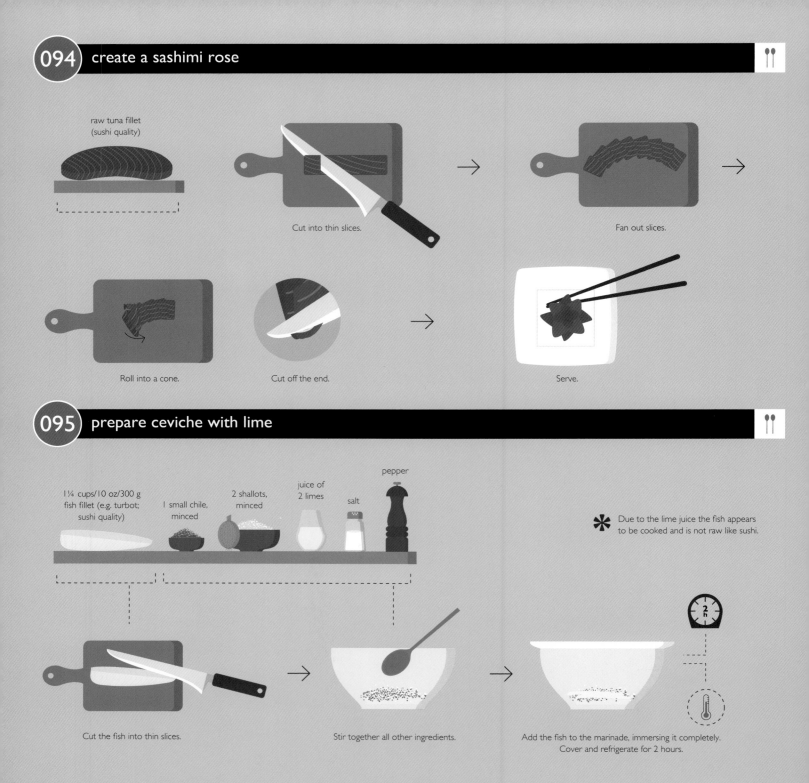

094 create a sashimi rose

raw tuna fillet
(sushi quality)

Cut into thin slices.

Fan out slices.

Roll into a cone.

Cut off the end.

Serve.

095 prepare ceviche with lime

1¼ cups/10 oz/300 g
fish fillet (e.g. turbot;
sushi quality)

1 small chile,
minced

2 shallots,
minced

juice of
2 limes

salt

pepper

✳ Due to the lime juice the fish appears
to be cooked and is not raw like sushi.

Cut the fish into thin slices.

Stir together all other ingredients.

Add the fish to the marinade, immersing it completely.
Cover and refrigerate for 2 hours.

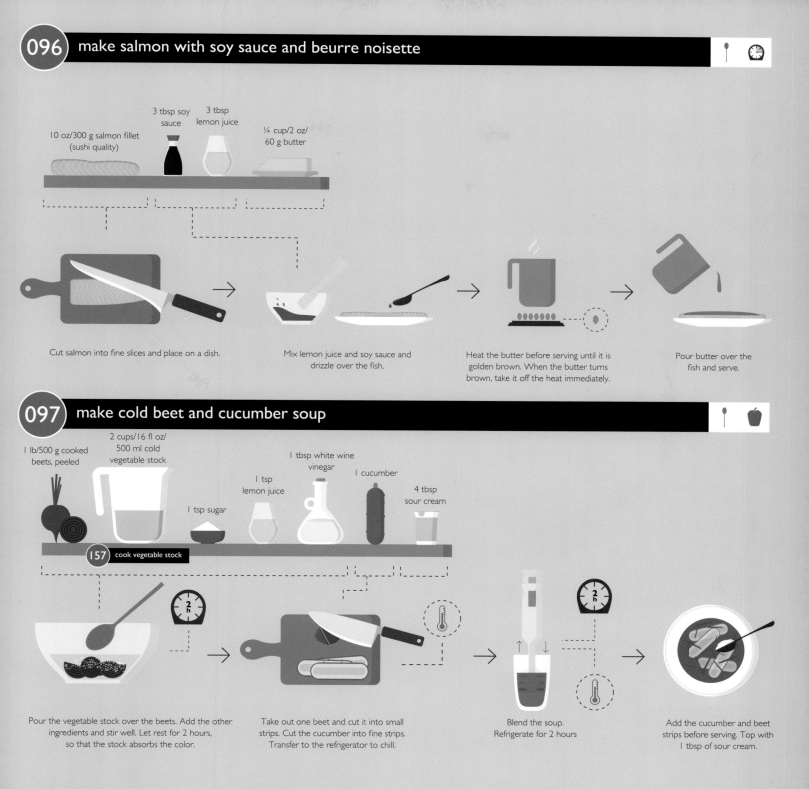

096 make salmon with soy sauce and beurre noisette

10 oz/300 g salmon fillet
(sushi quality)

3 tbsp soy
sauce

3 tbsp
lemon juice

¼ cup/2 oz/
60 g butter

Cut salmon into fine slices and place on a dish.

Mix lemon juice and soy sauce and drizzle over the fish.

Heat the butter before serving until it is golden brown. When the butter turns brown, take it off the heat immediately.

Pour butter over the fish and serve.

097 make cold beet and cucumber soup

1 lb/500 g cooked beets, peeled

2 cups/16 fl oz/
500 ml cold
vegetable stock

1 tsp sugar

1 tsp
lemon juice

1 tbsp white wine
vinegar

1 cucumber

4 tbsp
sour cream

157 cook vegetable stock

Pour the vegetable stock over the beets. Add the other ingredients and stir well. Let rest for 2 hours, so that the stock absorbs the color.

Take out one beet and cut it into small strips. Cut the cucumber into fine strips. Transfer to the refrigerator to chill.

Blend the soup.
Refrigerate for 2 hours

Add the cucumber and beet strips before serving. Top with 1 tbsp of sour cream.

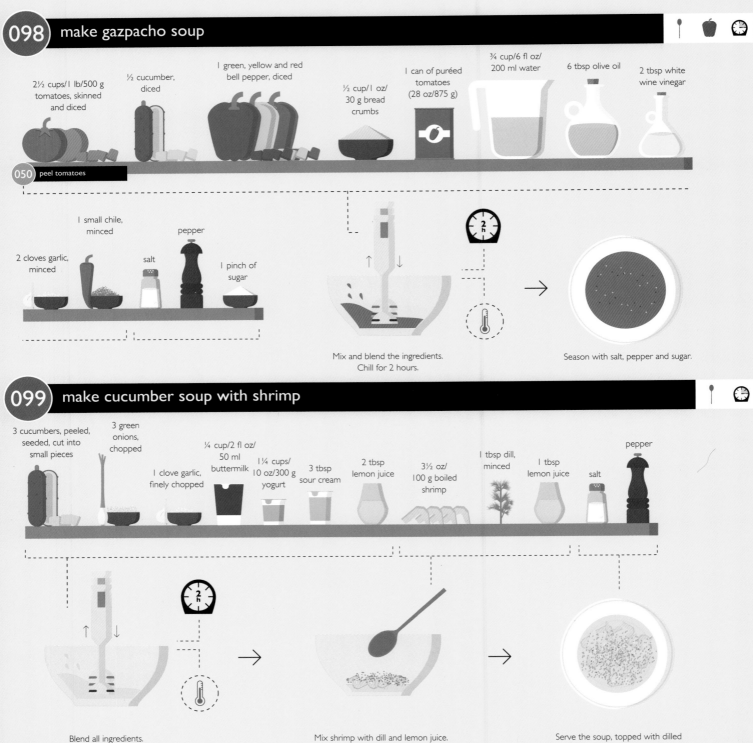

098 make gazpacho soup

2½ cups/1 lb/500 g tomatoes, skinned and diced

½ cucumber, diced

1 green, yellow and red bell pepper, diced

½ cup/1 oz/30 g bread crumbs

1 can of puréed tomatoes (28 oz/875 g)

¾ cup/6 fl oz/200 ml water

6 tbsp olive oil

2 tbsp white wine vinegar

050 peel tomatoes

2 cloves garlic, minced

1 small chile, minced

salt

pepper

1 pinch of sugar

2h

Mix and blend the ingredients. Chill for 2 hours.

Season with salt, pepper and sugar.

099 make cucumber soup with shrimp

3 cucumbers, peeled, seeded, cut into small pieces

3 green onions, chopped

1 clove garlic, finely chopped

¼ cup/2 fl oz/50 ml buttermilk

1¼ cups/10 oz/300 g yogurt

3 tbsp sour cream

2 tbsp lemon juice

3½ oz/100 g boiled shrimp

1 tbsp dill, minced

1 tbsp lemon juice

salt

pepper

2h

Blend all ingredients. Chill for 2 hours.

Mix shrimp with dill and lemon juice.

Serve the soup, topped with dilled shrimp; season with salt and pepper.

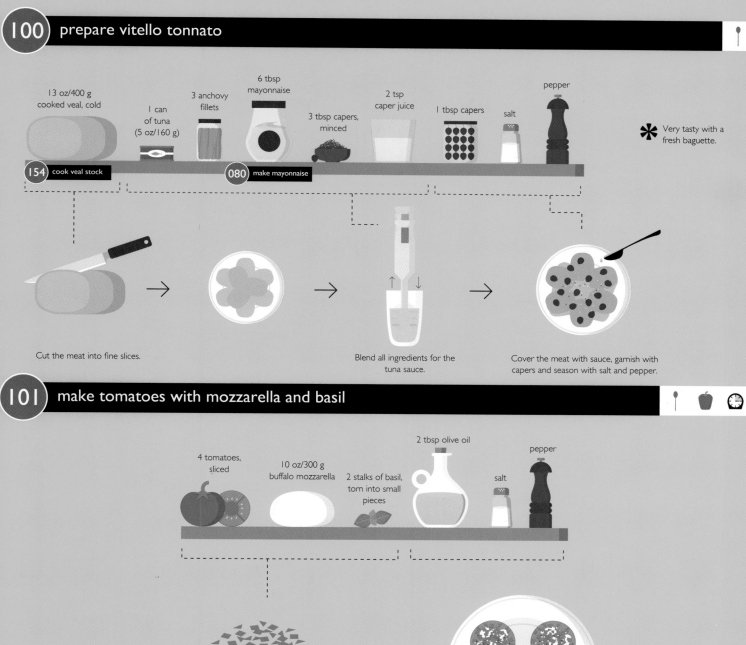

13 oz/400 g
cooked veal, cold

1 can
of tuna
(5 oz/160 g)

3 anchovy
fillets

6 tbsp
mayonnaise

3 tbsp capers,
minced

2 tsp
caper juice

1 tbsp capers

salt

pepper

154 cook veal stock

080 make mayonnaise

✳ Very tasty with a
fresh baguette.

Cut the meat into fine slices.

Blend all ingredients for the
tuna sauce.

Cover the meat with sauce, garnish with
capers and season with salt and pepper.

4 tomatoes,
sliced

10 oz/300 g
buffalo mozzarella

2 stalks of basil,
torn into small
pieces

2 tbsp olive oil

salt

pepper

Using your fingers, rip the
mozzarella into small pieces
and spread over the sliced
tomatoes. Garnish with basil.

Drizzle with olive oil
and season with
salt and pepper.

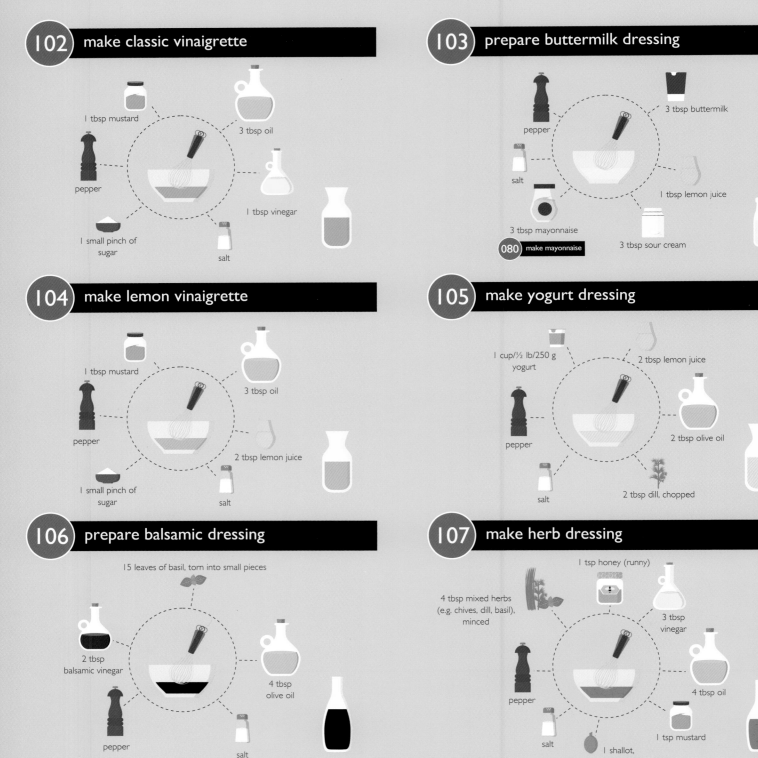

102 make classic vinaigrette

1 tbsp mustard

3 tbsp oil

pepper

1 tbsp vinegar

1 small pinch of sugar

salt

103 prepare buttermilk dressing

pepper

3 tbsp buttermilk

salt

1 tbsp lemon juice

3 tbsp mayonnaise

080 make mayonnaise

3 tbsp sour cream

104 make lemon vinaigrette

1 tbsp mustard

3 tbsp oil

pepper

2 tbsp lemon juice

1 small pinch of sugar

salt

105 make yogurt dressing

1 cup/½ lb/250 g yogurt

2 tbsp lemon juice

pepper

2 tbsp olive oil

salt

2 tbsp dill, chopped

106 prepare balsamic dressing

15 leaves of basil, torn into small pieces

2 tbsp balsamic vinegar

4 tbsp olive oil

pepper

salt

107 make herb dressing

1 tsp honey (runny)

4 tbsp mixed herbs (e.g. chives, dill, basil), minced

3 tbsp vinegar

4 tbsp oil

pepper

1 tsp mustard

salt

1 shallot, minced

108 prepare caesar dressing

2 cloves garlic, chopped

salt

pepper

1 egg yolk

juice of 1 lemon

2 tsp mustard

1 tbsp worcestershire sauce

1 tsp vinegar

2 anchovy fillets, minced

4 tbsp olive oil

109 prepare frisée with bacon and croutons

107 make herb dressing

1 head frisée lettuce

2 tbsp fried bacon pieces

2 tbsp croutons (fried cubes of white bread)

110 make a tomato salad

4 large tomatoes, sliced

106 prepare balsamic dressing

111 make a green salad

102 make classic vinaigrette

1 head lettuce, torn into small pieces

112 make a mushroom salad

104 make lemon vinaigrette

2¾ cups/8¼ oz/250 g mushrooms, sliced

113 make a spinach salad with pine nuts

8 cups/8 oz/250 g spinach

105 make yogurt dressing

2 tbsp toasted pine nuts

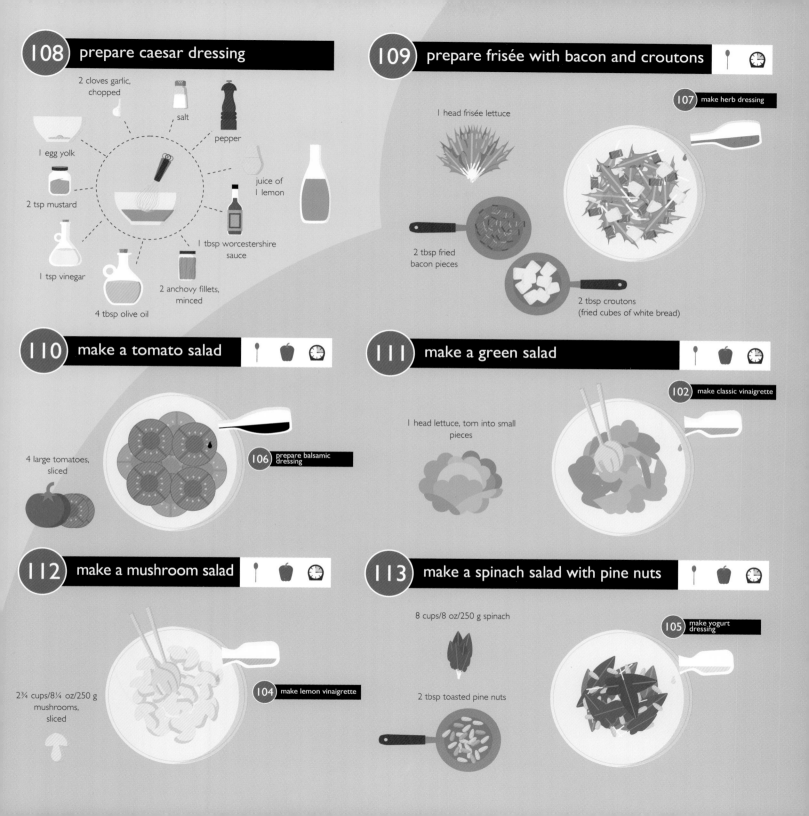

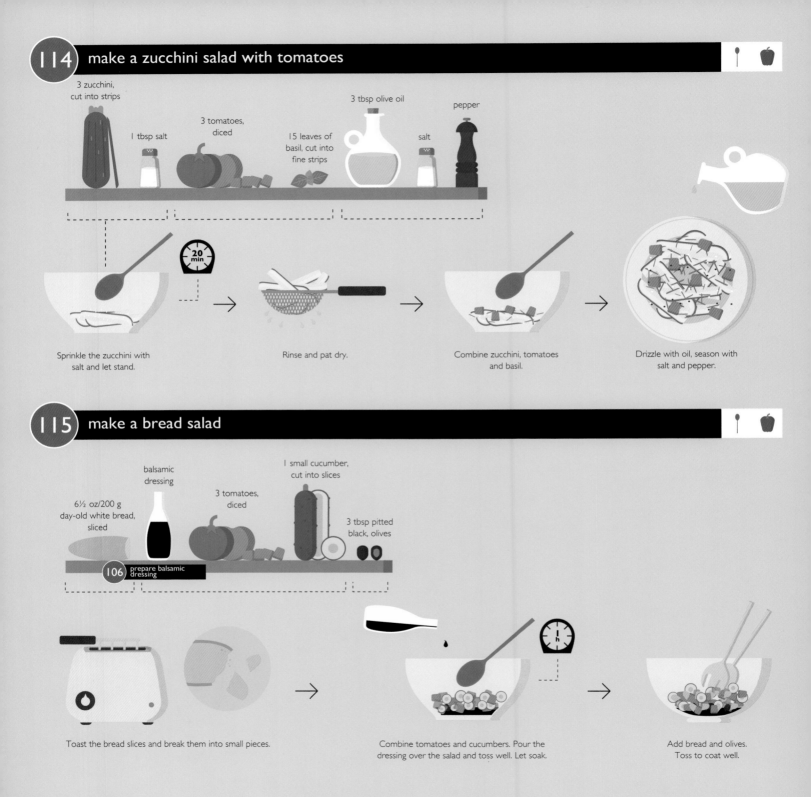

114 make a zucchini salad with tomatoes

3 zucchini,
cut into strips

1 tbsp salt

3 tomatoes,
diced

15 leaves of
basil, cut into
fine strips

3 tbsp olive oil

salt

pepper

20 min

Sprinkle the zucchini with
salt and let stand.

Rinse and pat dry.

Combine zucchini, tomatoes
and basil.

Drizzle with oil, season with
salt and pepper.

115 make a bread salad

6½ oz/200 g
day-old white bread,
sliced

balsamic
dressing

3 tomatoes,
diced

1 small cucumber,
cut into slices

3 tbsp pitted
black, olives

106 prepare balsamic
dressing

Toast the bread slices and break them into small pieces.

Combine tomatoes and cucumbers. Pour the
dressing over the salad and toss well. Let soak.

Add bread and olives.
Toss to coat well.

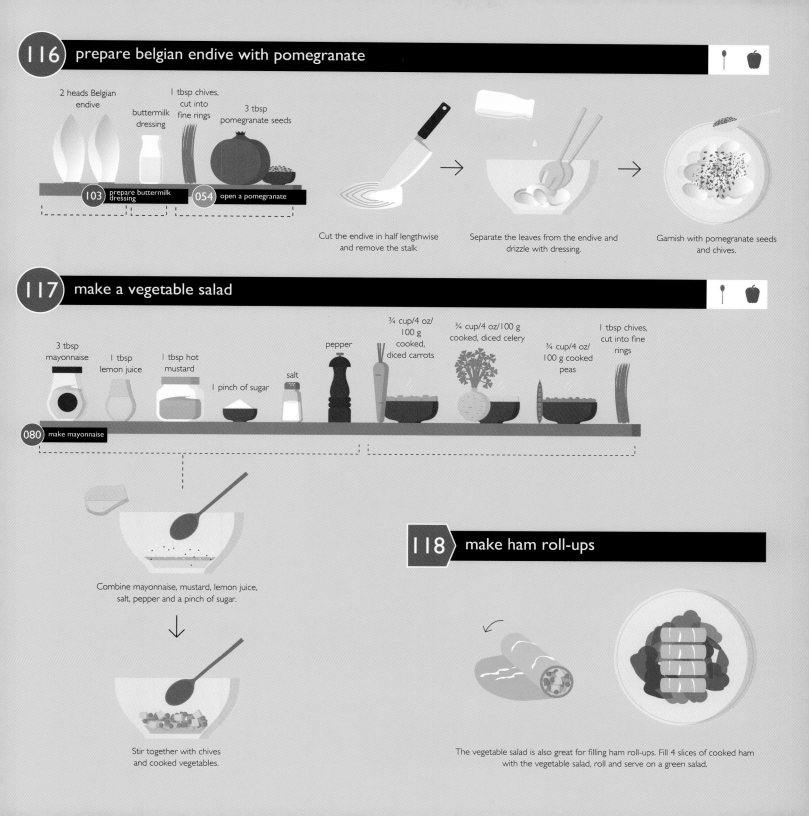

116 prepare belgian endive with pomegranate

2 heads Belgian endive

buttermilk dressing

1 tbsp chives, cut into fine rings

3 tbsp pomegranate seeds

103 prepare buttermilk dressing

054 open a pomegranate

Cut the endive in half lengthwise and remove the stalk

Separate the leaves from the endive and drizzle with dressing.

Garnish with pomegranate seeds and chives.

117 make a vegetable salad

3 tbsp mayonnaise

1 tbsp lemon juice

1 tbsp hot mustard

1 pinch of sugar

salt

pepper

¾ cup/4 oz/100 g cooked, diced carrots

¾ cup/4 oz/100 g cooked, diced celery

¾ cup/4 oz/100 g cooked peas

1 tbsp chives, cut into fine rings

080 make mayonnaise

Combine mayonnaise, mustard, lemon juice, salt, pepper and a pinch of sugar.

Stir together with chives and cooked vegetables.

118 make ham roll-ups

The vegetable salad is also great for filling ham roll-ups. Fill 4 slices of cooked ham with the vegetable salad, roll and serve on a green salad.

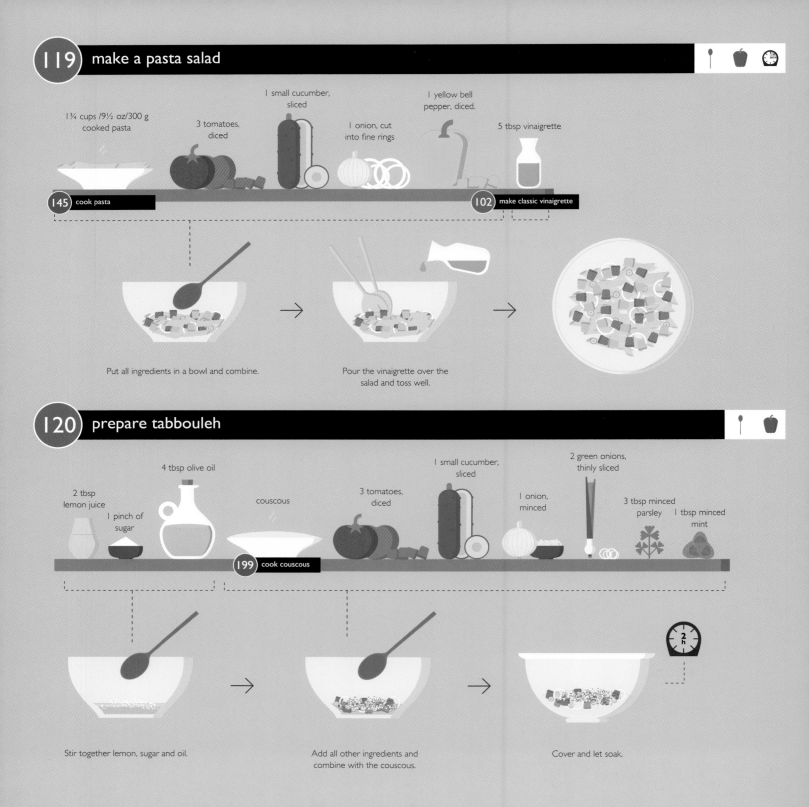

119 make a pasta salad

1¾ cups /9½ oz/300 g cooked pasta

3 tomatoes, diced

1 small cucumber, sliced

1 onion, cut into fine rings

1 yellow bell pepper, diced.

5 tbsp vinaigrette

145 cook pasta

102 make classic vinaigrette

Put all ingredients in a bowl and combine.

Pour the vinaigrette over the salad and toss well.

120 prepare tabbouleh

2 tbsp lemon juice

1 pinch of sugar

4 tbsp olive oil

couscous

3 tomatoes, diced

1 small cucumber, sliced

1 onion, minced

2 green onions, thinly sliced

3 tbsp minced parsley

1 tbsp minced mint

199 cook couscous

Stir together lemon, sugar and oil.

Add all other ingredients and combine with the couscous.

Cover and let soak.

121 make an egg salad

4 hard-boiled eggs, cut in half and sliced

3 pickled gherkins, diced

2 tbsp mayonnaise

1 tbsp minced chives

138 boil eggs

080 make mayonnaise

Combine all ingredients.
Let rest for 1 hour.

122 make an egg salad with vegetables

1 cup/⅓ lb/ 150 g cooked peas

¾ cup/4 oz/ 100 g cooked, diced carrots

2 tbsp capers

Carefully combine all ingredients.

123 make coleslaw

4 cups/12 oz/ 350 g green cabbage, grated

2 carrots, grated

buttermilk dressing

103 prepare buttermilk dressing

Combine grated cabbage and carrots.

Add the dressing and toss well;
cover and let rest for 2 hours.

124 make a caesar salad

2 cups/6½ oz/200 g romaine lettuce, torn into small pieces

4 tbsp croutons (toasted cubes of white bread)

6 tbsp caesar dressing

2 tbsp grated Parmesan

108 prepare caesar dressing

❋ Can be topped with grilled chicken breast, cut into slices.

Stir together salad and croutons.

Pour the dressing over the salad.

Sprinkle with Parmesan.

125 make a waldorf salad

1½ cups/6½ oz/ 200 g celery root strips

2 apples, peeled, cut into strips

3 tbsp chopped walnuts

3 tbsp mayonnaise

2 tbsp lemon juice

2 tbsp sour cream

salt

pepper

2 tbsp chopped walnuts

080 make mayonnaise

Combine apples, celeriac and chopped walnuts.

Stir together mayonnaise, lemon juice and sour cream; season with salt and pepper.

Pour the dressing over the salad and toss well. Cover and refrigerate.

Garnish with walnuts.

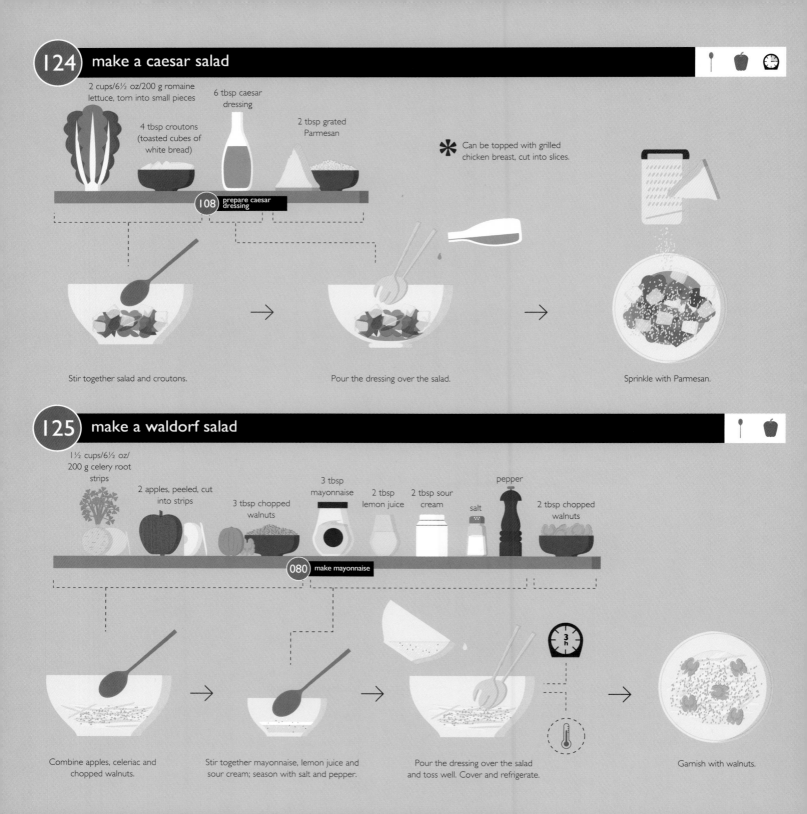

126 prepare buttercream

1 cup/8 oz/ 250 g unsalted butter

⅔ cup/5 oz/150 g sugar

2 egg yolks

Remove the butter and eggs from the refrigerator and let stand at room temperature for 2 hours. Beat butter and sugar until creamy.

Add the egg yolks, one at a time, and beat until combined.

127 prepare chocolate buttercream

Add 1 cup/2½ oz/150 g of melted chocolate and use as filling or frosting for a cake, such as a sponge roll.

375 make a sponge roll

128 prepare chocolate mousse

2½ cups/12½ oz/200 g dark chocolate (at least 60% cocoa), broken into pieces

4 eggs, separated

1 pinch of salt

3 tbsp soft butter

068 separate an egg

Melt the chocolate in a double boiler. Let cool.

Beat the egg whites with a pinch of salt until stiff peaks form.

Melt the butter. Let cool.

Whisk together the egg yolks and butter until creamy. Carefully add the melted chocolate.

Carefully fold in the beaten egg whites. Cover and refrigerate for at least 3 hours.

✳ Good to prepare ahead of time; chill in the refrigerator overnight.

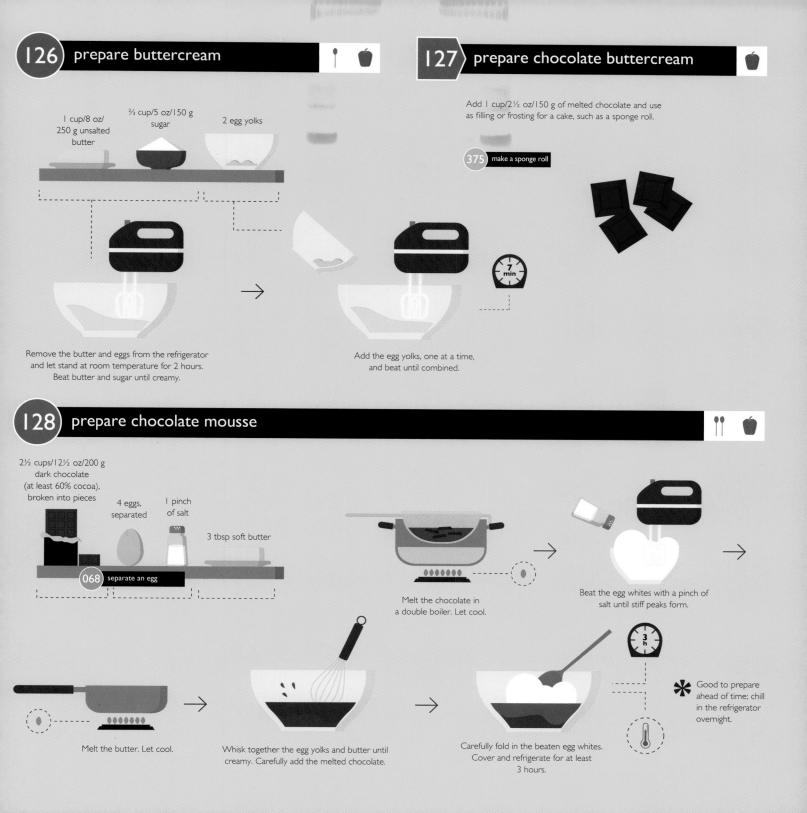

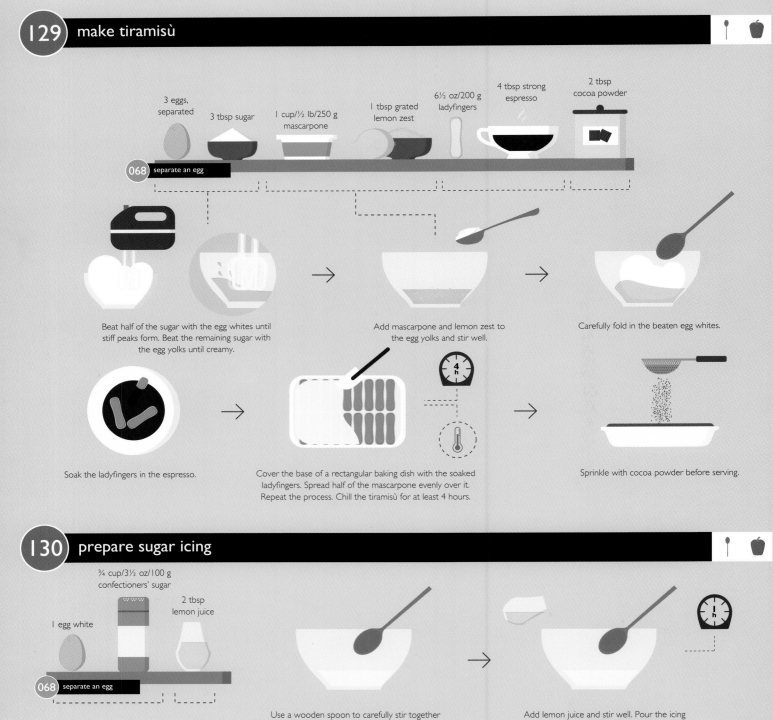

129 make tiramisù

3 eggs, separated

3 tbsp sugar

1 cup/½ lb/250 g mascarpone

1 tbsp grated lemon zest

6½ oz/200 g ladyfingers

4 tbsp strong espresso

2 tbsp cocoa powder

068 separate an egg

Beat half of the sugar with the egg whites until stiff peaks form. Beat the remaining sugar with the egg yolks until creamy.

Add mascarpone and lemon zest to the egg yolks and stir well.

Carefully fold in the beaten egg whites.

Soak the ladyfingers in the espresso.

Cover the base of a rectangular baking dish with the soaked ladyfingers. Spread half of the mascarpone evenly over it. Repeat the process. Chill the tiramisù for at least 4 hours.

Sprinkle with cocoa powder before serving.

130 prepare sugar icing

¾ cup/3½ oz/100 g confectioners' sugar

1 egg white

2 tbsp lemon juice

068 separate an egg

Use a wooden spoon to carefully stir together egg white and sugar. Do not beat.

Add lemon juice and stir well. Pour the icing over a cake and let it set for 1 hour.

prepare chocolate icing

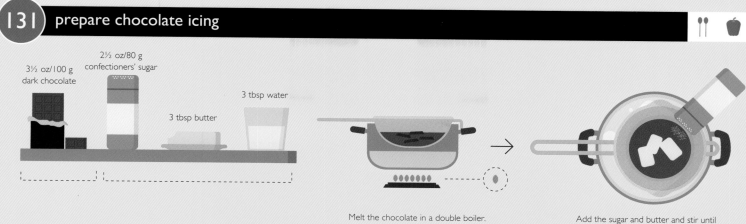

3½ oz/100 g
dark chocolate

2½ oz/80 g
confectioners' sugar

3 tbsp butter

3 tbsp water

Melt the chocolate in a double boiler.

Add the sugar and butter and stir until
combined. Add some water if needed.
Ice a cake while still warm.

ice a perfectly smooth cake

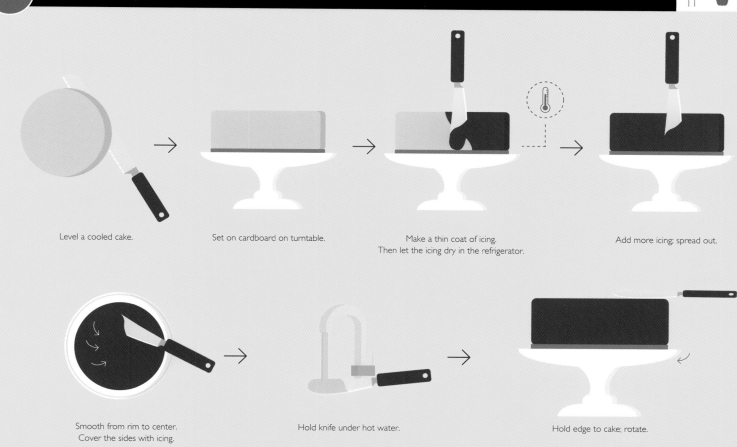

Level a cooled cake.

Set on cardboard on turntable.

Make a thin coat of icing.
Then let the icing dry in the refrigerator.

Add more icing; spread out.

Smooth from rim to center.
Cover the sides with icing.

Hold knife under hot water.

Hold edge to cake; rotate.

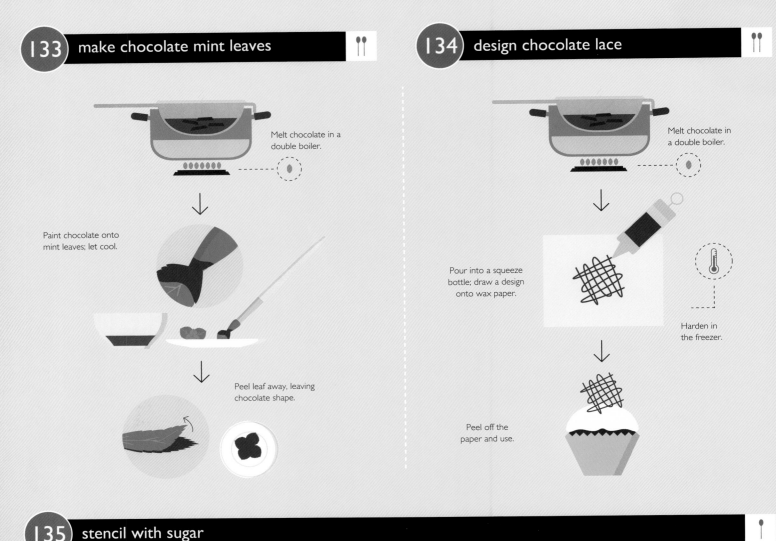

133 make chocolate mint leaves

Melt chocolate in a double boiler.

Paint chocolate onto mint leaves; let cool.

Peel leaf away, leaving chocolate shape.

134 design chocolate lace

Melt chocolate in a double boiler.

Pour into a squeeze bottle; draw a design onto wax paper.

Harden in the freezer.

Peel off the paper and use.

135 stencil with sugar

Set stencil onto cooled cake.

Sift confectioners' sugar over stencil.

136 prepare a fruit salad

juice of 1 lemon

juice of 1 orange

1 tbsp sugar

2 bananas, peeled, thinly sliced

2 apples, peeled, cored, diced

1 pear, peeled, cored, diced

2 tbsp raspberries

½ cup/3½ oz/ 100 g red grapes

¾ cup/3½ oz/100 g peeled, seeded, diced melon

4 mint leaves, slivered

Combine lemon juice, orange juice and sugar in a bowl.

Add fruit and stir well.

Garnish with mint leaves.

137 freeze smoothie pops

1 lb/500 g different fruit

2 tbsp peanut butter

¾ cup/6 fl oz/ 200 ml milk

Blend all ingredients.

Freeze.

8 h

cook

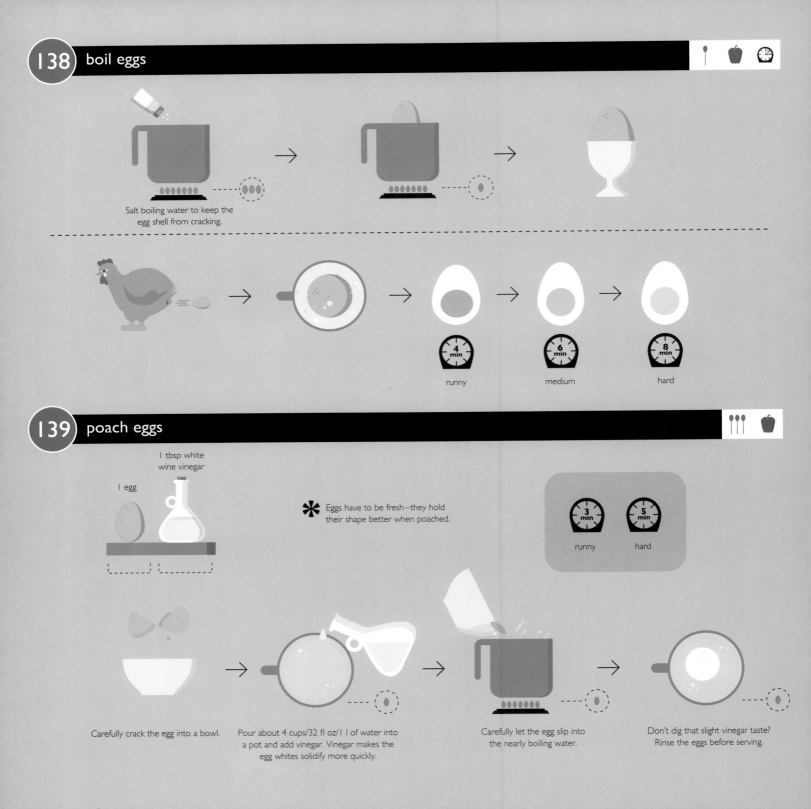

Salt boiling water to keep the
egg shell from cracking.

4 min runny

6 min medium

8 min hard

1 tbsp white
wine vinegar

1 egg

Eggs have to be fresh—they hold
their shape better when poached.

3 min runny

5 min hard

Carefully crack the egg into a bowl.

Pour about 4 cups/32 fl oz/1 l of water into
a pot and add vinegar. Vinegar makes the
egg whites solidify more quickly.

Carefully let the egg slip into
the nearly boiling water.

Don't dig that slight vinegar taste?
Rinse the eggs before serving.

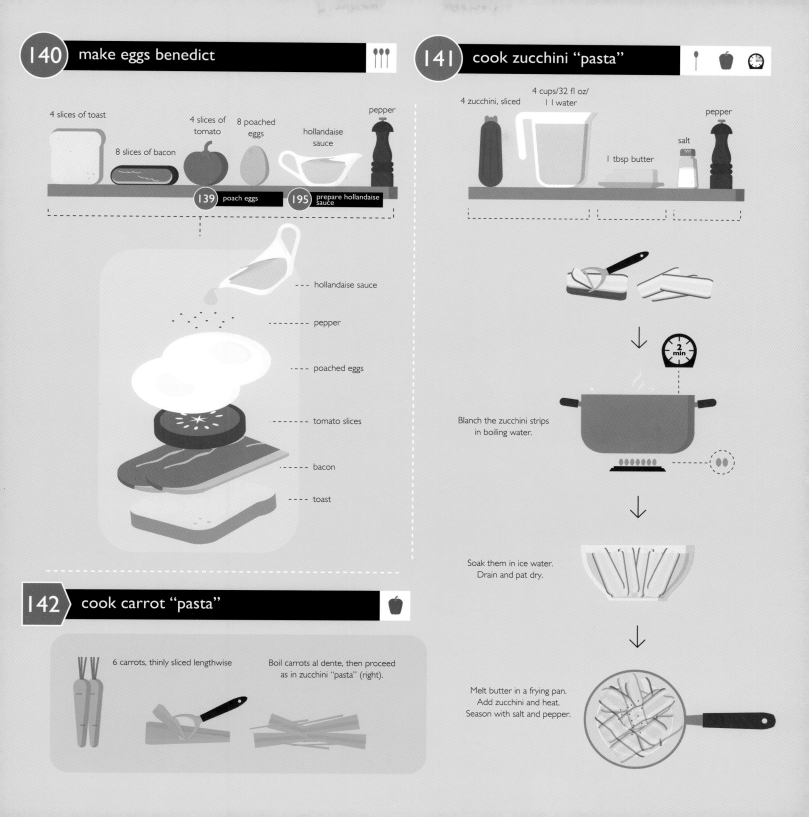

140 make eggs benedict

4 slices of toast

8 slices of bacon

4 slices of tomato

8 poached eggs

hollandaise sauce

pepper

139 poach eggs

195 prepare hollandaise sauce

- - - hollandaise sauce
- - - pepper
- - - poached eggs
- - - - - - tomato slices
- - - - bacon
- - - toast

141 cook zucchini "pasta"

4 zucchini, sliced

4 cups/32 fl oz/ 1 l water

1 tbsp butter

salt

pepper

2 min

Blanch the zucchini strips in boiling water.

Soak them in ice water. Drain and pat dry.

Melt butter in a frying pan. Add zucchini and heat. Season with salt and pepper.

142 cook carrot "pasta"

6 carrots, thinly sliced lengthwise

Boil carrots al dente, then proceed as in zucchini "pasta" (right).

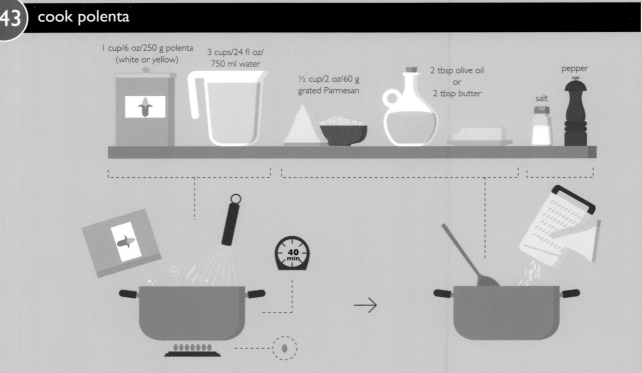

1 cup/6 oz/250 g polenta (white or yellow)

3 cups/24 fl oz/750 ml water

½ cup/2 oz/60 g grated Parmesan

2 tbsp olive oil or 2 tbsp butter

salt

pepper

40 min

Bring water to a boil; then gradually add the polenta. Let it simmer at low heat, stirring constantly.

When polenta is creamy, add cheese and oil or butter. Season with salt and pepper.

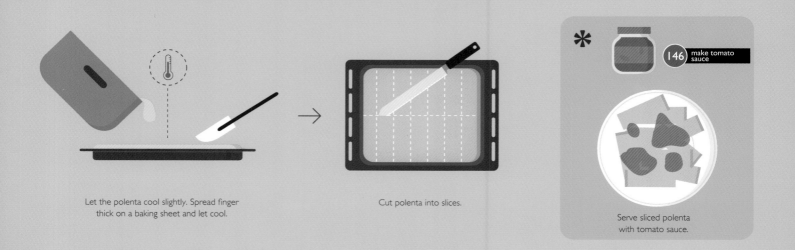

*

146 make tomato sauce

Let the polenta cool slightly. Spread finger thick on a baking sheet and let cool.

Cut polenta into slices.

Serve sliced polenta with tomato sauce.

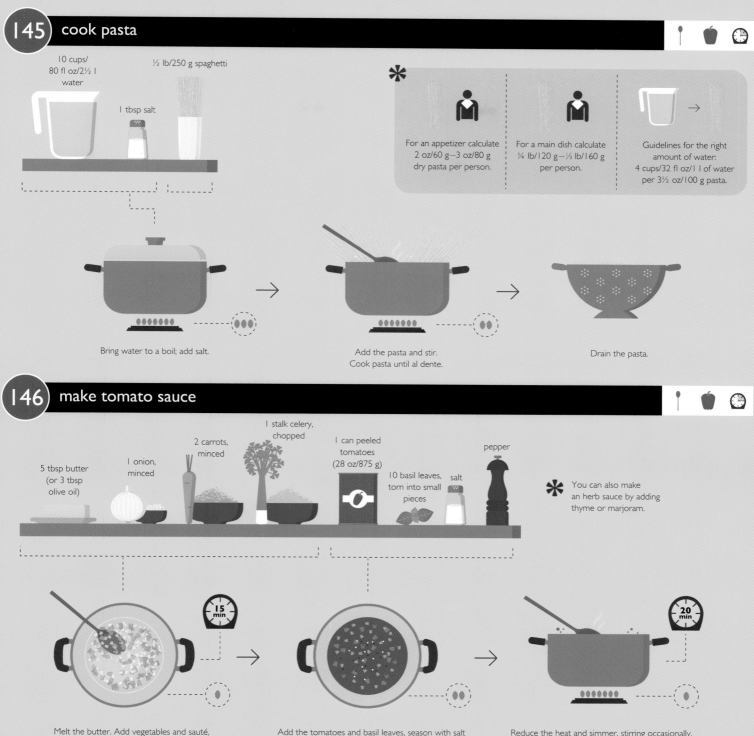

145 cook pasta

10 cups/ 80 fl oz/2½ l water

1 tbsp salt

½ lb/250 g spaghetti

For an appetizer calculate 2 oz/60 g—3 oz/80 g dry pasta per person.

For a main dish calculate ¼ lb/120 g—⅓ lb/160 g per person.

Guidelines for the right amount of water: 4 cups/32 fl oz/1 l of water per 3½ oz/100 g pasta.

Bring water to a boil; add salt.

Add the pasta and stir. Cook pasta until al dente.

Drain the pasta.

146 make tomato sauce

5 tbsp butter (or 3 tbsp olive oil)

1 onion, minced

2 carrots, minced

1 stalk celery, chopped

1 can peeled tomatoes (28 oz/875 g)

10 basil leaves, torn into small pieces

salt

pepper

You can also make an herb sauce by adding thyme or marjoram.

Melt the butter. Add vegetables and sauté, stirring occasionally.

Add the tomatoes and basil leaves, season with salt and pepper and cook until the sauce begins to bubble.

Reduce the heat and simmer, stirring occasionally.

15 min

20 min

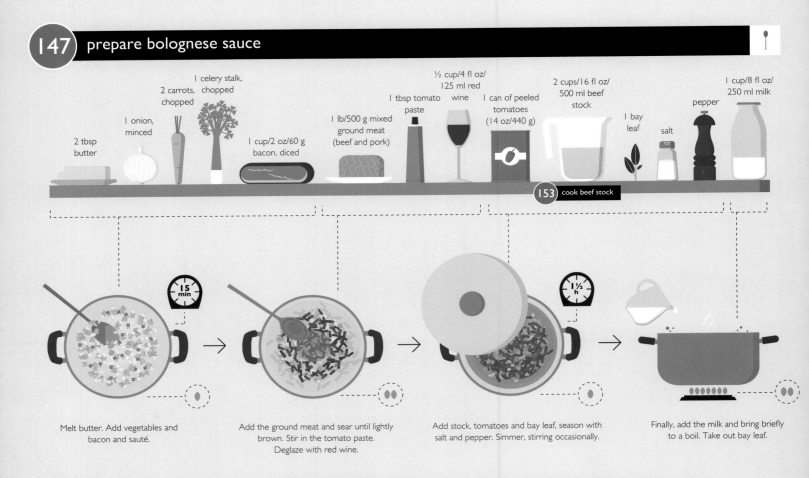

2 tbsp butter

1 onion, minced

2 carrots, chopped

1 celery stalk, chopped

1 cup/2 oz/60 g bacon, diced

1 lb/500 g mixed ground meat (beef and pork)

1 tbsp tomato paste

½ cup/4 fl oz/ 125 ml red wine

1 can of peeled tomatoes (14 oz/440 g)

2 cups/16 fl oz/ 500 ml beef stock

1 bay leaf

salt

pepper

1 cup/8 fl oz/ 250 ml milk

153 cook beef stock

15 min

1½ h

Melt butter. Add vegetables and bacon and sauté.

Add the ground meat and sear until lightly brown. Stir in the tomato paste. Deglaze with red wine.

Add stock, tomatoes and bay leaf, season with salt and pepper. Simmer, stirring occasionally.

Finally, add the milk and bring briefly to a boil. Take out bay leaf.

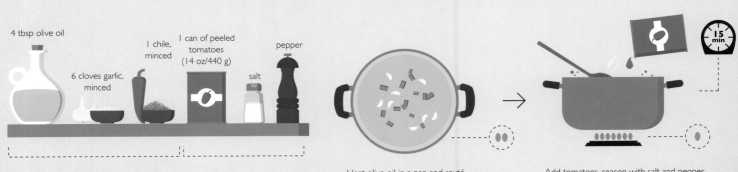

4 tbsp olive oil

6 cloves garlic, minced

1 chile, minced

1 can of peeled tomatoes (14 oz/440 g)

salt

pepper

15 min

Heat olive oil in a pan and sauté chile and garlic.

Add tomatoes, season with salt and pepper. Simmer at low heat.

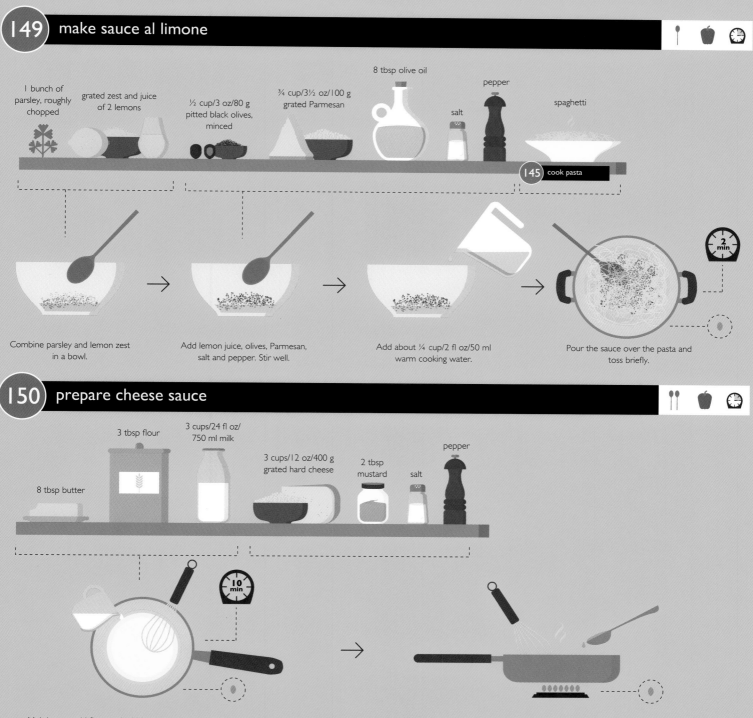

149 make sauce al limone

1 bunch of parsley, roughly chopped

grated zest and juice of 2 lemons

½ cup/3 oz/80 g pitted black olives, minced

¾ cup/3½ oz/100 g grated Parmesan

8 tbsp olive oil

salt

pepper

spaghetti

145 cook pasta

2 min

Combine parsley and lemon zest in a bowl.

Add lemon juice, olives, Parmesan, salt and pepper. Stir well.

Add about ¼ cup/2 fl oz/50 ml warm cooking water.

Pour the sauce over the pasta and toss briefly.

150 prepare cheese sauce

3 tbsp flour

3 cups/24 fl oz/ 750 ml milk

3 cups/12 oz/400 g grated hard cheese

2 tbsp mustard

salt

pepper

8 tbsp butter

10 min

Melt butter, add flour and whisk constantly until a golden paste forms. Gradually whisk in cold milk. Simmer, stirring frequently, until the mixture is thick and creamy, for about 10 minutes.

Add cheese and mustard, season with salt and pepper. Continue to simmer, stirring frequently, until the cheese is melted and the sauce is creamy.

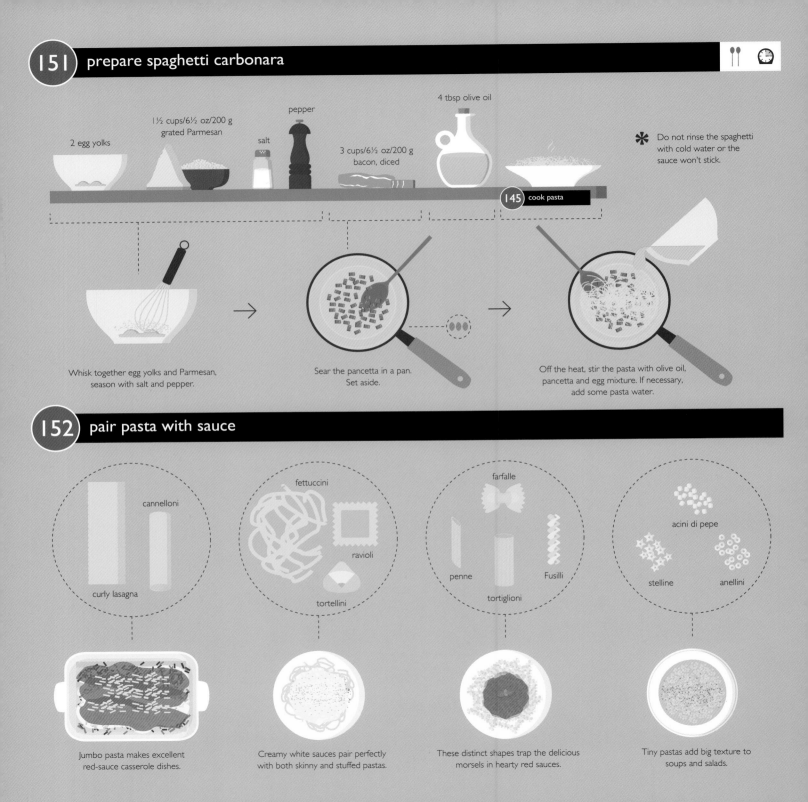

151 prepare spaghetti carbonara

2 egg yolks

1½ cups/6½ oz/200 g grated Parmesan

salt

pepper

3 cups/6½ oz/200 g bacon, diced

4 tbsp olive oil

✳ Do not rinse the spaghetti with cold water or the sauce won't stick.

145 cook pasta

Whisk together egg yolks and Parmesan, season with salt and pepper.

Sear the pancetta in a pan. Set aside.

Off the heat, stir the pasta with olive oil, pancetta and egg mixture. If necessary, add some pasta water.

152 pair pasta with sauce

cannelloni

curly lasagna

Jumbo pasta makes excellent red-sauce casserole dishes.

fettuccini

ravioli

tortellini

Creamy white sauces pair perfectly with both skinny and stuffed pastas.

farfalle

penne

tortiglioni

Fusilli

These distinct shapes trap the delicious morsels in hearty red sauces.

acini di pepe

stelline

anellini

Tiny pastas add big texture to soups and salads.

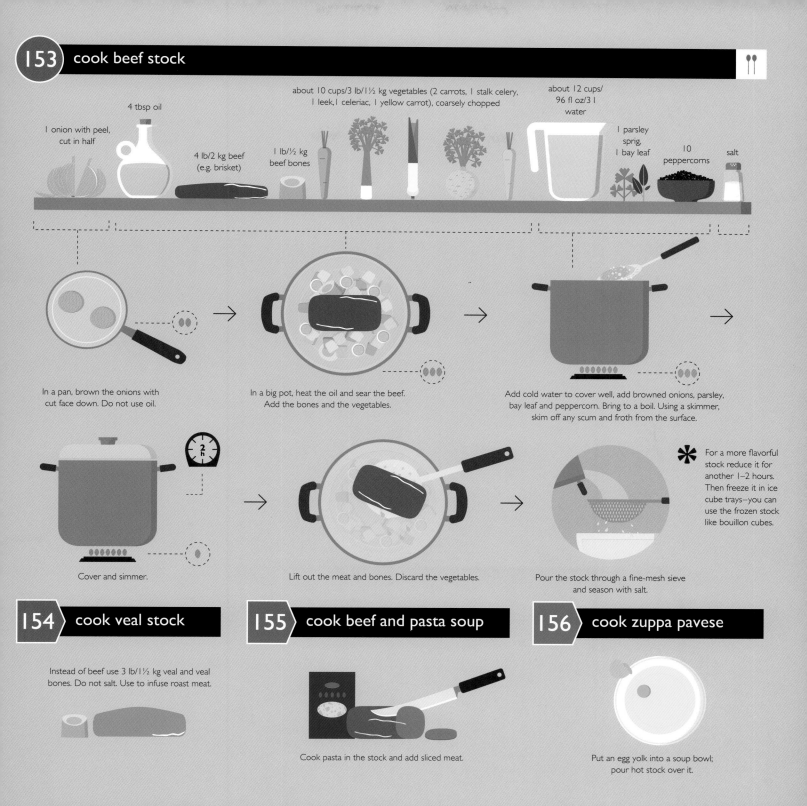

153 | cook beef stock

I onion with peel, cut in half

4 tbsp oil

4 lb/2 kg beef (e.g. brisket)

I lb/½ kg beef bones

about 10 cups/3 lb/1½ kg vegetables (2 carrots, I stalk celery, I leek, I celeriac, I yellow carrot), coarsely chopped

about 12 cups/ 96 fl oz/3 l water

I parsley sprig, I bay leaf

10 peppercorns

salt

In a pan, brown the onions with cut face down. Do not use oil.

In a big pot, heat the oil and sear the beef. Add the bones and the vegetables.

Add cold water to cover well, add browned onions, parsley, bay leaf and peppercorn. Bring to a boil. Using a skimmer, skim off any scum and froth from the surface.

Cover and simmer.

Lift out the meat and bones. Discard the vegetables.

Pour the stock through a fine-mesh sieve and season with salt.

✳ For a more flavorful stock reduce it for another 1–2 hours. Then freeze it in ice cube trays—you can use the frozen stock like bouillon cubes.

154 | cook veal stock

Instead of beef use 3 lb/1½ kg veal and veal bones. Do not salt. Use to infuse roast meat.

155 | cook beef and pasta soup

Cook pasta in the stock and add sliced meat.

156 | cook zuppa pavese

Put an egg yolk into a soup bowl; pour hot stock over it.

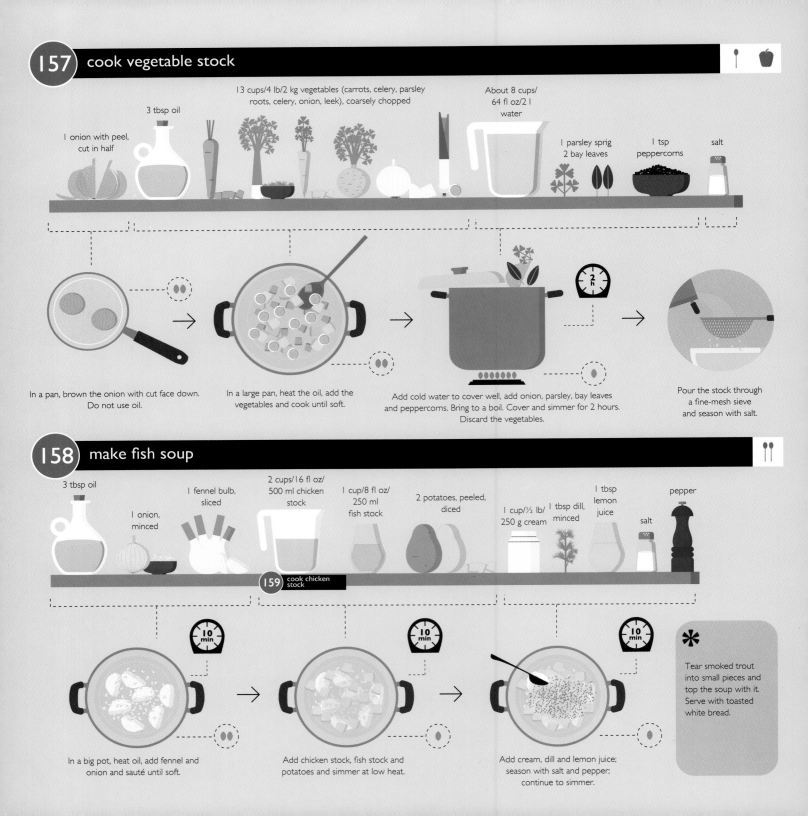

157 cook vegetable stock

I onion with peel, cut in half

3 tbsp oil

13 cups/4 lb/2 kg vegetables (carrots, celery, parsley roots, celery, onion, leek), coarsely chopped

About 8 cups/ 64 fl oz/2 l water

I parsley sprig
2 bay leaves

I tsp peppercorns

salt

In a pan, brown the onion with cut face down. Do not use oil.

In a large pan, heat the oil, add the vegetables and cook until soft.

Add cold water to cover well, add onion, parsley, bay leaves and peppercorns. Bring to a boil. Cover and simmer for 2 hours. Discard the vegetables.

Pour the stock through a fine-mesh sieve and season with salt.

158 make fish soup

3 tbsp oil

I onion, minced

I fennel bulb, sliced

2 cups/16 fl oz/ 500 ml chicken stock

I cup/8 fl oz/ 250 ml fish stock

2 potatoes, peeled, diced

I cup/½ lb/ 250 g cream

I tbsp dill, minced

I tbsp lemon juice

salt

pepper

159 cook chicken stock

In a big pot, heat oil, add fennel and onion and sauté until soft.

Add chicken stock, fish stock and potatoes and simmer at low heat.

Add cream, dill and lemon juice; season with salt and pepper; continue to simmer.

Tear smoked trout into small pieces and top the soup with it. Serve with toasted white bread.

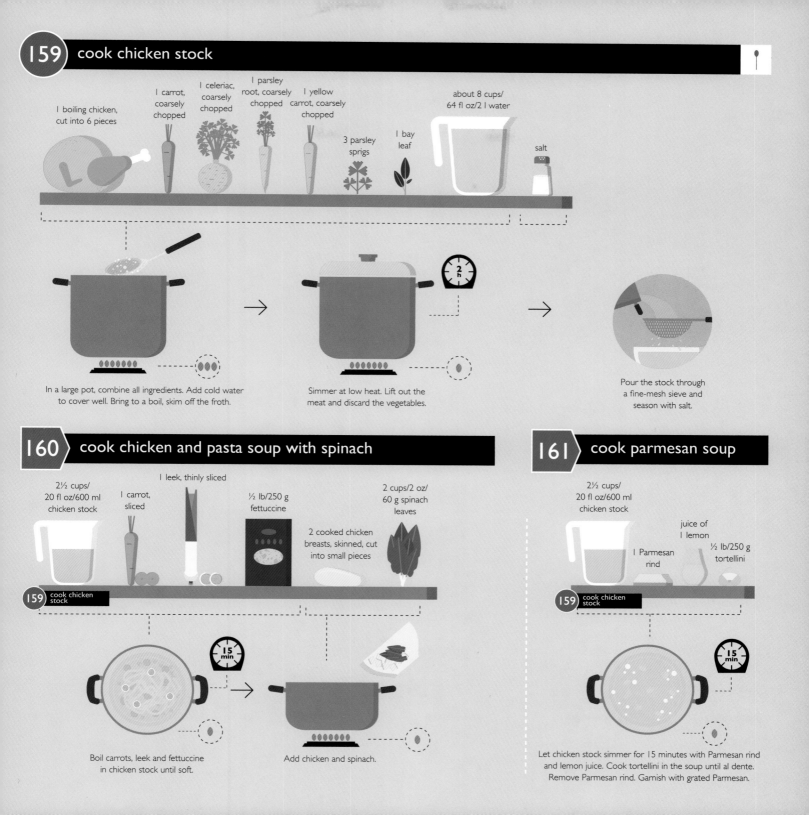

159 cook chicken stock

1 boiling chicken, cut into 6 pieces

1 carrot, coarsely chopped

1 celeriac, coarsely chopped

1 parsley root, coarsely chopped

1 yellow carrot, coarsely chopped

3 parsley sprigs

1 bay leaf

about 8 cups/ 64 fl oz/2 l water

salt

In a large pot, combine all ingredients. Add cold water to cover well. Bring to a boil, skim off the froth.

Simmer at low heat. Lift out the meat and discard the vegetables.

Pour the stock through a fine-mesh sieve and season with salt.

160 cook chicken and pasta soup with spinach

2½ cups/ 20 fl oz/600 ml chicken stock

1 carrot, sliced

1 leek, thinly sliced

½ lb/250 g fettuccine

2 cooked chicken breasts, skinned, cut into small pieces

2 cups/2 oz/ 60 g spinach leaves

159 cook chicken stock

Boil carrots, leek and fettuccine in chicken stock until soft.

Add chicken and spinach.

161 cook parmesan soup

2½ cups/ 20 fl oz/600 ml chicken stock

1 Parmesan rind

juice of 1 lemon

½ lb/250 g tortellini

159 cook chicken stock

Let chicken stock simmer for 15 minutes with Parmesan rind and lemon juice. Cook tortellini in the soup until al dente. Remove Parmesan rind. Garnish with grated Parmesan.

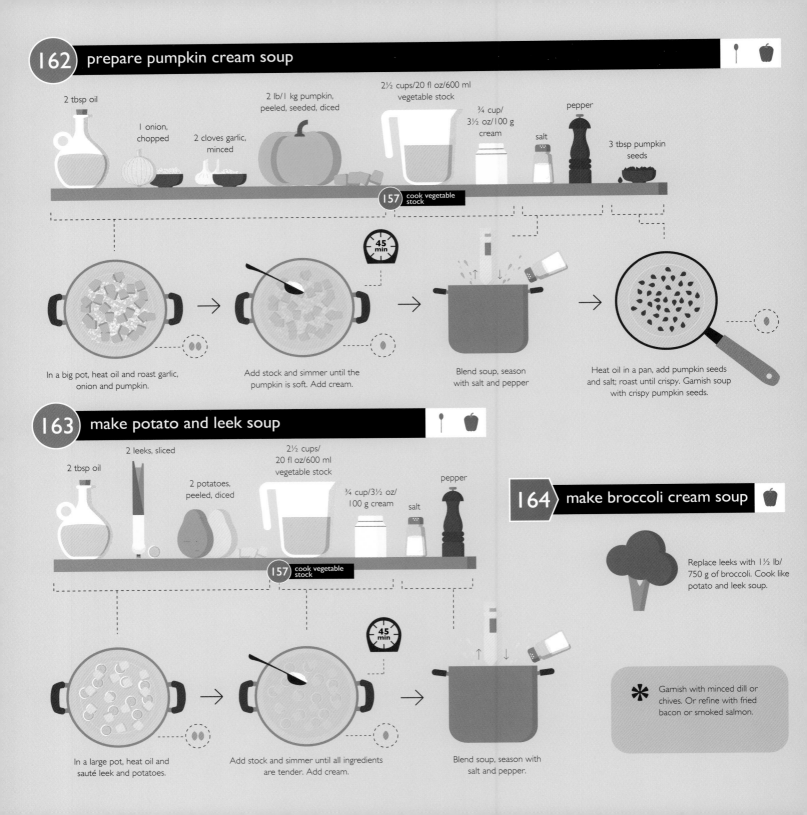

162 prepare pumpkin cream soup

2 tbsp oil

1 onion, chopped

2 cloves garlic, minced

2 lb/1 kg pumpkin, peeled, seeded, diced

2½ cups/20 fl oz/600 ml vegetable stock

¾ cup/3½ oz/100 g cream

salt

pepper

3 tbsp pumpkin seeds

157 cook vegetable stock

45 min

In a big pot, heat oil and roast garlic, onion and pumpkin.

Add stock and simmer until the pumpkin is soft. Add cream.

Blend soup, season with salt and pepper

Heat oil in a pan, add pumpkin seeds and salt; roast until crispy. Garnish soup with crispy pumpkin seeds.

163 make potato and leek soup

2 tbsp oil

2 leeks, sliced

2 potatoes, peeled, diced

2½ cups/20 fl oz/600 ml vegetable stock

¾ cup/3½ oz/100 g cream

salt

pepper

157 cook vegetable stock

45 min

In a large pot, heat oil and sauté leek and potatoes.

Add stock and simmer until all ingredients are tender. Add cream.

Blend soup, season with salt and pepper.

164 make broccoli cream soup

Replace leeks with 1½ lb/750 g of broccoli. Cook like potato and leek soup.

✳ Garnish with minced dill or chives. Or refine with fried bacon or smoked salmon.

165 make carrot soup with ginger

2 tbsp oil

1 onion, minced

2 cloves garlic, minced

4 cups/2 lb/1 kg carrots, sliced

1 small piece of ginger, peeled, sliced

2½ cups/20 fl oz/600 ml vegetable stock

157 cook vegetable stock

¾ cup/3½ oz/100 g cream

salt

pepper

35 min

In a big pot, heat oil and sauté onions, carrots, garlic and ginger.

Add stock and simmer until carrots are tender. Add cream.

Blend soup, season with salt and pepper.

166 cook red lentil soup with chile

2 tbsp oil

1 onion, chopped

1 chile, finely minced

¾ cup/6½ oz/200 g red lentils

1 carrot, diced

1 tomato, skinned, seeds removed, diced

4 tbsp lemon juice

3¼ cups/26 fl oz/800 ml vegetable stock

salt

pepper

045 dice a chile pepper

050 peel tomatoes

157 cook vegetable stock

40 min

In a large sauce pan, heat oil and sauté onion, chile, lentils, carrots and tomatoes.

Add lemon juice and stock and simmer until lentils are very tender.

Blend soup, season with salt and pepper.

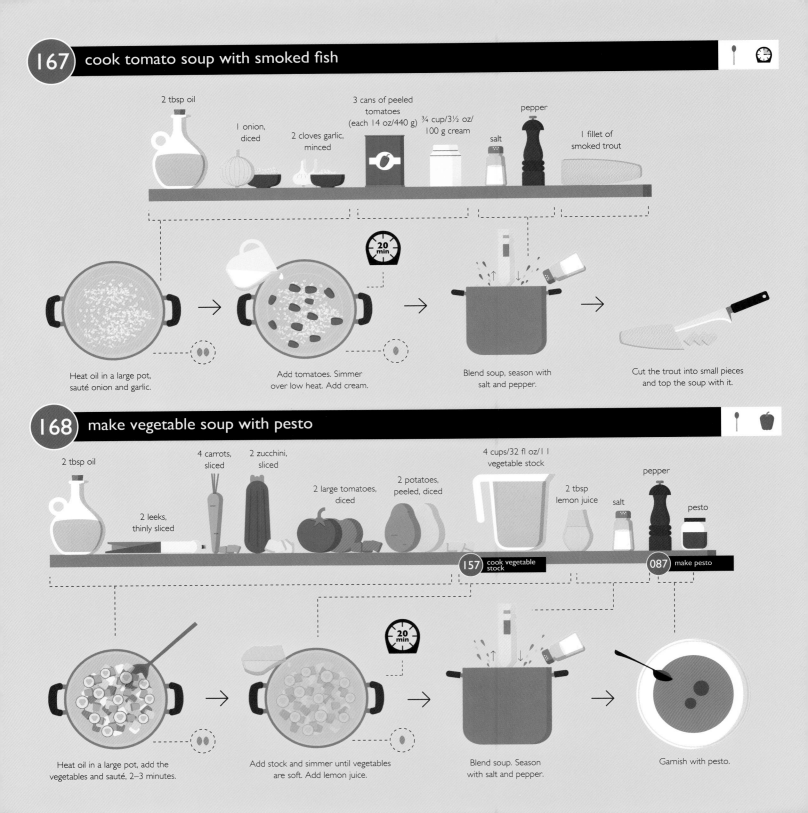

2 tbsp oil

1 onion, diced

2 cloves garlic, minced

3 cans of peeled tomatoes (each 14 oz/440 g)

¾ cup/3½ oz/ 100 g cream

salt

pepper

1 fillet of smoked trout

20 min

Heat oil in a large pot, sauté onion and garlic.

Add tomatoes. Simmer over low heat. Add cream.

Blend soup, season with salt and pepper.

Cut the trout into small pieces and top the soup with it.

168 make vegetable soup with pesto

2 tbsp oil

2 leeks, thinly sliced

4 carrots, sliced

2 zucchini, sliced

2 large tomatoes, diced

2 potatoes, peeled, diced

4 cups/32 fl oz/1 l vegetable stock

2 tbsp lemon juice

salt

pepper

pesto

157 cook vegetable stock

087 make pesto

20 min

Heat oil in a large pot, add the vegetables and sauté, 2–3 minutes.

Add stock and simmer until vegetables are soft. Add lemon juice.

Blend soup. Season with salt and pepper.

Garnish with pesto.

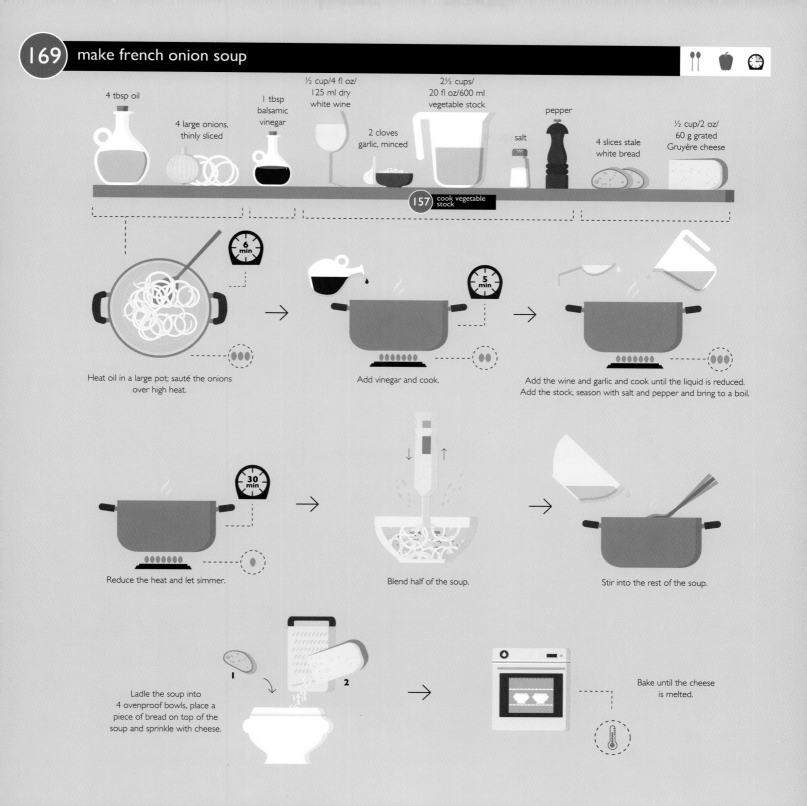

4 tbsp oil

4 large onions, thinly sliced

1 tbsp balsamic vinegar

½ cup/4 fl oz/ 125 ml dry white wine

2 cloves garlic, minced

2½ cups/ 20 fl oz/600 ml vegetable stock

salt

pepper

4 slices stale white bread

½ cup/2 oz/ 60 g grated Gruyère cheese

157 cook vegetable stock

6 min

Heat oil in a large pot; sauté the onions over high heat.

5 min

Add vinegar and cook.

Add the wine and garlic and cook until the liquid is reduced. Add the stock, season with salt and pepper and bring to a boil.

30 min

Reduce the heat and let simmer.

Blend half of the soup.

Stir into the rest of the soup.

Ladle the soup into 4 ovenproof bowls, place a piece of bread on top of the soup and sprinkle with cheese.

1

2

Bake until the cheese is melted.

4 tbsp olive oil

2 carrots, chopped

2 large onions, minced

2 potatoes, peeled, diced

2 zucchini, sliced

3 thyme sprigs, leaves plucked off

4 cups/ 32 fl oz/ 1 l water

¾ cup/6½ oz/ 200 g canned peeled tomatoes

½ head cabbage, shredded

1½ cups/ 13 oz/400 g canned white beans, drained

4 slices rustic bread, torn into pieces

5 cups/5 oz/ 150 g spinach leaves

salt

pepper

15 min

Heat oil in a large pot; sauté the vegetables with the thyme until softened.

45 min

Stir in tomatoes, cabbage and water. Simmer over low heat.

10 min

Stir in beans and cook over low heat. Season with salt and pepper.

Cover and refrigerate overnight.

20 min

Add bread and spinach to the soup and simmer at low heat; stir to break up the bread.

❋ Drizzle generously with olive oil before serving.

171 make miso soup

3 cups/24 fl oz/750 ml
water

about 3 inch/8 cm
kombu seaweed

1 tbsp bonito
flakes

2 tbsp white
miso paste

❋ Use 3–4 shiitake mushrooms
instead of bonito flakes for
a vegetarian miso soup.

In a large pot, bring water to a boil and
add kombu seaweed; cook until soft.

Remove from the heat and
take out the seaweed.

Stir in the bonito flakes
and simmer.

5 min

Mix the miso paste with 6 tbsp of the
hot liquid until a smooth paste forms.

Stir the miso mixture into the soup
and heat—do not let it boil!

172 make miso soup with tofu

3 cups/3 oz/100 g
spinach leaves

3½ oz/100 g
diced tofu

Heat diced tofu and spinach
in the soup until warm.

173 make miso soup with halibut

2 green onions,
thinly sliced

5 min

4 fillets of halibut
about ⅓ lb/
150 g

Heat 2 tbsp of oil in a pan. Fry the halibut fillets for about
5 minutes on each side. Add to the soup and garnish with onions.

174 make miso soup with rice vermicelli

6½ oz/200 g
rice vermicelli

3 cups/3 oz/
100 g
spinach leaves

6½ oz/200 g cooked chicken
breast, cut into bite-size pieces

Add rice vermicelli, chicken and spinach
to the soup and simmer until warm.

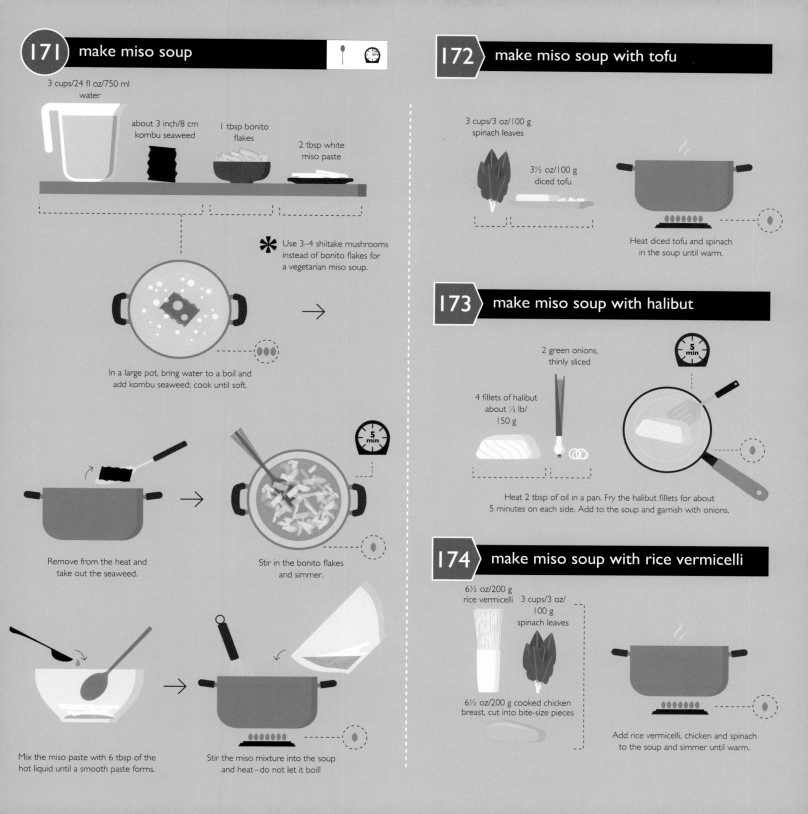

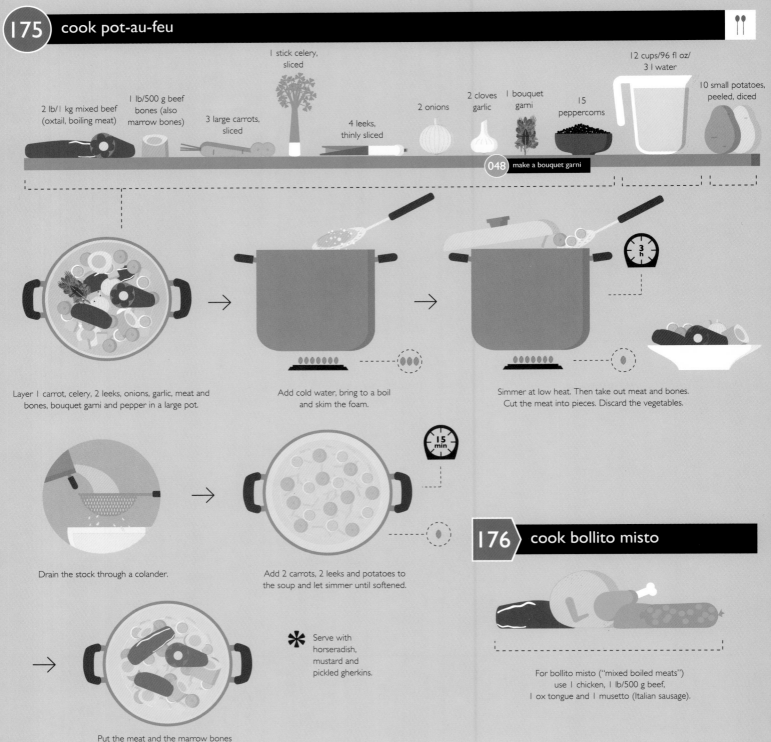

2 lb/1 kg mixed beef (oxtail, boiling meat)

1 lb/500 g beef bones (also marrow bones)

3 large carrots, sliced

1 stick celery, sliced

4 leeks, thinly sliced

2 onions

2 cloves garlic

1 bouquet garni

15 peppercorns

12 cups/96 fl oz/ 3 l water

10 small potatoes, peeled, diced

048   make a bouquet garni

3 h

Layer 1 carrot, celery, 2 leeks, onions, garlic, meat and bones, bouquet garni and pepper in a large pot.

Add cold water, bring to a boil and skim the foam.

Simmer at low heat. Then take out meat and bones. Cut the meat into pieces. Discard the vegetables.

15 min

Drain the stock through a colander.

Add 2 carrots, 2 leeks and potatoes to the soup and let simmer until softened.

✳ Serve with horseradish, mustard and pickled gherkins.

Put the meat and the marrow bones back in the soup and heat.

176   cook bollito misto

For bollito misto ("mixed boiled meats") use 1 chicken, 1 lb/500 g beef, 1 ox tongue and 1 musetto (Italian sausage).

177 cook rice

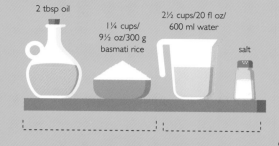

2 tbsp oil

1¼ cups/ 9½ oz/300 g basmati rice

2½ cups/20 fl oz/ 600 ml water

salt

12 min

5 min

Heat oil in a pot, add rice and stir constantly until the rice is translucent.

Add water and salt, stir and simmer at low heat until the liquid is completely absorbed.

Let rest, then fluff the rice with a fork.

178 cook saffron pilaf rice

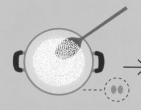

1 pinch of saffron

1 onion, chopped

1 tbsp paprika powder

1½ cups/ 12 fl oz/400 ml chicken stock

1 cinnamon stick

salt

pepper

159 cook chicken stock

Cook the rice as described above in the chicken stock together with the spices.

179 cook rice and pea soup with chicken

Boil the rice as described above. Add ¾ cup/4 oz/ 100 g boiled peas and ⅓ lb/ 150 g cooked and thinly sliced chicken breast to the rice.

180 make sushi rice

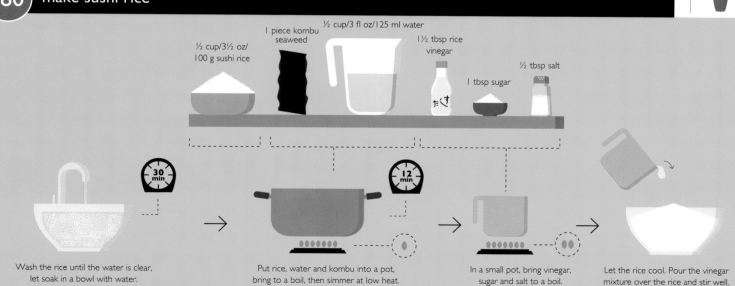

½ cup/3½ oz/ 100 g sushi rice

1 piece kombu seaweed

½ cup/3 fl oz/125 ml water

1½ tbsp rice vinegar

1 tbsp sugar

½ tbsp salt

30 min

12 min

Wash the rice until the water is clear, let soak in a bowl with water.

Put rice, water and kombu into a pot, bring to a boil, then simmer at low heat.

In a small pot, bring vinegar, sugar and salt to a boil.

Let the rice cool. Pour the vinegar mixture over the rice and stir well.

181 make risotto

3 tbsp butter

1 onion, minced

1½ cups/11 oz/ 350 g risotto rice (Arborio, Canaroli)

½ cup/4 fl oz/ 125 ml white wine

about 4 cups/ 32 fl oz/1 l vegetable stock (or chicken stock)

salt

pepper

3 tbsp grated Parmesan

157 cook vegetable stock

159 cook chicken stock

5 min

Heat half of the butter in a pot, add onions and cook until softened.

Add rice and stir constantly until the rice is translucent. Pour in the wine and stir until completely absorbed.

15 min

Add the stock gradually, simmer, stirring until most of the liquid has been absorbed before adding more stock. The rice should be tender but slightly firm at the center.

Add Parmesan and the rest of the butter. Season with salt and pepper. The risotto should be creamy. If necessary, add more stock.

182 make risotto alla milanese

½ cup/4 fl oz/ 125 ml white wine

20 saffron threads

Cook the saffron in wine and add to the risotto.

183 make champagne risotto

½ cup/4 fl oz/ 125 ml champagne

Use champagne instead of wine. Add a small amount of champagne before serving.

184 make red wine risotto

¾ cup/6 fl oz/ 200 ml red wine

6½ oz/200 g fried salsiccia, sliced

Use red wine instead of white wine. Add the salsiccia right before serving.

185 make asparagus risotto

6½ oz/200 g asparagus

½ cup/4 fl oz/ 125 ml white wine

15 min

Peel asparagus and boil the peel in wine. Take out the peel and add the liquid to the risotto.

Cut asparagus into small pieces. Add asparagus pieces 10 minutes before cooking time ends.

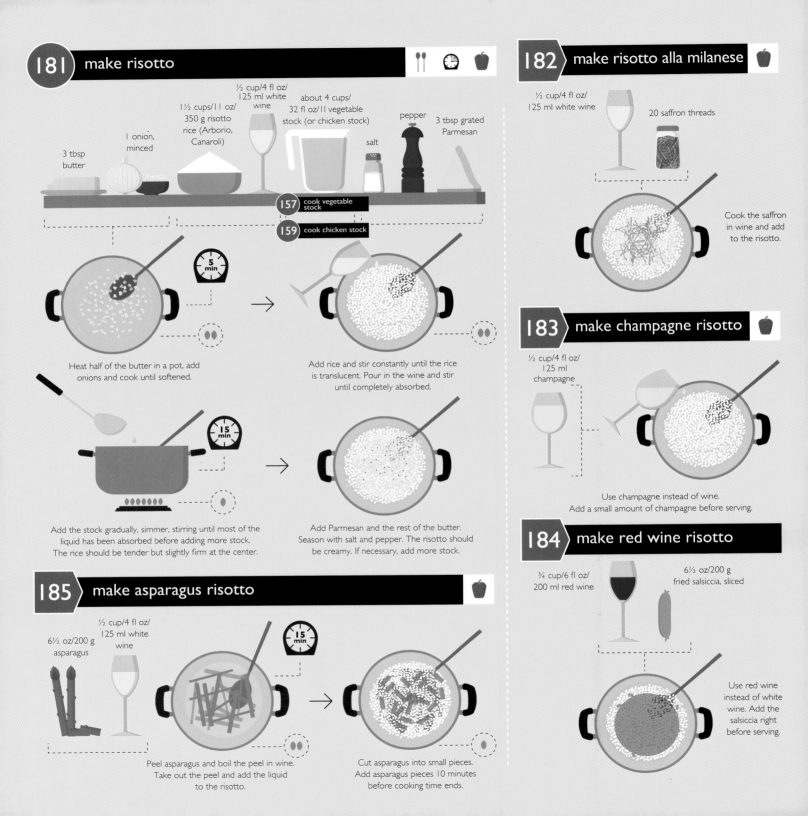

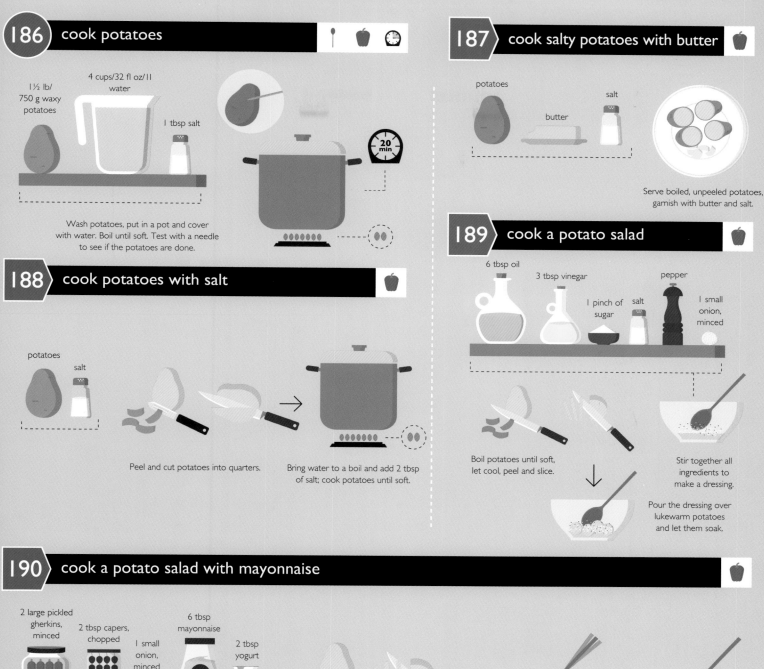

186 cook potatoes

1 ½ lb/ 750 g waxy potatoes

4 cups/32 fl oz/1l water

1 tbsp salt

20 min

Wash potatoes, put in a pot and cover with water. Boil until soft. Test with a needle to see if the potatoes are done.

187 cook salty potatoes with butter

potatoes

butter

salt

Serve boiled, unpeeled potatoes, garnish with butter and salt.

188 cook potatoes with salt

potatoes

salt

Peel and cut potatoes into quarters.

Bring water to a boil and add 2 tbsp of salt; cook potatoes until soft.

189 cook a potato salad

6 tbsp oil

3 tbsp vinegar

1 pinch of sugar

salt

pepper

1 small onion, minced

Boil potatoes until soft, let cool, peel and slice.

Stir together all ingredients to make a dressing.

Pour the dressing over lukewarm potatoes and let them soak.

190 cook a potato salad with mayonnaise

2 large pickled gherkins, minced

2 tbsp capers, chopped

1 small onion, minced

6 tbsp mayonnaise

2 tbsp yogurt

080 make mayonnaise

Boil unpeeled potatoes until tender. Let them cool, peel and cut into slices.

Stir together all ingredients and add to the potatoes.

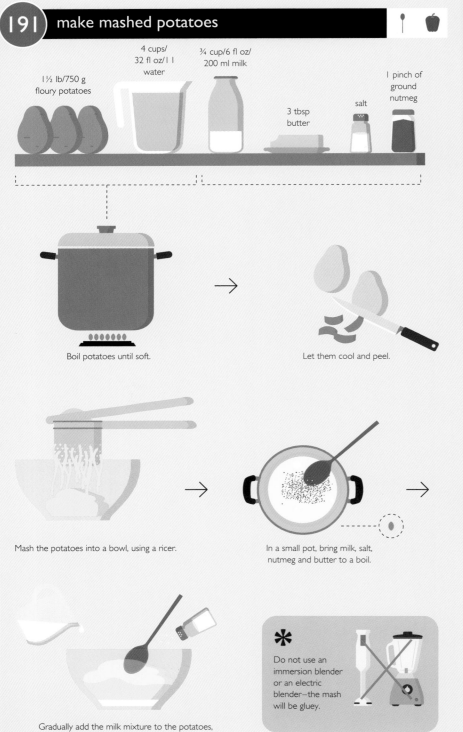

191 make mashed potatoes

1½ lb/750 g floury potatoes

4 cups/ 32 fl oz/1 l water

¾ cup/6 fl oz/ 200 ml milk

3 tbsp butter

salt

1 pinch of ground nutmeg

Boil potatoes until soft.

Let them cool and peel.

Mash the potatoes into a bowl, using a ricer.

In a small pot, bring milk, salt, nutmeg and butter to a boil.

Gradually add the milk mixture to the potatoes, the mashed potatoes should be smooth and creamy. Season with salt if necessary.

✳ Do not use an immersion blender or an electric blender—the mash will be gluey.

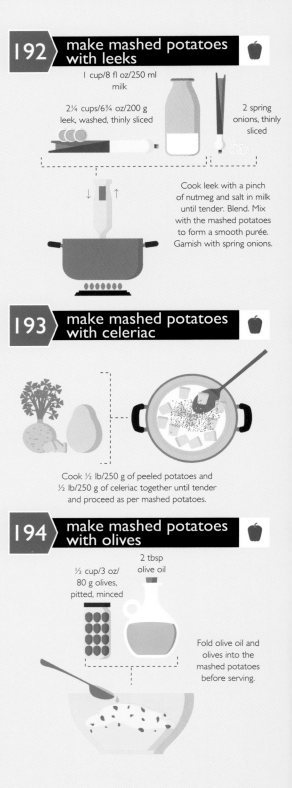

192 make mashed potatoes with leeks

1 cup/8 fl oz/250 ml milk

2¼ cups/6¾ oz/200 g leek, washed, thinly sliced

2 spring onions, thinly sliced

Cook leek with a pinch of nutmeg and salt in milk until tender. Blend. Mix with the mashed potatoes to form a smooth purée. Garnish with spring onions.

193 make mashed potatoes with celeriac

Cook ½ lb/250 g of peeled potatoes and ½ lb/250 g of celeriac together until tender and proceed as per mashed potatoes.

194 make mashed potatoes with olives

½ cup/3 oz/ 80 g olives, pitted, minced

2 tbsp olive oil

Fold olive oil and olives into the mashed potatoes before serving.

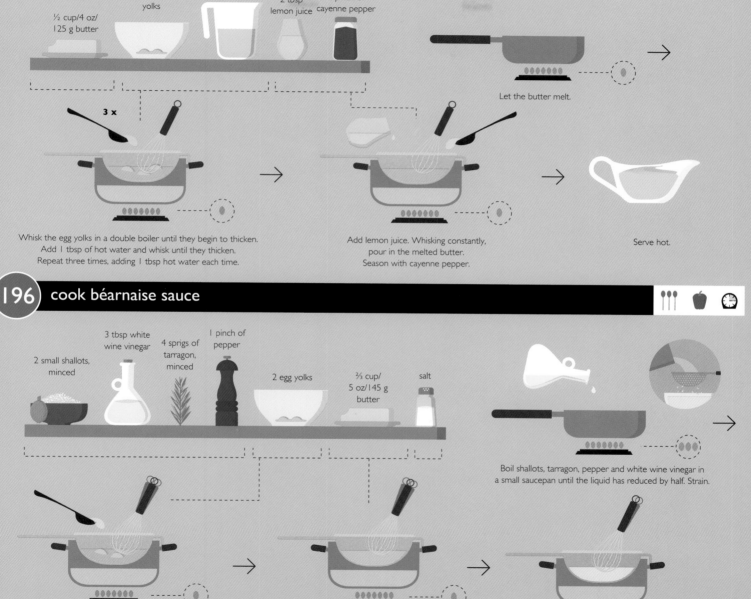

195 prepare hollandaise sauce

½ cup/4 oz/ 125 g butter

3 egg yolks

hot water

2 tbsp lemon juice

1 pinch of cayenne pepper

Let the butter melt.

3 x

Whisk the egg yolks in a double boiler until they begin to thicken.
Add 1 tbsp of hot water and whisk until they thicken.
Repeat three times, adding 1 tbsp hot water each time.

Add lemon juice. Whisking constantly,
pour in the melted butter.
Season with cayenne pepper.

Serve hot.

196 cook béarnaise sauce

2 small shallots, minced

3 tbsp white wine vinegar

4 sprigs of tarragon, minced

1 pinch of pepper

2 egg yolks

⅔ cup/ 5 oz/145 g butter

salt

Boil shallots, tarragon, pepper and white wine vinegar in
a small saucepan until the liquid has reduced by half. Strain.

Whisk the egg yolks in a double boiler until
they begin to thicken. Constantly whisking,
add the vinegar mixture.

Add two thirds of the butter in small pieces
and keep whisking.

Remove from the heat and add the last third
of the butter. The sauce should be fluffy
but thick. Season with salt.

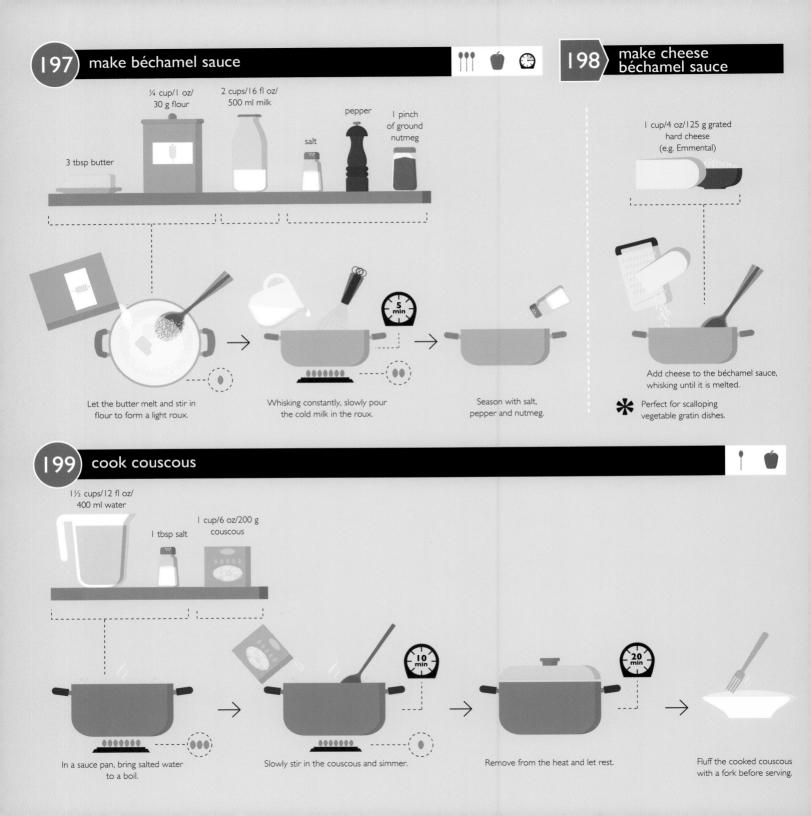

197 make béchamel sauce

3 tbsp butter

¼ cup/1 oz/ 30 g flour

2 cups/16 fl oz/ 500 ml milk

salt

pepper

1 pinch of ground nutmeg

Let the butter melt and stir in flour to form a light roux.

5 min

Whisking constantly, slowly pour the cold milk in the roux.

Season with salt, pepper and nutmeg.

198 make cheese béchamel sauce

1 cup/4 oz/125 g grated hard cheese (e.g. Emmental)

Add cheese to the béchamel sauce, whisking until it is melted.

✳ Perfect for scalloping vegetable gratin dishes.

199 cook couscous

1½ cups/12 fl oz/ 400 ml water

1 tbsp salt

1 cup/6 oz/200 g couscous

In a sauce pan, bring salted water to a boil.

10 min

Slowly stir in the couscous and simmer.

20 min

Remove from the heat and let rest.

Fluff the cooked couscous with a fork before serving.

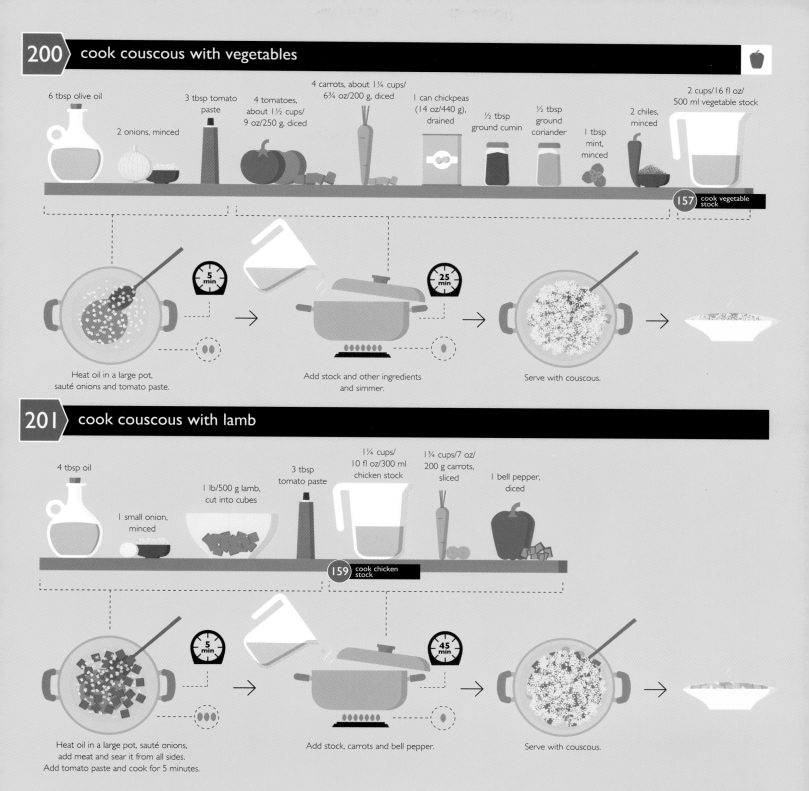

200 cook couscous with vegetables

6 tbsp olive oil

2 onions, minced

3 tbsp tomato paste

4 tomatoes, about 1½ cups/ 9 oz/250 g, diced

4 carrots, about 1¼ cups/ 6¾ oz/200 g, diced

1 can chickpeas (14 oz/440 g), drained

½ tbsp ground cumin

½ tbsp ground coriander

1 tbsp mint, minced

2 chiles, minced

2 cups/16 fl oz/ 500 ml vegetable stock

157 cook vegetable stock

5 min

25 min

Heat oil in a large pot, sauté onions and tomato paste.

Add stock and other ingredients and simmer.

Serve with couscous.

201 cook couscous with lamb

4 tbsp oil

1 small onion, minced

1 lb/500 g lamb, cut into cubes

3 tbsp tomato paste

1¼ cups/ 10 fl oz/300 ml chicken stock

1¾ cups/7 oz/ 200 g carrots, sliced

1 bell pepper, diced

159 cook chicken stock

5 min

45 min

Heat oil in a large pot, sauté onions, add meat and sear it from all sides. Add tomato paste and cook for 5 minutes.

Add stock, carrots and bell pepper.

Serve with couscous.

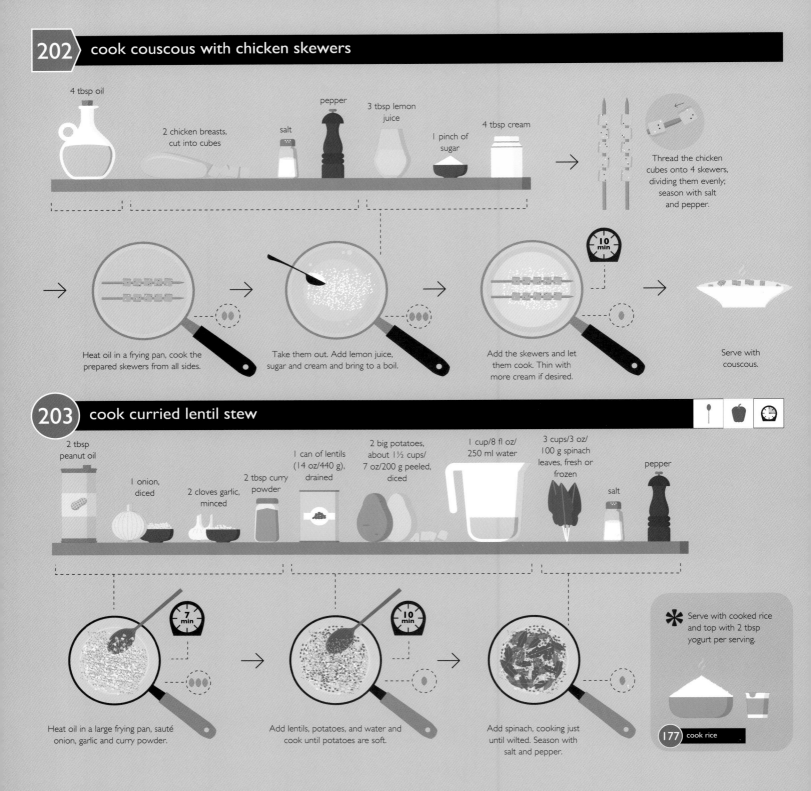

202 | cook couscous with chicken skewers

4 tbsp oil

2 chicken breasts, cut into cubes

salt

pepper

3 tbsp lemon juice

1 pinch of sugar

4 tbsp cream

Thread the chicken cubes onto 4 skewers, dividing them evenly; season with salt and pepper.

Heat oil in a frying pan, cook the prepared skewers from all sides.

Take them out. Add lemon juice, sugar and cream and bring to a boil.

10 min
Add the skewers and let them cook. Thin with more cream if desired.

Serve with couscous.

203 | cook curried lentil stew

2 tbsp peanut oil

1 onion, diced

2 cloves garlic, minced

2 tbsp curry powder

1 can of lentils (14 oz/440 g), drained

2 big potatoes, about 1½ cups/ 7 oz/200 g peeled, diced

1 cup/8 fl oz/ 250 ml water

3 cups/3 oz/ 100 g spinach leaves, fresh or frozen

salt

pepper

7 min
Heat oil in a large frying pan, sauté onion, garlic and curry powder.

10 min
Add lentils, potatoes, and water and cook until potatoes are soft.

Add spinach, cooking just until wilted. Season with salt and pepper.

✳ Serve with cooked rice and top with 2 tbsp yogurt per serving.

177 cook rice

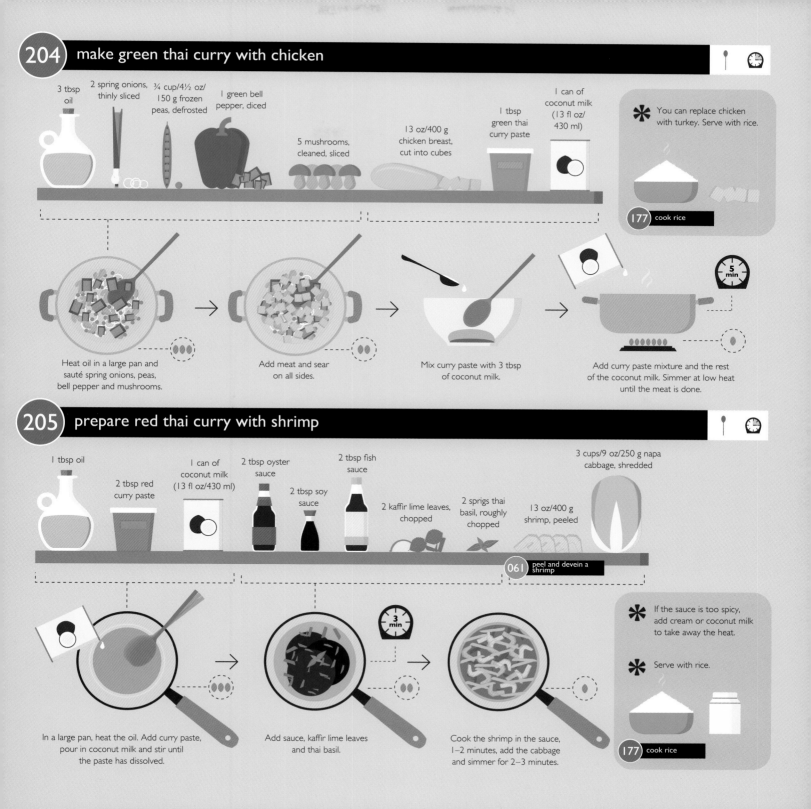

204 make green thai curry with chicken

3 tbsp oil

2 spring onions, thinly sliced

¾ cup/4½ oz/150 g frozen peas, defrosted

1 green bell pepper, diced

5 mushrooms, cleaned, sliced

13 oz/400 g chicken breast, cut into cubes

1 tbsp green thai curry paste

1 can of coconut milk (13 fl oz/430 ml)

❋ You can replace chicken with turkey. Serve with rice.

177 cook rice

Heat oil in a large pan and sauté spring onions, peas, bell pepper and mushrooms.

Add meat and sear on all sides.

Mix curry paste with 3 tbsp of coconut milk.

5 min

Add curry paste mixture and the rest of the coconut milk. Simmer at low heat until the meat is done.

205 prepare red thai curry with shrimp

1 tbsp oil

2 tbsp red curry paste

1 can of coconut milk (13 fl oz/430 ml)

2 tbsp oyster sauce

2 tbsp soy sauce

2 tbsp fish sauce

2 kaffir lime leaves, chopped

2 sprigs thai basil, roughly chopped

13 oz/400 g shrimp, peeled

3 cups/9 oz/250 g napa cabbage, shredded

061 peel and devein a shrimp

In a large pan, heat the oil. Add curry paste, pour in coconut milk and stir until the paste has dissolved.

3 min

Add sauce, kaffir lime leaves and thai basil.

Cook the shrimp in the sauce, 1–2 minutes, add the cabbage and simmer for 2–3 minutes.

❋ If the sauce is too spicy, add cream or coconut milk to take away the heat.

❋ Serve with rice.

177 cook rice

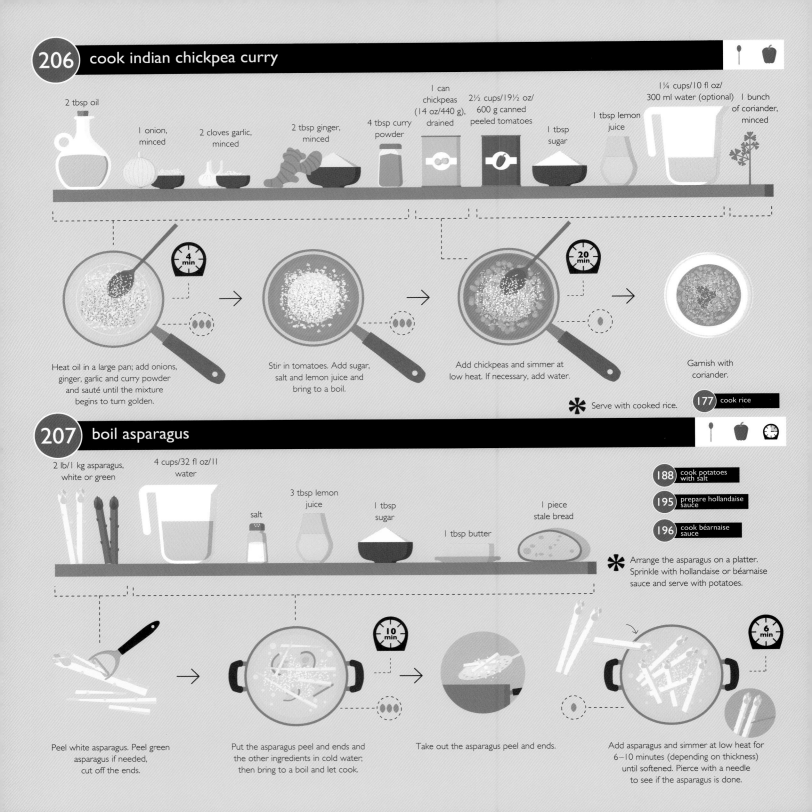

206 cook indian chickpea curry

2 tbsp oil

1 onion, minced

2 cloves garlic, minced

2 tbsp ginger, minced

4 tbsp curry powder

1 can chickpeas (14 oz/440 g), drained

2½ cups/19½ oz/ 600 g canned peeled tomatoes

1 tbsp sugar

1 tbsp lemon juice

1¼ cups/10 fl oz/ 300 ml water (optional)

1 bunch of coriander, minced

4 min

20 min

Heat oil in a large pan; add onions, ginger, garlic and curry powder and sauté until the mixture begins to turn golden.

Stir in tomatoes. Add sugar, salt and lemon juice and bring to a boil.

Add chickpeas and simmer at low heat. If necessary, add water.

Garnish with coriander.

✳ Serve with cooked rice.

177 cook rice

207 boil asparagus

2 lb/1 kg asparagus, white or green

4 cups/32 fl oz/1l water

salt

3 tbsp lemon juice

1 tbsp sugar

1 tbsp butter

1 piece stale bread

188 cook potatoes with salt

195 prepare hollandaise sauce

196 cook béarnaise sauce

✳ Arrange the asparagus on a platter. Sprinkle with hollandaise or béarnaise sauce and serve with potatoes.

10 min

6 min

Peel white asparagus. Peel green asparagus if needed, cut off the ends.

Put the asparagus peel and ends and the other ingredients in cold water; then bring to a boil and let cook.

Take out the asparagus peel and ends.

Add asparagus and simmer at low heat for 6–10 minutes (depending on thickness) until softened. Pierce with a needle to see if the asparagus is done.

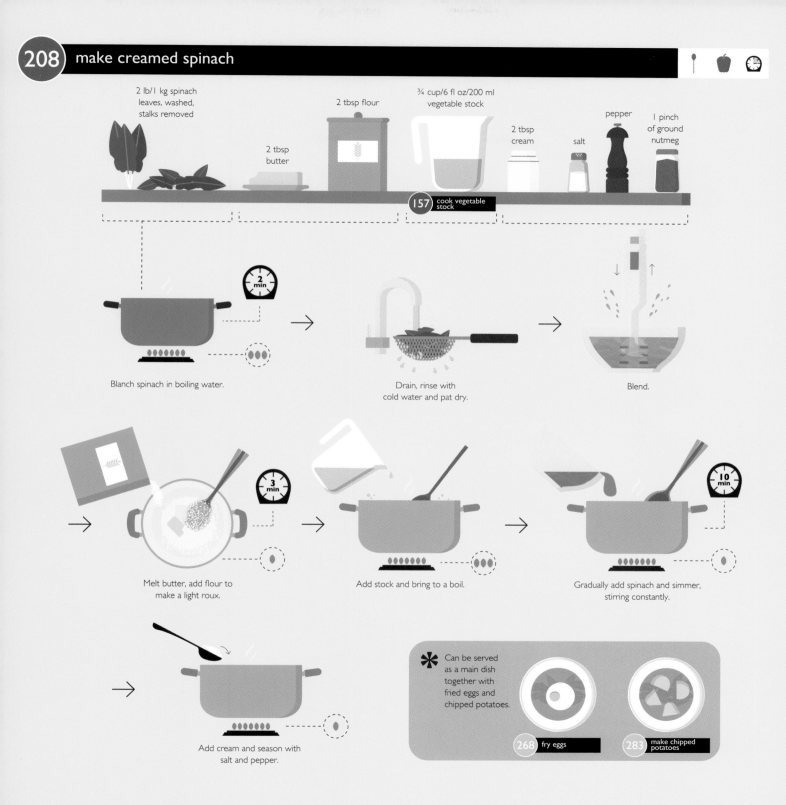

2 lb/1 kg spinach leaves, washed, stalks removed

2 tbsp butter

2 tbsp flour

¾ cup/6 fl oz/200 ml vegetable stock

2 tbsp cream

salt

pepper

1 pinch of ground nutmeg

157 cook vegetable stock

2 min

Blanch spinach in boiling water.

Drain, rinse with cold water and pat dry.

Blend.

3 min

Melt butter, add flour to make a light roux.

Add stock and bring to a boil.

10 min

Gradually add spinach and simmer, stirring constantly.

Add cream and season with salt and pepper.

✳ Can be served as a main dish together with fried eggs and chipped potatoes.

268 fry eggs

283 make chipped potatoes

1 lb/500 g green beans, ends cut off

4 cups/32 fl oz/1 l water

1 tbsp salt

4 tbsp olive oil

1 tsp white wine vinegar

* Prosciutto chips lend a crunchy texture: Cut prosciutto into fine slices and fry in a pan until crispy. Break into small pieces and sprinkle over the green beans.

4 min

Bring salted water to a boil, blanch the green beans.

Drain, rinse with cold water and drain again.

Heat oil in a pan, add beans and turn them lightly at low heat. Add vinegar.

¾ cup/6½ oz/ 200 g dried white beans

6 cups/48 fl oz/ 1½ l water

4 tbsp oil

2 cloves garlic, minced

5 sage leaves, minced

1 large tomato, peeled, diced

pepper

salt

050 peel tomatoes

12 h

Let the beans soak in 4 cups/32 fl oz/1 l of cold water overnight.

1 h

Boil the beans in 2 cups/16 fl oz/500 ml of water.

1 min

Heat oil, sauté garlic and sage.

3 min

Add tomato dices and continue to simmer. Season with salt and pepper.

Drain the beans and add them to the tomatoes. Season with salt if needed.

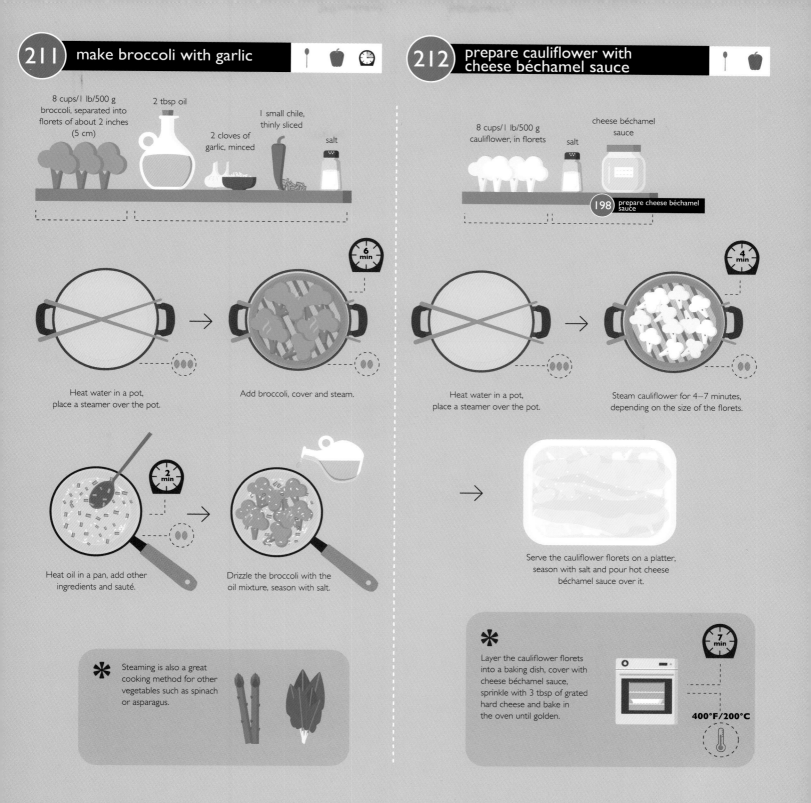

211 make broccoli with garlic

8 cups/1 lb/500 g broccoli, separated into florets of about 2 inches (5 cm)

2 tbsp oil

2 cloves of garlic, minced

1 small chile, thinly sliced

salt

6 min — Heat water in a pot, place a steamer over the pot.

Add broccoli, cover and steam.

2 min — Heat oil in a pan, add other ingredients and sauté.

Drizzle the broccoli with the oil mixture, season with salt.

✱ Steaming is also a great cooking method for other vegetables such as spinach or asparagus.

212 prepare cauliflower with cheese béchamel sauce

8 cups/1 lb/500 g cauliflower, in florets

salt

cheese béchamel sauce

198 prepare cheese béchamel sauce

Heat water in a pot, place a steamer over the pot.

4 min — Steam cauliflower for 4–7 minutes, depending on the size of the florets.

Serve the cauliflower florets on a platter, season with salt and pour hot cheese béchamel sauce over it.

✱ Layer the cauliflower florets into a baking dish, cover with cheese béchamel sauce, sprinkle with 3 tbsp of grated hard cheese and bake in the oven until golden.

7 min

400°F/200°C

213 poach salmon

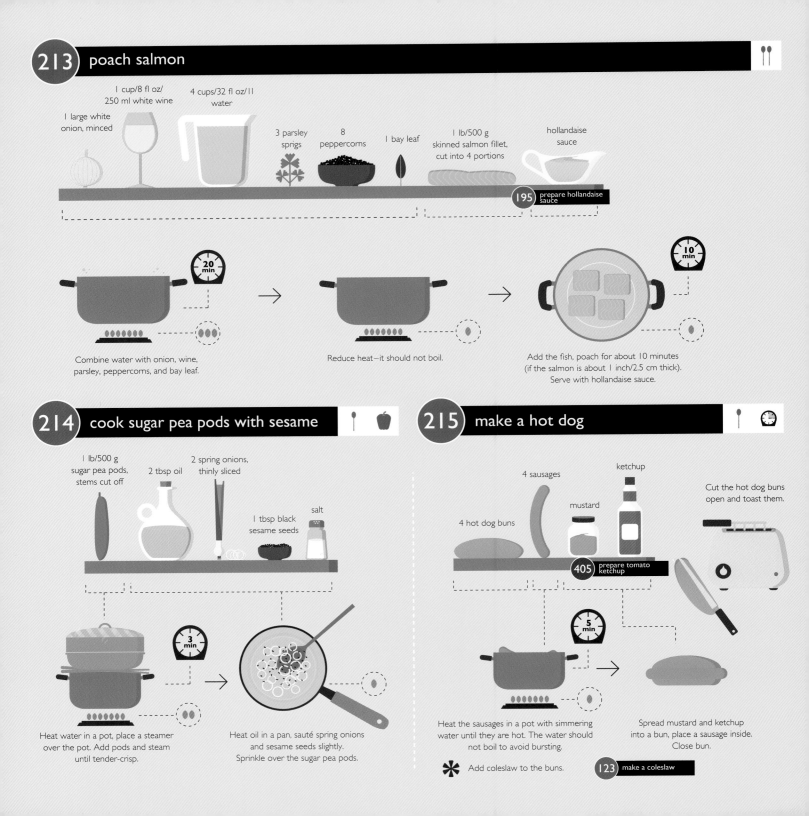

1 large white onion, minced

1 cup/8 fl oz/250 ml white wine

4 cups/32 fl oz/1 l water

3 parsley sprigs

8 peppercorns

1 bay leaf

1 lb/500 g skinned salmon fillet, cut into 4 portions

hollandaise sauce

195 prepare hollandaise sauce

Combine water with onion, wine, parsley, peppercorns, and bay leaf.

20 min

Reduce heat—it should not boil.

Add the fish, poach for about 10 minutes (if the salmon is about 1 inch/2.5 cm thick). Serve with hollandaise sauce.

10 min

214 cook sugar pea pods with sesame

1 lb/500 g sugar pea pods, stems cut off

2 tbsp oil

2 spring onions, thinly sliced

1 tbsp black sesame seeds

salt

Heat water in a pot, place a steamer over the pot. Add pods and steam until tender-crisp.

3 min

Heat oil in a pan, sauté spring onions and sesame seeds slightly. Sprinkle over the sugar pea pods.

215 make a hot dog

4 sausages

ketchup

mustard

4 hot dog buns

Cut the hot dog buns open and toast them.

405 prepare tomato ketchup

Heat the sausages in a pot with simmering water until they are hot. The water should not boil to avoid bursting.

5 min

Spread mustard and ketchup into a bun, place a sausage inside. Close bun.

✳ Add coleslaw to the buns.

123 make a coleslaw

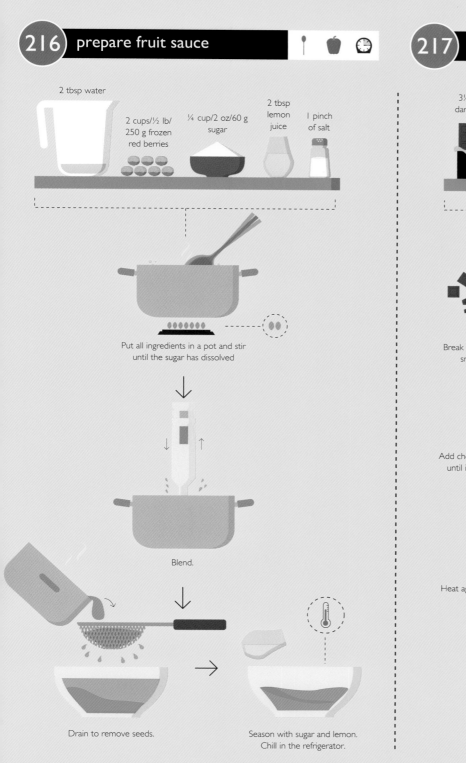

2 tbsp water

2 cups/½ lb/
250 g frozen
red berries

¼ cup/2 oz/60 g
sugar

2 tbsp
lemon
juice

I pinch
of salt

Put all ingredients in a pot and stir
until the sugar has dissolved

Blend.

Drain to remove seeds.

Season with sugar and lemon.
Chill in the refrigerator.

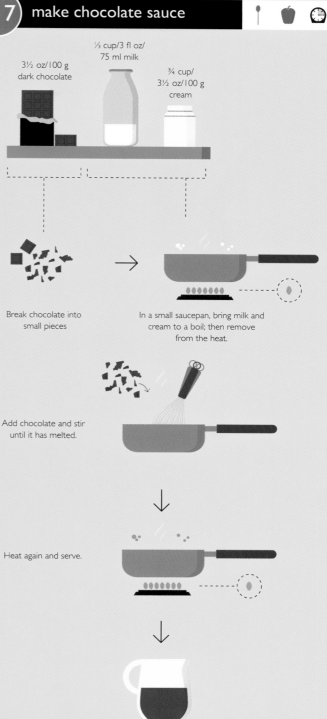

3½ oz/100 g
dark chocolate

⅓ cup/3 fl oz/
75 ml milk

¾ cup/
3½ oz/100 g
cream

Break chocolate into
small pieces

In a small saucepan, bring milk and
cream to a boil; then remove
from the heat.

Add chocolate and stir
until it has melted.

Heat again and serve.

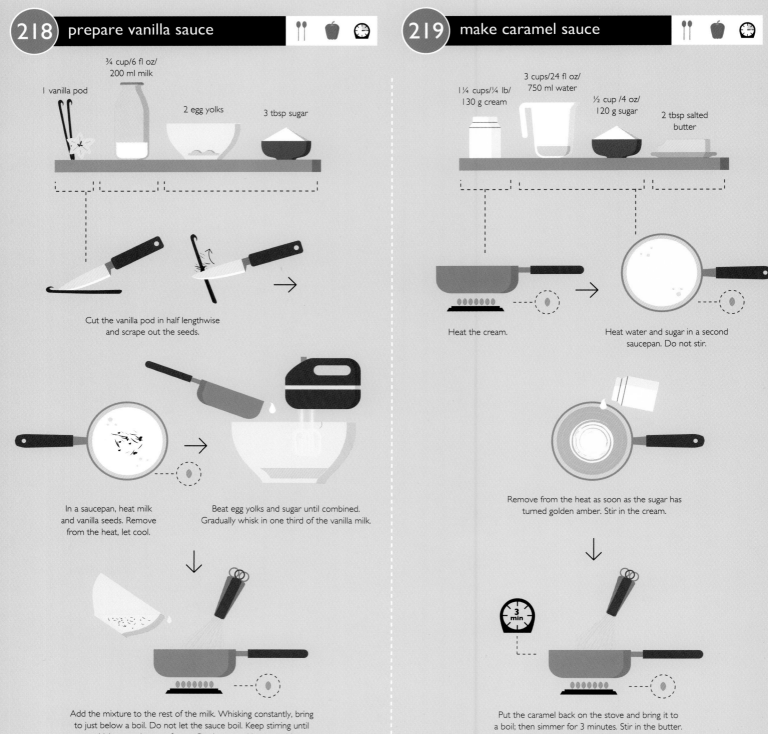

218 prepare vanilla sauce

1 vanilla pod

¾ cup/6 fl oz/ 200 ml milk

2 egg yolks

3 tbsp sugar

Cut the vanilla pod in half lengthwise and scrape out the seeds.

In a saucepan, heat milk and vanilla seeds. Remove from the heat, let cool.

Beat egg yolks and sugar until combined. Gradually whisk in one third of the vanilla milk.

Add the mixture to the rest of the milk. Whisking constantly, bring to just below a boil. Do not let the sauce boil. Keep stirring until a thick, smooth sauce forms. Can be served hot or cold.

219 make caramel sauce

1 ¼ cups/¼ lb/ 130 g cream

3 cups/24 fl oz/ 750 ml water

½ cup /4 oz/ 120 g sugar

2 tbsp salted butter

Heat the cream.

Heat water and sugar in a second saucepan. Do not stir.

Remove from the heat as soon as the sugar has turned golden amber. Stir in the cream.

3 min

Put the caramel back on the stove and bring it to a boil; then simmer for 3 minutes. Stir in the butter. The sauce thickens when it is cold.

220 make chocolate pudding

1½ oz/50 g chocolate, broken to pieces

2 cups/16 fl oz/ 500 ml milk

1 tbsp cocoa powder

3 tbsp sugar

2 tbsp cornstarch

Heat 1¼ cups/10 fl oz/300 ml milk, add the chocolate, stirring until it is melted.

Whisk the rest of the ingredients and ¾ cup/6 fl oz/200 ml milk until just combined.

Stir into the hot mixture. Bring to a boil, stirring constantly. Then simmer at low heat until the mixture thickens.

Ladle into pudding moulds and let cool.

221 prepare vanilla pudding

2 cups/16 fl oz/ 500 ml milk

1 vanilla pod

¼ cup / 2 oz/60 g) sugar

3 egg yolks

¼ cup/2 oz/ 30 g cornstarch

Cut vanilla in half lengthwise, scrape out the seeds.

Warm milk and vanilla seeds.

Whisk egg yolks and sugar until creamy.

Whisk in the cornstarch and add 5 tbsp of hot milk.

Whisk the mixture into the hot milk and cook until it comes to a boil and thickens.

Ladle into pudding moulds and let cool.

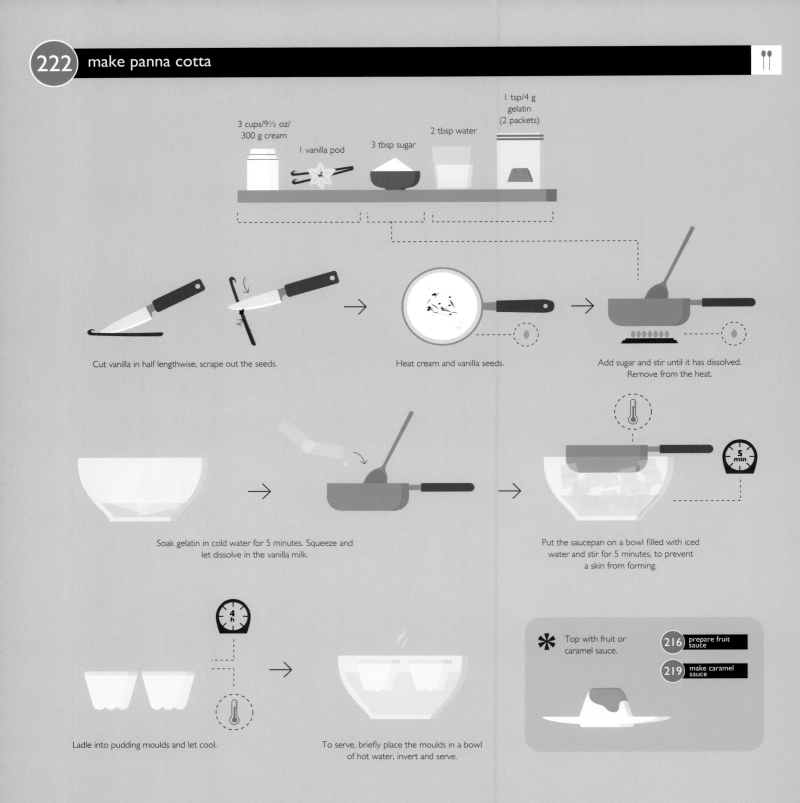

3 cups/9½ oz/ 300 g cream

1 vanilla pod

3 tbsp sugar

2 tbsp water

1 tsp/4 g gelatin (2 packets)

Cut vanilla in half lengthwise, scrape out the seeds.

Heat cream and vanilla seeds.

Add sugar and stir until it has dissolved. Remove from the heat.

Soak gelatin in cold water for 5 minutes. Squeeze and let dissolve in the vanilla milk.

Put the saucepan on a bowl filled with iced water and stir for 5 minutes, to prevent a skin from forming.

5 min

Ladle into pudding moulds and let cool.

4 h

To serve, briefly place the moulds in a bowl of hot water, invert and serve.

Top with fruit or caramel sauce.

216 prepare fruit sauce

219 make caramel sauce

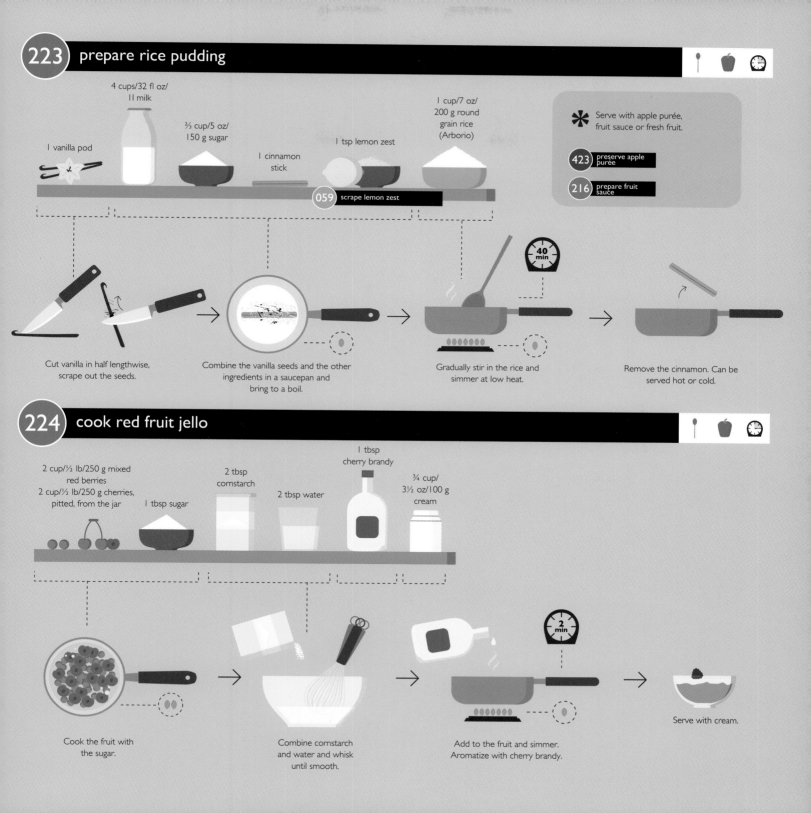

223 prepare rice pudding

I vanilla pod

4 cups/32 fl oz/
1l milk

⅔ cup/5 oz/
150 g sugar

I cinnamon
stick

I tsp lemon zest

I cup/7 oz/
200 g round
grain rice
(Arborio)

059 scrape lemon zest

Serve with apple purée,
fruit sauce or fresh fruit.

423 preserve apple purée

216 prepare fruit sauce

40 min

Cut vanilla in half lengthwise,
scrape out the seeds.

Combine the vanilla seeds and the other
ingredients in a saucepan and
bring to a boil.

Gradually stir in the rice and
simmer at low heat.

Remove the cinnamon. Can be
served hot or cold.

224 cook red fruit jello

2 cup/½ lb/250 g mixed
red berries
2 cup/½ lb/250 g cherries,
pitted, from the jar

I tbsp sugar

2 tbsp
cornstarch

2 tbsp water

I tbsp
cherry brandy

¾ cup/
3½ oz/100 g
cream

2 min

Cook the fruit with
the sugar.

Combine cornstarch
and water and whisk
until smooth.

Add to the fruit and simmer.
Aromatize with cherry brandy.

Serve with cream.

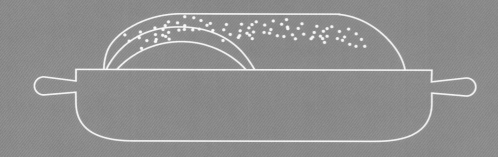

roast

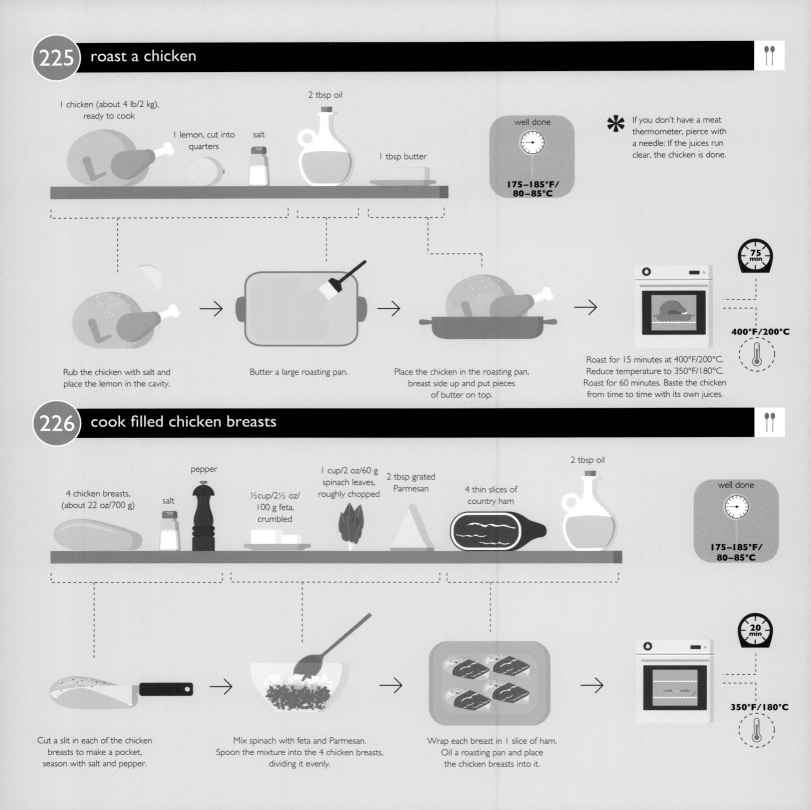

225 roast a chicken

1 chicken (about 4 lb/2 kg), ready to cook

1 lemon, cut into quarters

salt

2 tbsp oil

1 tbsp butter

well done
175–185°F/ 80–85°C

If you don't have a meat thermometer, pierce with a needle: If the juices run clear, the chicken is done.

Rub the chicken with salt and place the lemon in the cavity.

Butter a large roasting pan.

Place the chicken in the roasting pan, breast side up and put pieces of butter on top.

75 min

400°F/200°C

Roast for 15 minutes at 400°F/200°C. Reduce temperature to 350°F/180°C. Roast for 60 minutes. Baste the chicken from time to time with its own juices.

226 cook filled chicken breasts

4 chicken breasts, (about 22 oz/700 g)

salt

pepper

½ cup/2½ oz/ 100 g feta, crumbled

1 cup/2 oz/60 g spinach leaves, roughly chopped

2 tbsp grated Parmesan

4 thin slices of country ham

2 tbsp oil

well done
175–185°F/ 80–85°C

Cut a slit in each of the chicken breasts to make a pocket, season with salt and pepper.

Mix spinach with feta and Parmesan. Spoon the mixture into the 4 chicken breasts, dividing it evenly.

Wrap each breast in 1 slice of ham. Oil a roasting pan and place the chicken breasts into it.

20 min

350°F/180°C

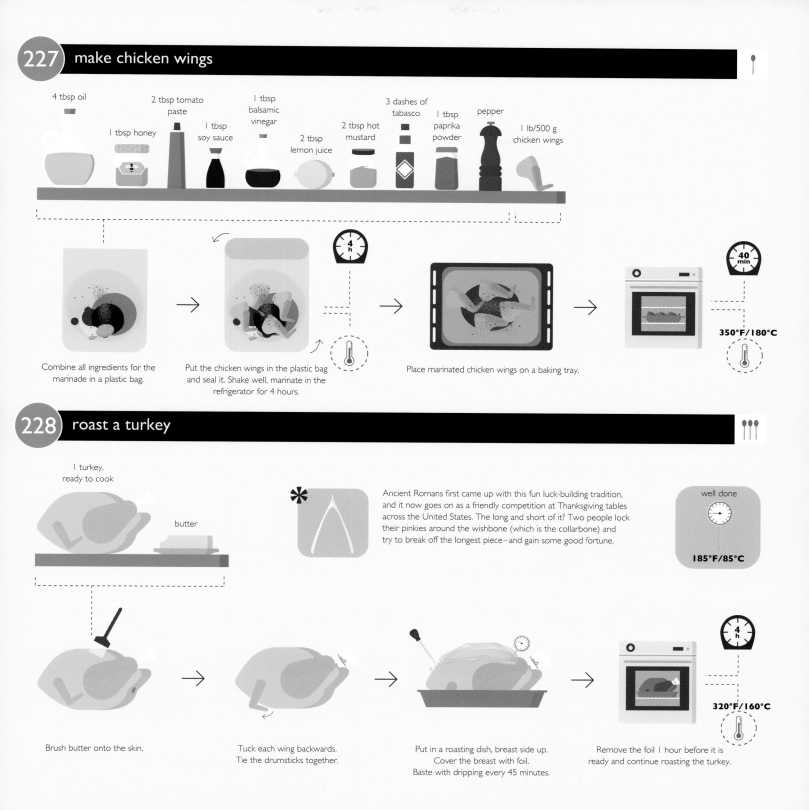

227 make chicken wings

4 tbsp oil

1 tbsp honey

2 tbsp tomato paste

1 tbsp soy sauce

1 tbsp balsamic vinegar

2 tbsp lemon juice

2 tbsp hot mustard

3 dashes of tabasco

1 tbsp paprika powder

pepper

1 lb/500 g chicken wings

Combine all ingredients for the marinade in a plastic bag.

Put the chicken wings in the plastic bag and seal it. Shake well, marinate in the refrigerator for 4 hours.

4 h

Place marinated chicken wings on a baking tray.

40 min

350°F/180°C

228 roast a turkey

1 turkey, ready to cook

butter

Ancient Romans first came up with this fun luck-building tradition, and it now goes on as a friendly competition at Thanksgiving tables across the United States. The long and short of it? Two people lock their pinkies around the wishbone (which is the collarbone) and try to break off the longest piece—and gain some good fortune.

well done

185°F/85°C

Brush butter onto the skin.

Tuck each wing backwards. Tie the drumsticks together.

Put in a roasting dish, breast side up. Cover the breast with foil. Baste with dripping every 45 minutes.

Remove the foil 1 hour before it is ready and continue roasting the turkey.

4 h

320°F/160°C

229 cook roast beef

3 lb/1½ kg roast beef

1 tbsp oil

salt

pepper

2 cups/16 fl oz/500 ml beef stock

153 cook beef stock

rare
125–131°F/52–55°C
medium rare
140–149°F/60–65°C
well done
158+°F/70+°C

Brush the roast on all sides with oil, season with salt and pepper.

Place into a roasting pan, add the roast and sear on all sides. Add stock.

Cover the meat with foil and roast in the oven at 350°F/180°C for 1 hour.

Remove foil, roast for 30 more minutes until the meat has the desired core temperature.

1½
350°F/180°C

230 roast a porterhouse steak

2 tbsp butter

salt

1 porterhouse steak (about 2 lb/1 kg, 1¼ inch/3 cm thick)

In a roasting pan, melt the butter over high heat.

Sear the steak on one side. Turn the steak and immediately place the pan in the oven.

rare
125–131°F/52–55°C
medium rare
140–149°F/60–65°C
well done
158+°F/70+°C

10 min
450°F/230°C

After 10 minutes the steak is medium rare.

Let rest in a warm place for 5 minutes. Cut the loin and the tenderloin from the bone before serving and cut the meat into slices.

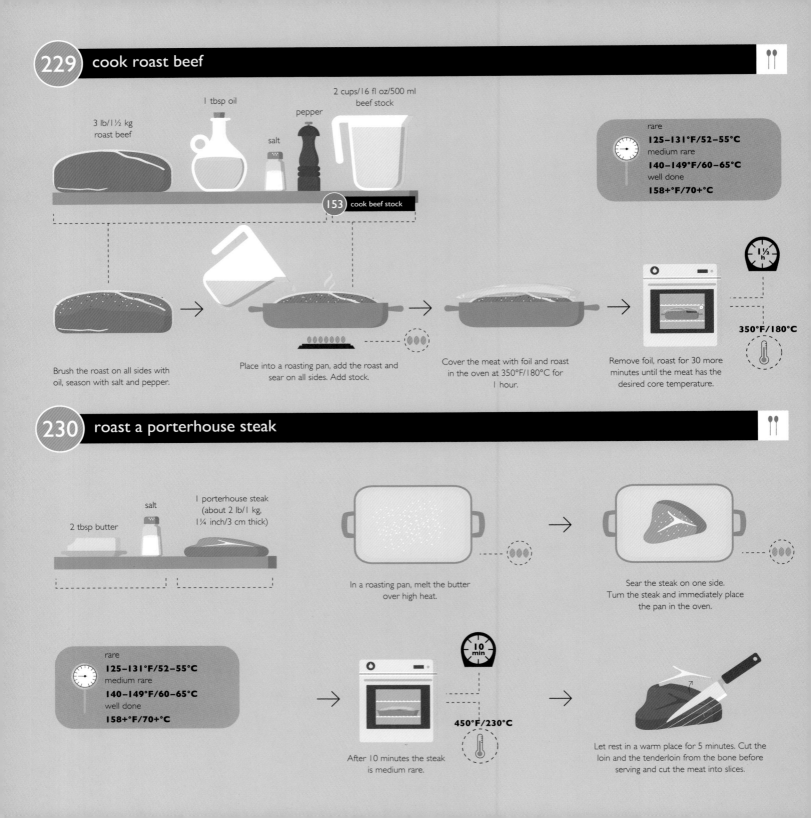

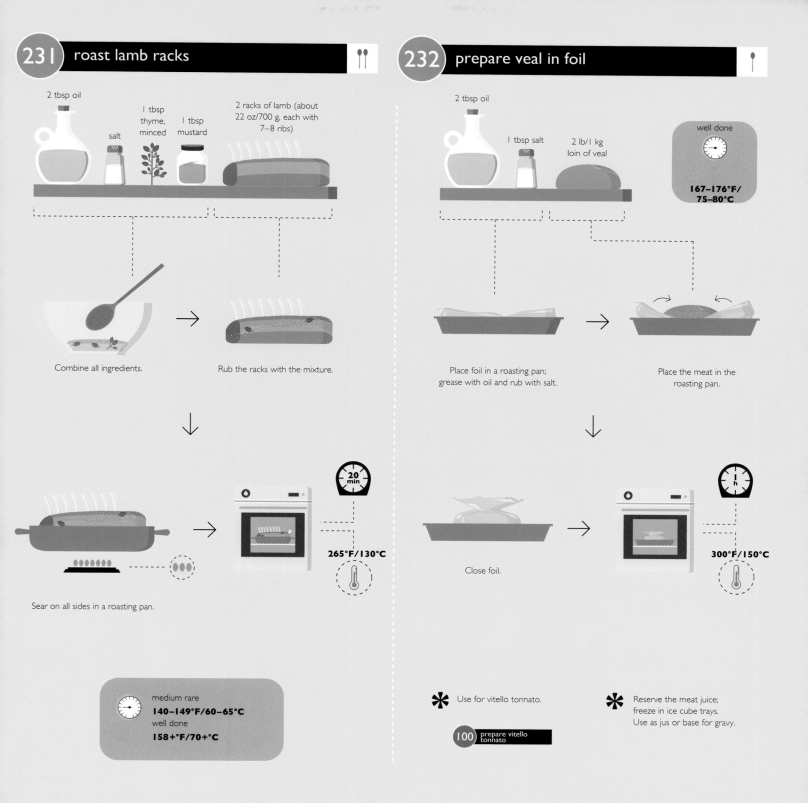

231 roast lamb racks

2 tbsp oil

salt

1 tbsp thyme, minced

1 tbsp mustard

2 racks of lamb (about 22 oz/700 g, each with 7–8 ribs)

Combine all ingredients.

Rub the racks with the mixture.

Sear on all sides in a roasting pan.

20 min

265°F/130°C

medium rare
140–149°F/60–65°C
well done
158+°F/70+°C

232 prepare veal in foil

2 tbsp oil

1 tbsp salt

2 lb/1 kg loin of veal

well done
167–176°F/75–80°C

Place foil in a roasting pan; grease with oil and rub with salt.

Place the meat in the roasting pan.

Close foil.

300°F/150°C

✳ Use for vitello tonnato.

100 prepare vitello tonnato

✳ Reserve the meat juice; freeze in ice cube trays. Use as jus or base for gravy.

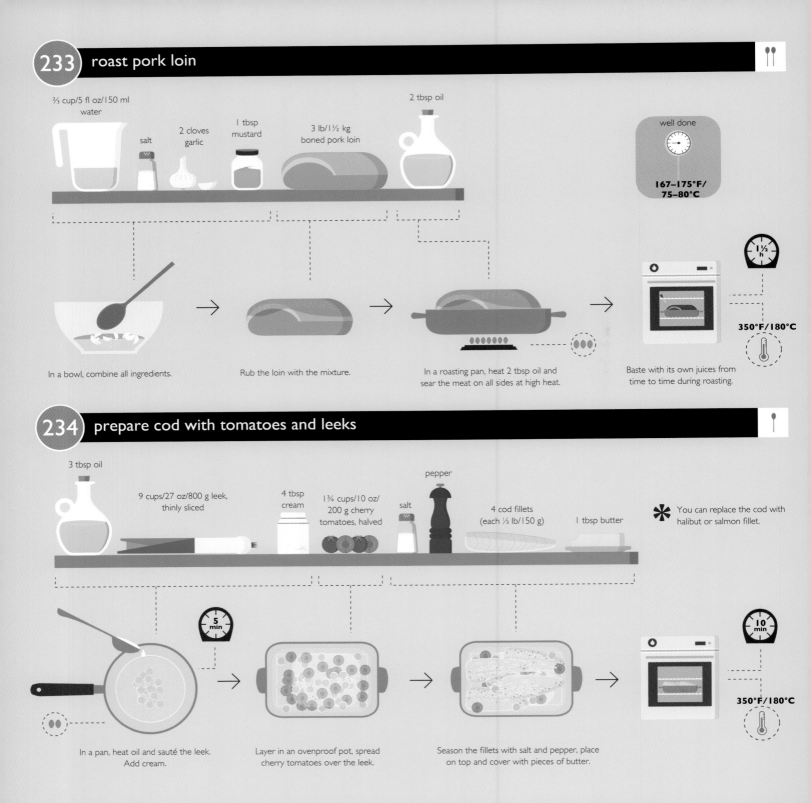

233 roast pork loin

⅔ cup/5 fl oz/150 ml water

salt

2 cloves garlic

1 tbsp mustard

3 lb/1½ kg boned pork loin

2 tbsp oil

well done

167–175°F/ 75–80°C

In a bowl, combine all ingredients.

Rub the loin with the mixture.

In a roasting pan, heat 2 tbsp oil and sear the meat on all sides at high heat.

1½ h

350°F/180°C

Baste with its own juices from time to time during roasting.

234 prepare cod with tomatoes and leeks

3 tbsp oil

9 cups/27 oz/800 g leek, thinly sliced

4 tbsp cream

1¾ cups/10 oz/ 200 g cherry tomatoes, halved

salt

pepper

4 cod fillets (each ⅓ lb/150 g)

1 tbsp butter

✳ You can replace the cod with halibut or salmon fillet.

In a pan, heat oil and sauté the leek. Add cream.

5 min

Layer in an ovenproof pot, spread cherry tomatoes over the leek.

Season the fillets with salt and pepper, place on top and cover with pieces of butter.

10 min

350°F/180°C

235 stuff vegetables

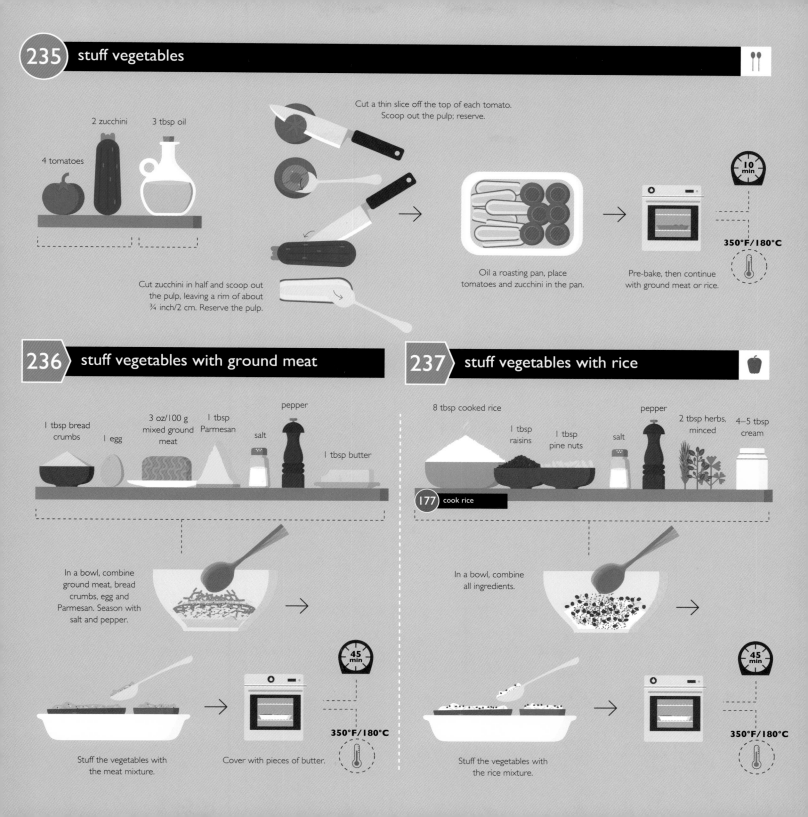

4 tomatoes

2 zucchini

3 tbsp oil

Cut a thin slice off the top of each tomato.
Scoop out the pulp; reserve.

Cut zucchini in half and scoop out
the pulp, leaving a rim of about
¾ inch/2 cm. Reserve the pulp.

Oil a roasting pan, place
tomatoes and zucchini in the pan.

Pre-bake, then continue
with ground meat or rice.

10 min

350°F/180°C

236 stuff vegetables with ground meat

1 tbsp bread crumbs

1 egg

3 oz/100 g mixed ground meat

1 tbsp Parmesan

salt

pepper

1 tbsp butter

In a bowl, combine
ground meat, bread
crumbs, egg and
Parmesan. Season with
salt and pepper.

Stuff the vegetables with
the meat mixture.

Cover with pieces of butter.

45 min

350°F/180°C

237 stuff vegetables with rice

8 tbsp cooked rice

1 tbsp raisins

1 tbsp pine nuts

salt

pepper

2 tbsp herbs, minced

4–5 tbsp cream

177 cook rice

In a bowl, combine
all ingredients.

Stuff the vegetables with
the rice mixture.

45 min

350°F/180°C

238 make bruschetta

8 slices of
white bread

4 tbsp olive oil

2 cups/13 oz/
400 g cherry
tomatoes,
cut in half

12 leaves of basil,
minced

salt

✳ For garlic bruschetta rub the warm bread with half a garlic clove, sprinkle with olive oil and season with salt and pepper.

3 min

400°F/200°C

Cover a baking tray with parchment paper; place the bread slices on it.

Drizzle with olive oil and roast until crispy.

Stir together cherry tomatoes and basil; season with salt.

Top the crispy bruschetta with the seasoned tomatoes.

239 cook sweet potato french fries

1 lb/500 g sweet potatoes, peeled, cut into strips

2 tbsp
sunflower oil

1 tbsp ground
caraway

salt

pepper

✳ A perfect side dish for roasted meat.

30 min

400°F/200°C

Put potato strips in a bowl, drizzle with oil, sprinkle with caraway and season with salt and pepper.

Line a baking tray with parchment paper; arrange potato strips on it.

Turn every 10 minutes.

Season with salt before serving.

240 cook brussels sprouts in the oven

1 lb/500 g brussels sprouts, trimmed, cut in half

3 tbsp olive oil

salt

pepper

3 tbsp hazelnuts, roughly chopped

1 tbsp white wine vinegar

2 tbsp hazelnut oil

Place brussels sprouts in a bowl, drizzle with oil and season with salt and pepper.

Line a baking tray with parchment paper and spread out brussels sprouts.

30 min

400°F/200°C

Turn the sprouts a few times while roasting.

Sprinkle cooked sprouts with hazelnuts and drizzle with vinegar and hazelnut oil.

241 make a frittata

6 eggs

4 cloves garlic, crushed

3 tbsp grated Parmesan

salt

pepper

2 tbsp oil

Whisk the eggs with garlic, salt, pepper and Parmesan

Grease a baking dish with 2 tbsp of oil and add egg mixture.

15 min

320°F/160°C

Cook in the stove until eggs solidify.

242 make roasted tomatoes

2 cups/12 oz/375 g cherry tomatoes (yellow and red)

2 tbsp shallots, minced

3 tbsp olive oil

salt

pepper

Place tomatoes, shallots and oil into a baking dish, season with salt and pepper.

15 min

400°F/200°C

Turn a few times while roasting.

✳ A perfect topping for bruschetta.

238 make bruschetta

2 small fennel heads, trimmed and cut into quarters

8 baby carrots, cut in half

9½ oz/300 g baby potatoes, cleaned, cut in half

9½ oz/300 g celeriac, peeled and cut into chunks

4 tbsp oil

1 tbsp thyme, minced

1 tbsp rosemary, chopped

salt

pepper

✱ This makes a great side dish for sliced polenta.

144 prepare sliced polenta

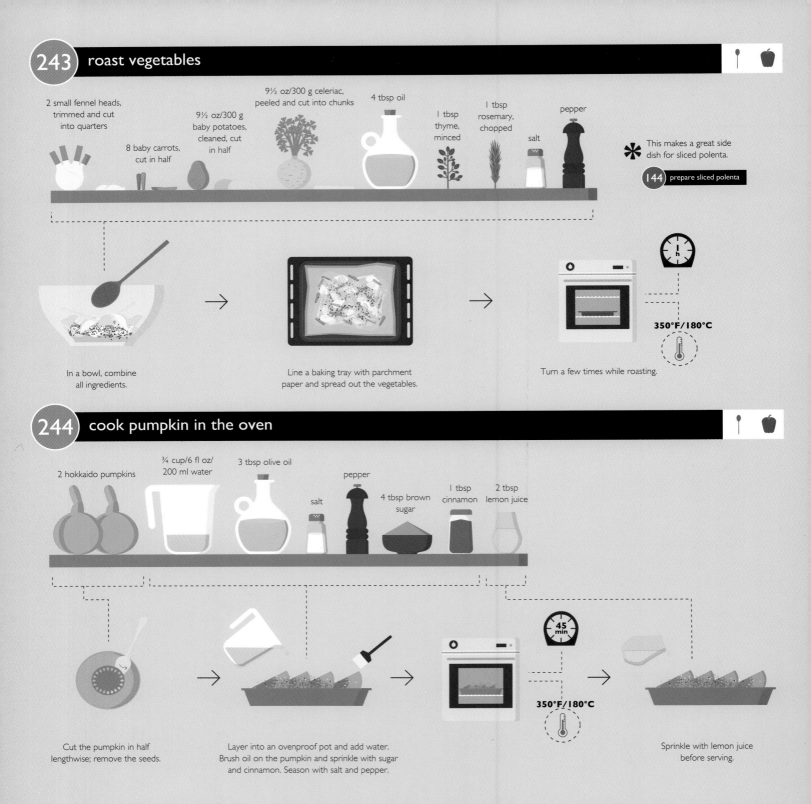

In a bowl, combine all ingredients.

Line a baking tray with parchment paper and spread out the vegetables.

Turn a few times while roasting.

350°F/180°C

2 hokkaido pumpkins

¾ cup/6 fl oz/ 200 ml water

3 tbsp olive oil

salt

pepper

4 tbsp brown sugar

1 tbsp cinnamon

2 tbsp lemon juice

Cut the pumpkin in half lengthwise; remove the seeds.

Layer into an ovenproof pot and add water. Brush oil on the pumpkin and sprinkle with sugar and cinnamon. Season with salt and pepper.

45 min

350°F/180°C

Sprinkle with lemon juice before serving.

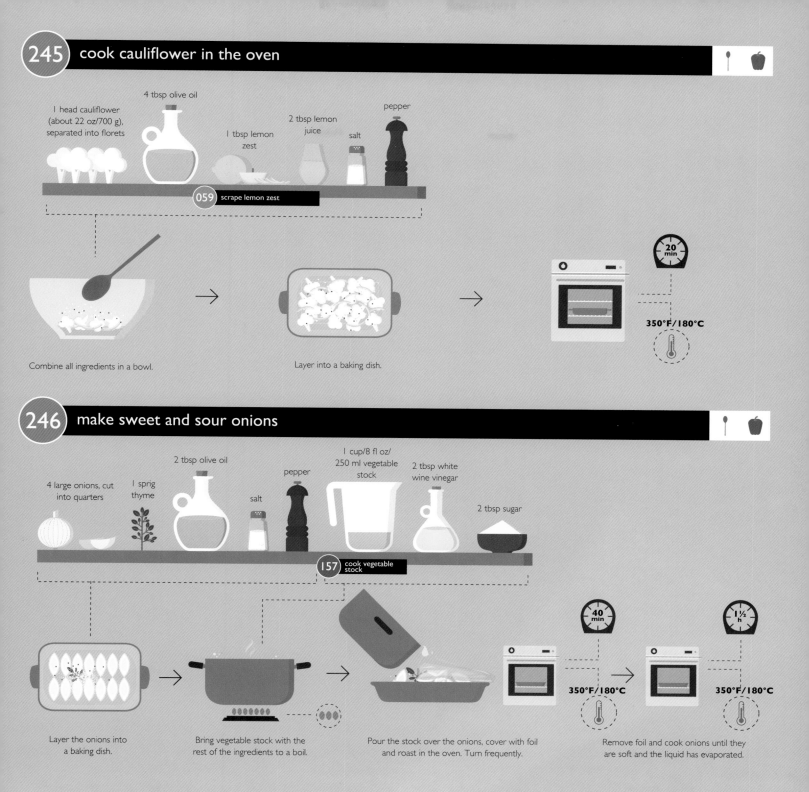

245 cook cauliflower in the oven

1 head cauliflower (about 22 oz/700 g), separated into florets

4 tbsp olive oil

1 tbsp lemon zest

2 tbsp lemon juice

salt

pepper

059 scrape lemon zest

Combine all ingredients in a bowl.

Layer into a baking dish.

20 min

350°F/180°C

246 make sweet and sour onions

4 large onions, cut into quarters

1 sprig thyme

2 tbsp olive oil

salt

pepper

1 cup/8 fl oz/ 250 ml vegetable stock

2 tbsp white wine vinegar

2 tbsp sugar

157 cook vegetable stock

Layer the onions into a baking dish.

Bring vegetable stock with the rest of the ingredients to a boil.

Pour the stock over the onions, cover with foil and roast in the oven. Turn frequently.

40 min

350°F/180°C

Remove foil and cook onions until they are soft and the liquid has evaporated.

1½ h

350°F/180°C

stew

10 saffron threads

2 tbsp water

2 onions, minced

2 tbsp parsley, minced

1 tbsp coriander, minced

5 tbsp lemon juice

1 tsp grated caraway

1 tsp ginger, chopped

salt

6 tbsp olive oil

4 chicken legs

✳ Serve with couscous or tabbouleh.

✳ If you don't have a tagine you can use an ovenproof pot instead.

199 cook couscous

120 prepare tabbouleh

2 tbsp oil

2 lemons, sliced

⅔ cup/5 fl oz/ 150 ml chicken stock

4 tbsp pitted green olives

1 tbsp parsley, minced

159 cook chicken stock

Soak saffron in hot water.

Blend the other ingredients to make a paste.

Marinate the chicken legs with the paste.

Heat oil in a tagine, roast lemon slices and remove them.

Sear chicken for 4 minutes, then remove it. Deglaze with chicken stock, scraping the bottom with a wooden spoon to dislodge any brown bits.

Add marinade, lemon and chicken legs. Cover and braise at low heat (or in the oven at 350°F/180°C).

Add olives and continue braising uncovered. Garnish with parsley.

248 make tagine with lamb

19½ oz/600 g lamb shoulder, cut into cubes

157 cook vegetable stock

Replace chicken stock with vegetable stock and coriander with thyme.

Add black instead of green olives and 2 tbsp of sun-dried tomatoes. Do not use saffron.

249 make tagine with veal

19½ oz/600 g veal shoulder, cut into cubes

Use about 2 tbsp of dried plums instead of lemons. Roast like the lemons. Sprinkle with sesame seeds before serving.

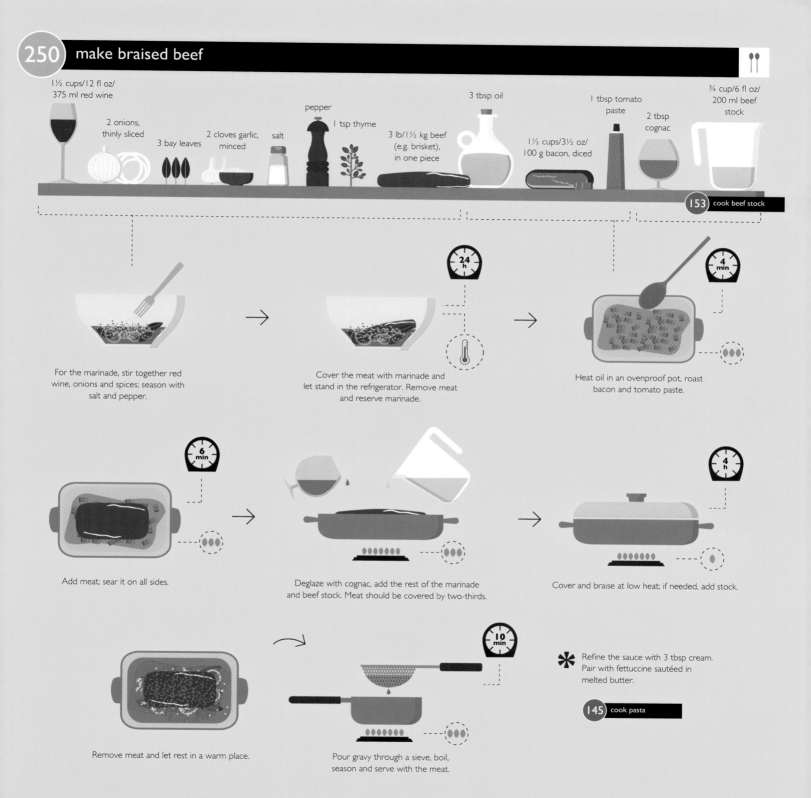

1½ cups/12 fl oz/ 375 ml red wine

2 onions, thinly sliced

3 bay leaves

2 cloves garlic, minced

salt

pepper

1 tsp thyme

3 lb/1½ kg beef (e.g. brisket), in one piece

3 tbsp oil

1½ cups/3½ oz/ 100 g bacon, diced

1 tbsp tomato paste

2 tbsp cognac

¾ cup/6 fl oz/ 200 ml beef stock

153 cook beef stock

24 h

4 min

For the marinade, stir together red wine, onions and spices; season with salt and pepper.

Cover the meat with marinade and let stand in the refrigerator. Remove meat and reserve marinade.

Heat oil in an ovenproof pot, roast bacon and tomato paste.

6 min

4 h

Add meat; sear it on all sides.

Deglaze with cognac, add the rest of the marinade and beef stock. Meat should be covered by two-thirds.

Cover and braise at low heat; if needed, add stock.

10 min

Remove meat and let rest in a warm place.

Pour gravy through a sieve, boil, season and serve with the meat.

✱ Refine the sauce with 3 tbsp cream. Pair with fettuccine sautéed in melted butter.

145 cook pasta

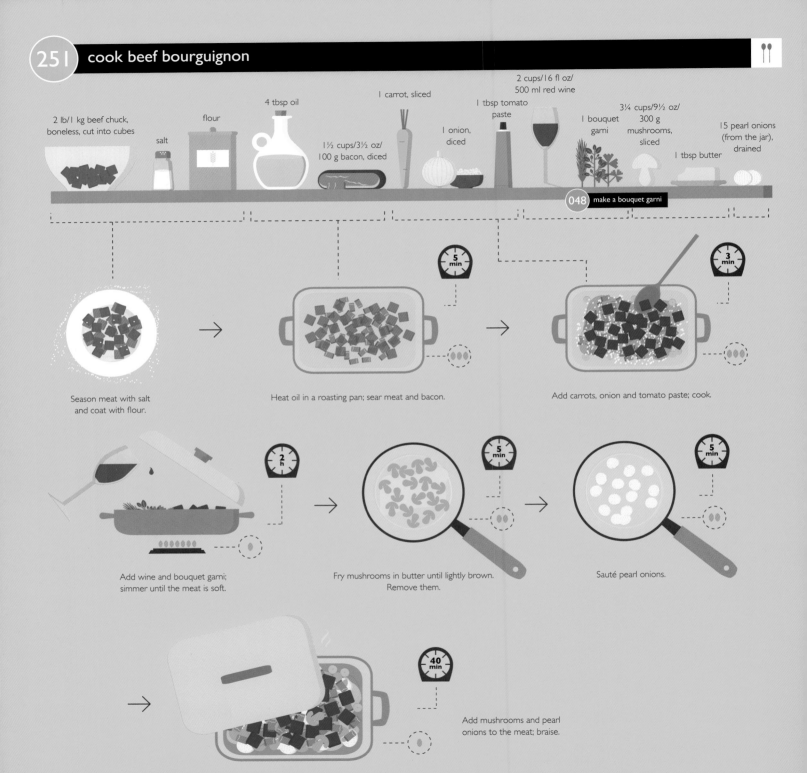

2 lb/1 kg beef chuck, boneless, cut into cubes

salt

flour

4 tbsp oil

1½ cups/3½ oz/ 100 g bacon, diced

1 carrot, sliced

1 onion, diced

1 tbsp tomato paste

2 cups/16 fl oz/ 500 ml red wine

1 bouquet garni

3¼ cups/9½ oz/ 300 g mushrooms, sliced

1 tbsp butter

15 pearl onions (from the jar), drained

048 make a bouquet garni

Season meat with salt and coat with flour.

5 min

Heat oil in a roasting pan; sear meat and bacon.

3 min

Add carrots, onion and tomato paste; cook.

2 h

Add wine and bouquet garni; simmer until the meat is soft.

5 min

Fry mushrooms in butter until lightly brown. Remove them.

5 min

Sauté pearl onions.

40 min

Add mushrooms and pearl onions to the meat; braise.

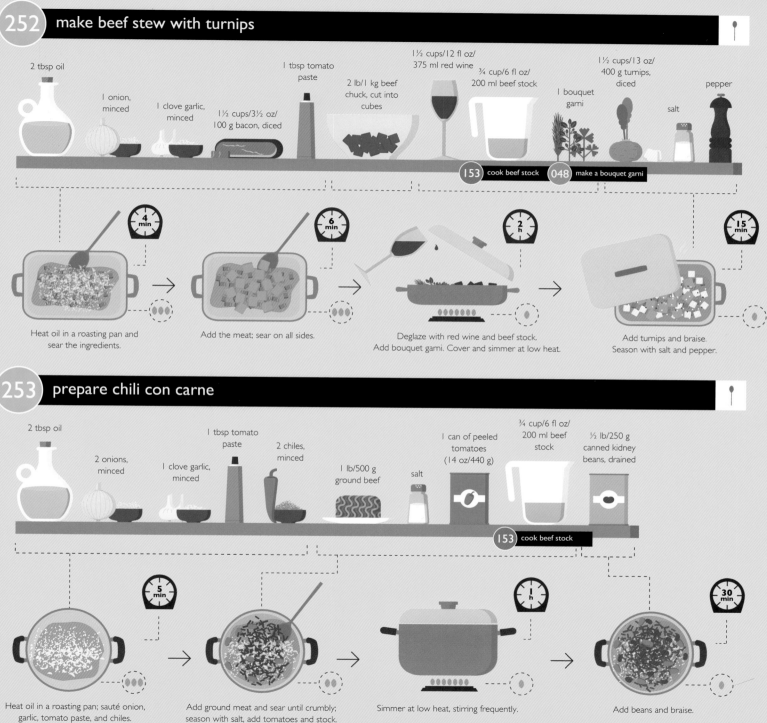

252 make beef stew with turnips

2 tbsp oil

1 onion, minced

1 clove garlic, minced

1½ cups/3½ oz/100 g bacon, diced

1 tbsp tomato paste

2 lb/1 kg beef chuck, cut into cubes

1½ cups/12 fl oz/375 ml red wine

¾ cup/6 fl oz/200 ml beef stock

1 bouquet garni

1½ cups/13 oz/400 g turnips, diced

salt

pepper

153 cook beef stock **048** make a bouquet garni

4 min — Heat oil in a roasting pan and sear the ingredients.

6 min — Add the meat; sear on all sides.

2 h — Deglaze with red wine and beef stock. Add bouquet garni. Cover and simmer at low heat.

15 min — Add turnips and braise. Season with salt and pepper.

253 prepare chili con carne

2 tbsp oil

2 onions, minced

1 clove garlic, minced

1 tbsp tomato paste

2 chiles, minced

1 lb/500 g ground beef

salt

1 can of peeled tomatoes (14 oz/440 g)

¾ cup/6 fl oz/200 ml beef stock

½ lb/250 g canned kidney beans, drained

153 cook beef stock

5 min — Heat oil in a roasting pan; sauté onion, garlic, tomato paste, and chiles.

— Add ground meat and sear until crumbly; season with salt, add tomatoes and stock.

1 h — Simmer at low heat, stirring frequently.

30 min — Add beans and braise.

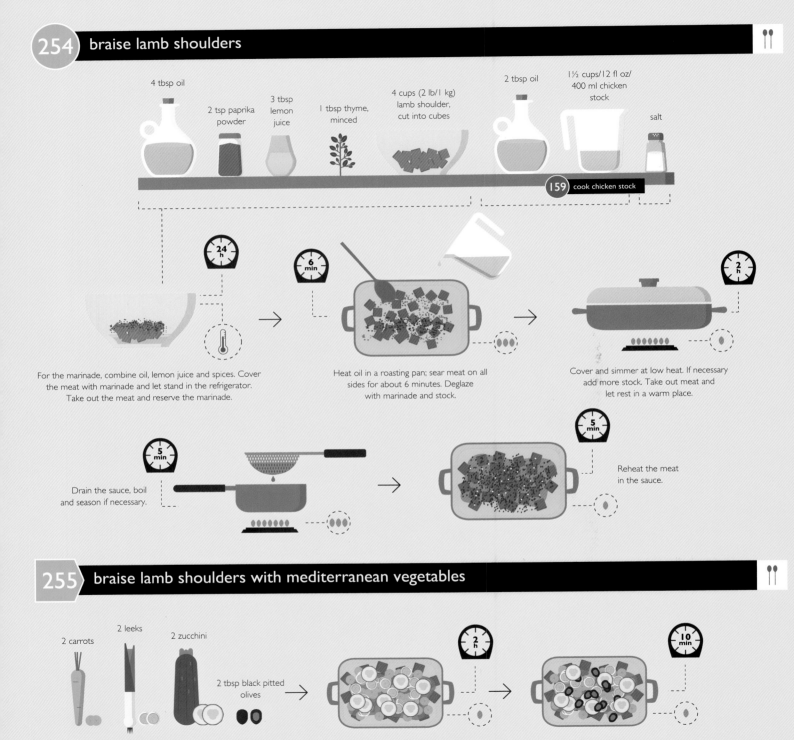

4 tbsp oil

2 tsp paprika powder

3 tbsp lemon juice

1 tbsp thyme, minced

4 cups (2 lb/1 kg) lamb shoulder, cut into cubes

2 tbsp oil

1½ cups/12 fl oz/ 400 ml chicken stock

salt

159 cook chicken stock

For the marinade, combine oil, lemon juice and spices. Cover the meat with marinade and let stand in the refrigerator. Take out the meat and reserve the marinade.

Heat oil in a roasting pan; sear meat on all sides for about 6 minutes. Deglaze with marinade and stock.

Cover and simmer at low heat. If necessary add more stock. Take out meat and let rest in a warm place.

Drain the sauce, boil and season if necessary.

Reheat the meat in the sauce.

2 carrots

2 leeks

2 zucchini

2 tbsp black pitted olives

(everything sliced)

Braise lamb with zucchini, carrots and leek.

Add 2 tbsp of olives.

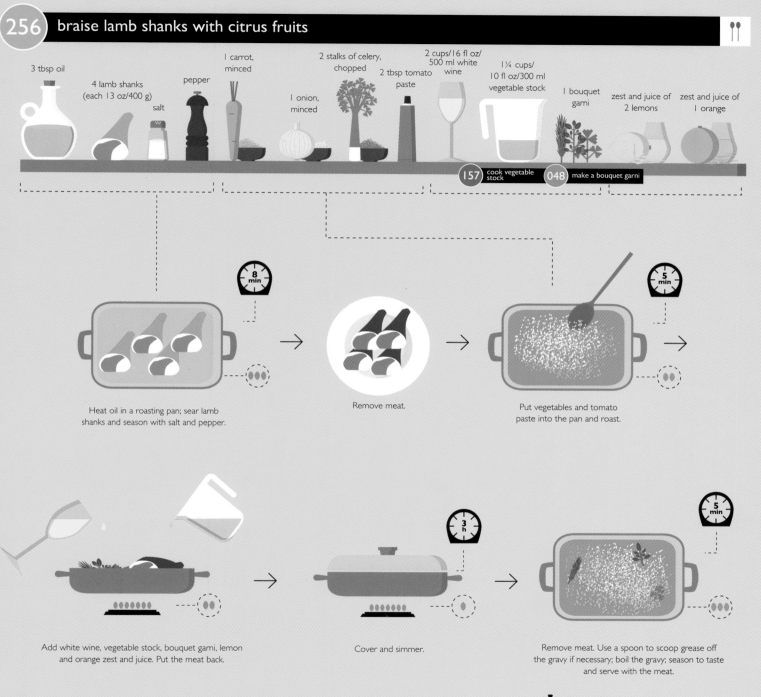

3 tbsp oil

4 lamb shanks (each 13 oz/400 g)

salt

pepper

1 carrot, minced

1 onion, minced

2 stalks of celery, chopped

2 tbsp tomato paste

2 cups/16 fl oz/ 500 ml white wine

1¼ cups/ 10 fl oz/300 ml vegetable stock

1 bouquet garni

zest and juice of 2 lemons

zest and juice of 1 orange

157 cook vegetable stock

048 make a bouquet garni

8 min

Heat oil in a roasting pan; sear lamb shanks and season with salt and pepper.

Remove meat.

5 min

Put vegetables and tomato paste into the pan and roast.

Add white wine, vegetable stock, bouquet garni, lemon and orange zest and juice. Put the meat back.

3 h

Cover and simmer.

5 min

Remove meat. Use a spoon to scoop grease off the gravy if necessary; boil the gravy; season to taste and serve with the meat.

 Sliced polenta is a perfect side dish.

144 prepare sliced polenta

2 lb/1 kg
veal (chuck),
in one piece

salt

pepper

3 tbsp oil

1 carrot,
minced

1 onion,
minced

2 tbsp tomato
paste

¾ cup/6 fl oz/
200 ml milk

1 cup/½ lb/
250 g cream

1 tbsp hot
mustard
(dijon)

141 cook zucchini "pasta"

❋ Zucchini "pasta" makes
a great side dish.

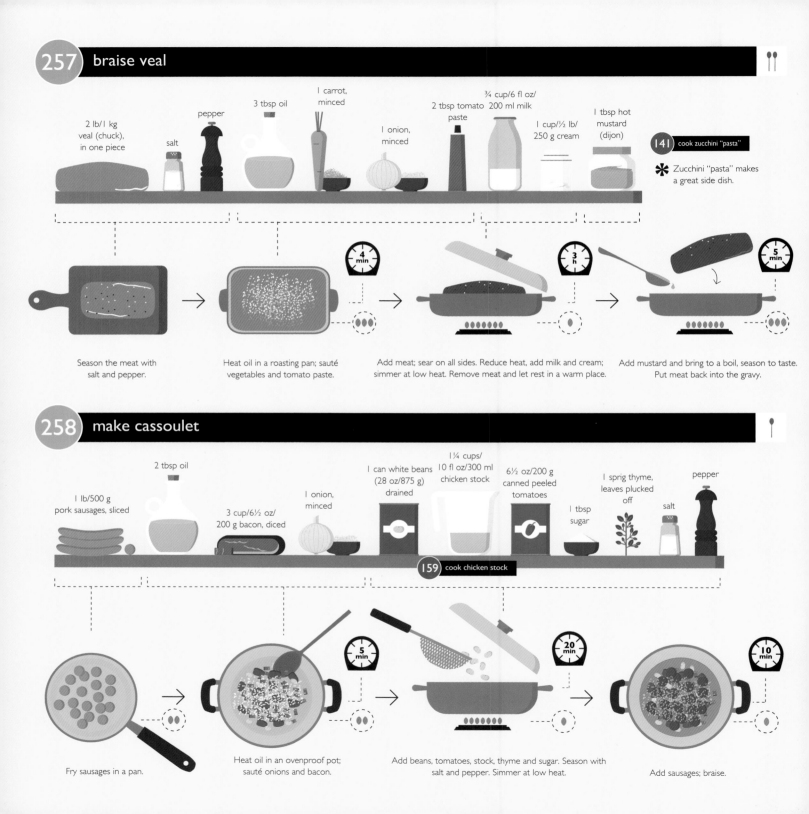

4 min

3 h

5 min

Season the meat with
salt and pepper.

Heat oil in a roasting pan; sauté
vegetables and tomato paste.

Add meat; sear on all sides. Reduce heat, add milk and cream;
simmer at low heat. Remove meat and let rest in a warm place.

Add mustard and bring to a boil, season to taste.
Put meat back into the gravy.

2 tbsp oil

1 lb/500 g
pork sausages, sliced

3 cup/6½ oz/
200 g bacon, diced

1 onion,
minced

1 can white beans
(28 oz/875 g)
drained

1¼ cups/
10 fl oz/300 ml
chicken stock

6½ oz/200 g
canned peeled
tomatoes

1 tbsp
sugar

1 sprig thyme,
leaves plucked
off

salt

pepper

159 cook chicken stock

5 min

20 min

10 min

Fry sausages in a pan.

Heat oil in an ovenproof pot;
sauté onions and bacon.

Add beans, tomatoes, stock, thyme and sugar. Season with
salt and pepper. Simmer at low heat.

Add sausages; braise.

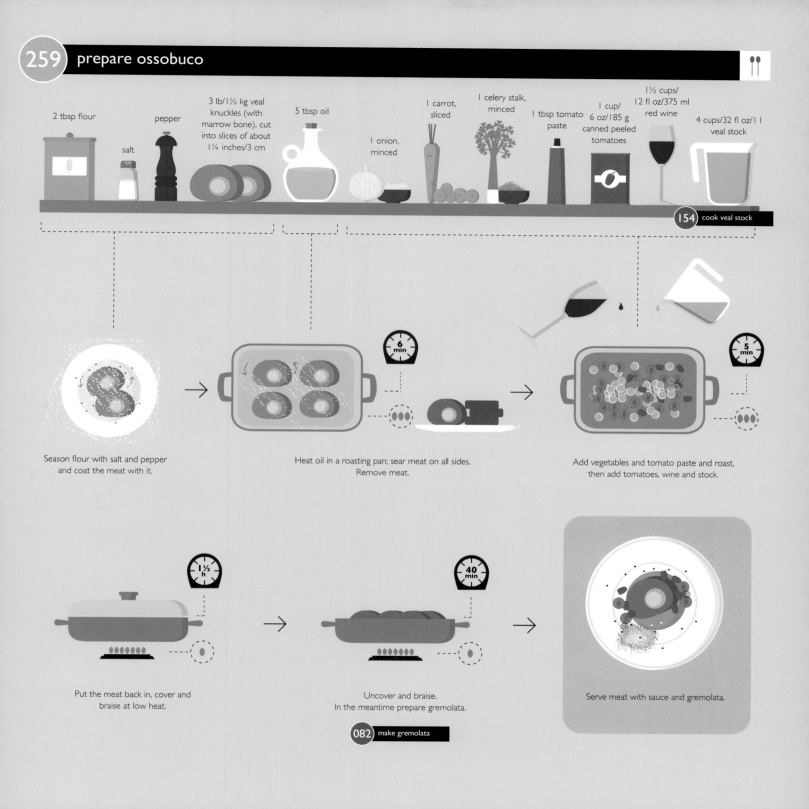

2 tbsp flour

salt

pepper

3 lb/1½ kg veal knuckles (with marrow bone), cut into slices of about 1¼ inches/3 cm

5 tbsp oil

1 onion, minced

1 carrot, sliced

1 celery stalk, minced

1 tbsp tomato paste

1 cup/ 6 oz/185 g canned peeled tomatoes

1½ cups/ 12 fl oz/375 ml red wine

4 cups/32 fl oz/1 l veal stock

154 | cook veal stock

Season flour with salt and pepper and coat the meat with it.

6 min

Heat oil in a roasting pan; sear meat on all sides. Remove meat.

5 min

Add vegetables and tomato paste and roast, then add tomatoes, wine and stock.

1½ h

Put the meat back in, cover and braise at low heat.

40 min

Uncover and braise. In the meantime prepare gremolata.

082 | make gremolata

Serve meat with sauce and gremolata.

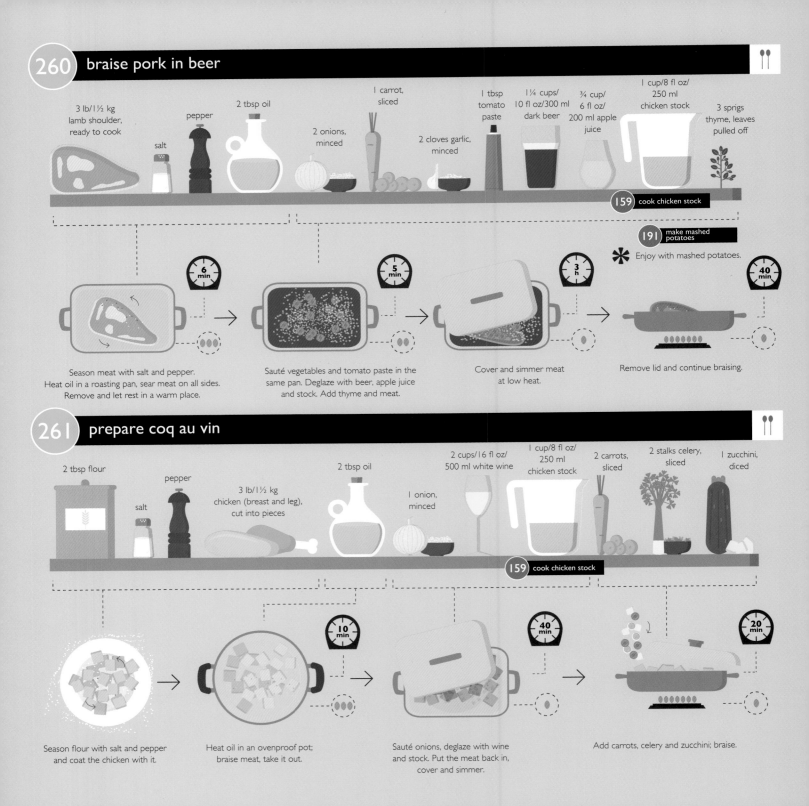

260 braise pork in beer

3 lb/1½ kg lamb shoulder, ready to cook

salt

pepper

2 tbsp oil

2 onions, minced

1 carrot, sliced

2 cloves garlic, minced

1 tbsp tomato paste

1¼ cups/ 10 fl oz/300 ml dark beer

¾ cup/ 6 fl oz/ 200 ml apple juice

1 cup/8 fl oz/ 250 ml chicken stock

3 sprigs thyme, leaves pulled off

159 cook chicken stock

191 make mashed potatoes

✳ Enjoy with mashed potatoes.

6 min

5 min

3 h

40 min

Season meat with salt and pepper. Heat oil in a roasting pan, sear meat on all sides. Remove and let rest in a warm place.

Sauté vegetables and tomato paste in the same pan. Deglaze with beer, apple juice and stock. Add thyme and meat.

Cover and simmer meat at low heat.

Remove lid and continue braising.

261 prepare coq au vin

2 tbsp flour

salt

pepper

3 lb/1½ kg chicken (breast and leg), cut into pieces

2 tbsp oil

1 onion, minced

2 cups/16 fl oz/ 500 ml white wine

1 cup/8 fl oz/ 250 ml chicken stock

2 carrots, sliced

2 stalks celery, sliced

1 zucchini, diced

159 cook chicken stock

10 min

40 min

20 min

Season flour with salt and pepper and coat the chicken with it.

Heat oil in an ovenproof pot; braise meat, take it out.

Sauté onions, deglaze with wine and stock. Put the meat back in, cover and simmer.

Add carrots, celery and zucchini; braise.

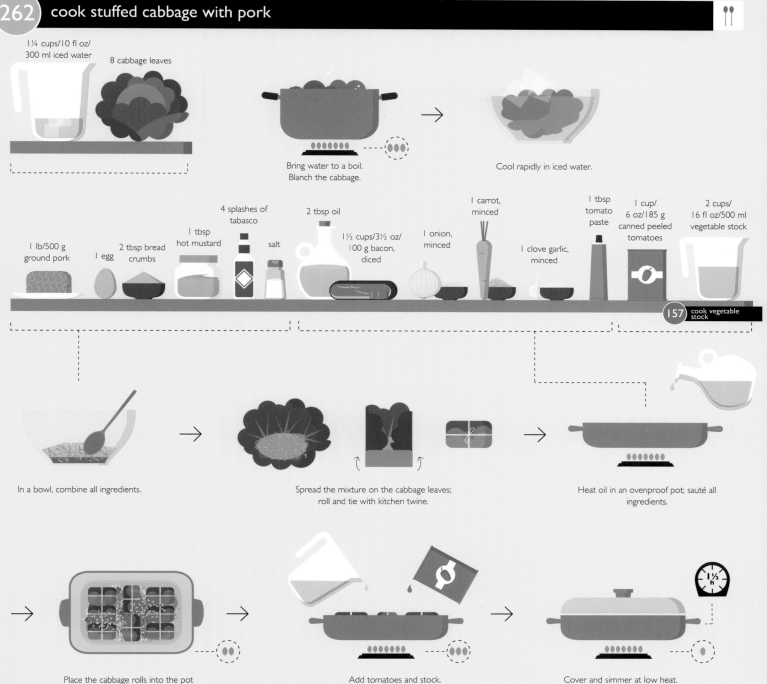

1¼ cups/10 fl oz/ 300 ml iced water

8 cabbage leaves

Bring water to a boil. Blanch the cabbage.

Cool rapidly in iced water.

1 lb/500 g ground pork

1 egg

2 tbsp bread crumbs

1 tbsp hot mustard

4 splashes of tabasco

salt

2 tbsp oil

1½ cups/3½ oz/ 100 g bacon, diced

1 onion, minced

1 carrot, minced

1 clove garlic, minced

1 tbsp tomato paste

1 cup/ 6 oz/185 g canned peeled tomatoes

2 cups/ 16 fl oz/500 ml vegetable stock

157 cook vegetable stock

In a bowl, combine all ingredients.

Spread the mixture on the cabbage leaves; roll and tie with kitchen twine.

Heat oil in an ovenproof pot; sauté all ingredients.

Place the cabbage rolls into the pot with the open side facing down.

Add tomatoes and stock.

1½ h

Cover and simmer at low heat.

✳ Serve along with potatoes.

188 cook potatoes with salt

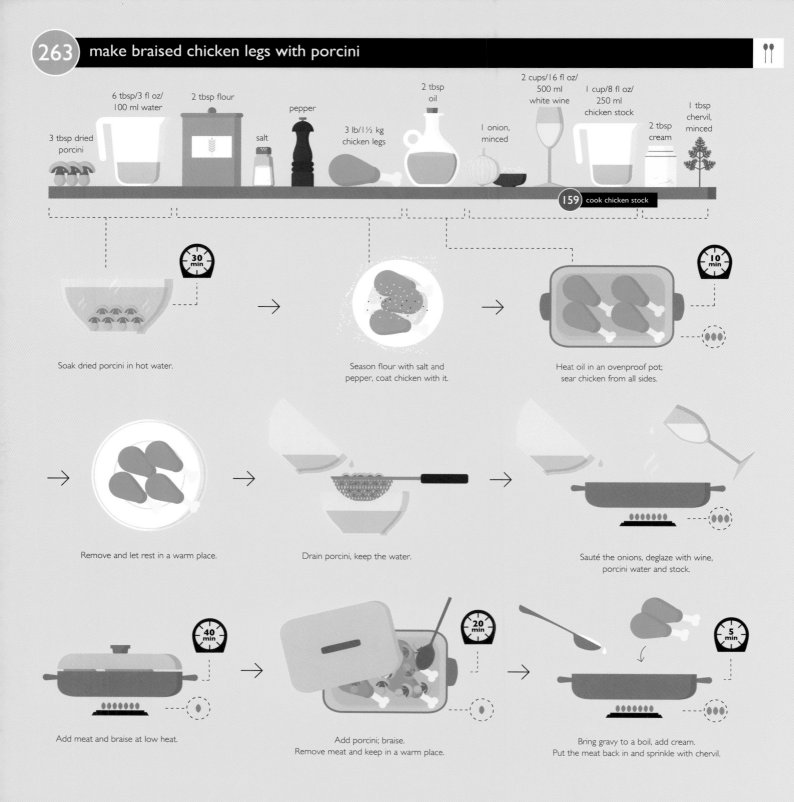

3 tbsp dried porcini

6 tbsp/3 fl oz/ 100 ml water

2 tbsp flour

salt

pepper

3 lb/1½ kg chicken legs

2 tbsp oil

1 onion, minced

2 cups/16 fl oz/ 500 ml white wine

1 cup/8 fl oz/ 250 ml chicken stock

2 tbsp cream

1 tbsp chervil, minced

159 cook chicken stock

30 min

Soak dried porcini in hot water.

Season flour with salt and pepper, coat chicken with it.

10 min

Heat oil in an ovenproof pot; sear chicken from all sides.

Remove and let rest in a warm place.

Drain porcini, keep the water.

Sauté the onions, deglaze with wine, porcini water and stock.

40 min

Add meat and braise at low heat.

20 min

Add porcini; braise.
Remove meat and keep in a warm place.

5 min

Bring gravy to a boil, add cream.
Put the meat back in and sprinkle with chervil.

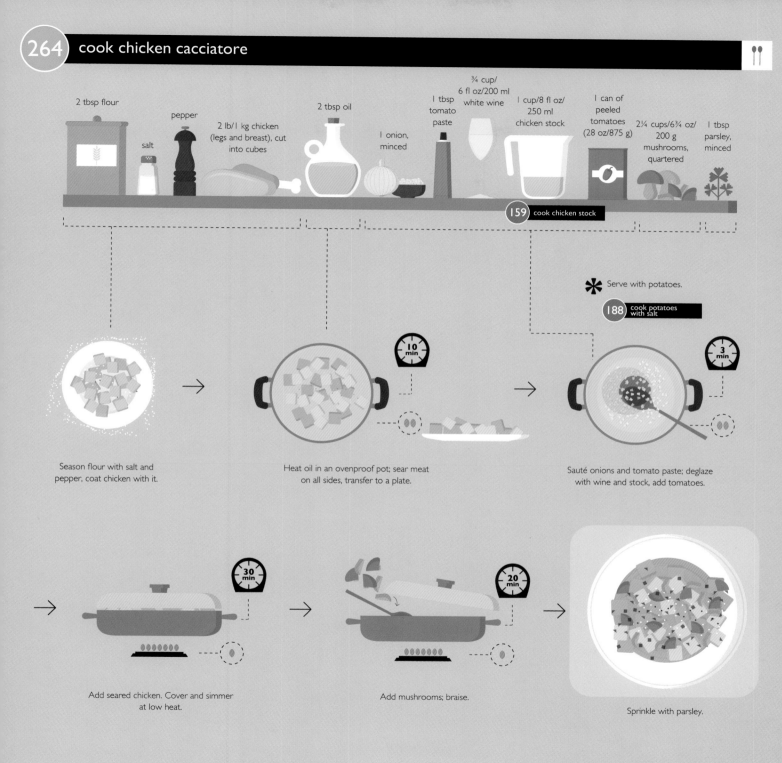

2 tbsp flour

salt

pepper

2 lb/1 kg chicken (legs and breast), cut into cubes

2 tbsp oil

1 onion, minced

1 tbsp tomato paste

¾ cup/ 6 fl oz/200 ml white wine

1 cup/8 fl oz/ 250 ml chicken stock

1 can of peeled tomatoes (28 oz/875 g)

2¼ cups/6¾ oz/ 200 g mushrooms, quartered

1 tbsp parsley, minced

159 cook chicken stock

Serve with potatoes.

188 cook potatoes with salt

Season flour with salt and pepper, coat chicken with it.

10 min

Heat oil in an ovenproof pot; sear meat on all sides, transfer to a plate.

3 min

Sauté onions and tomato paste; deglaze with wine and stock, add tomatoes.

30 min

Add seared chicken. Cover and simmer at low heat.

20 min

Add mushrooms; braise.

Sprinkle with parsley.

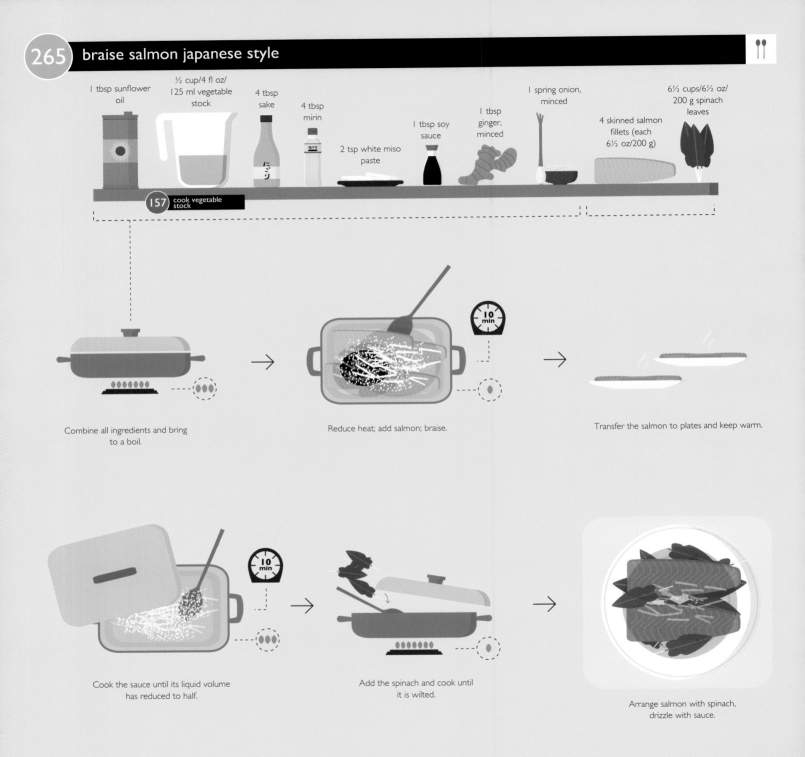

1 tbsp sunflower oil

½ cup/4 fl oz/ 125 ml vegetable stock

4 tbsp sake

4 tbsp mirin

2 tsp white miso paste

1 tbsp soy sauce

1 tbsp ginger, minced

1 spring onion, minced

4 skinned salmon fillets (each 6½ oz/200 g)

6½ cups/6½ oz/ 200 g spinach leaves

157 | cook vegetable stock

Combine all ingredients and bring to a boil.

Reduce heat; add salmon; braise.

Transfer the salmon to plates and keep warm.

Cook the sauce until its liquid volume has reduced to half.

Add the spinach and cook until it is wilted.

Arrange salmon with spinach, drizzle with sauce.

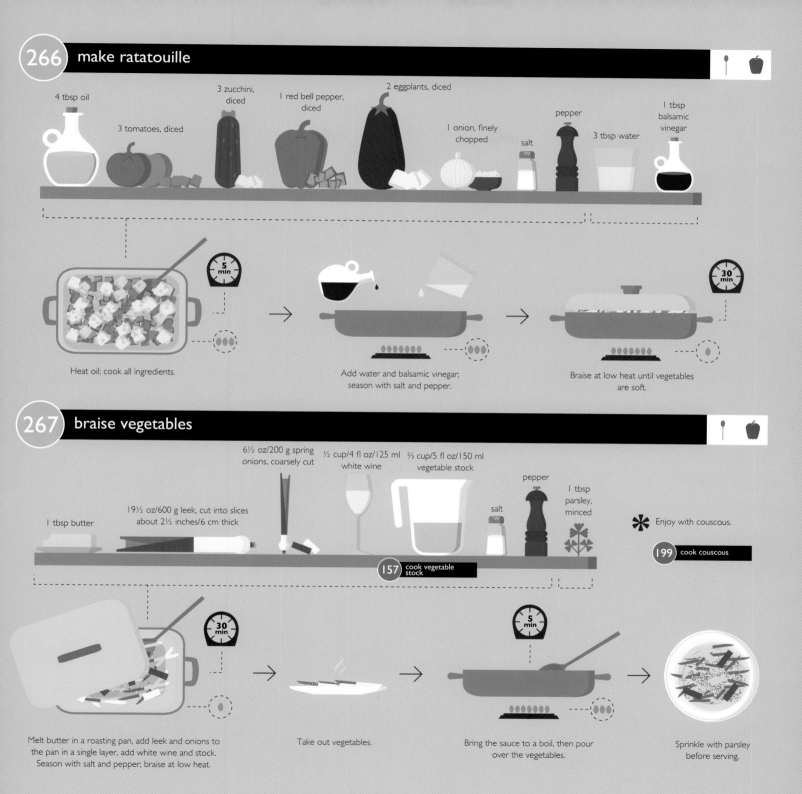

266 make ratatouille

4 tbsp oil

3 tomatoes, diced

3 zucchini, diced

1 red bell pepper, diced

2 eggplants, diced

1 onion, finely chopped

salt

pepper

3 tbsp water

1 tbsp balsamic vinegar

5 min

30 min

Heat oil; cook all ingredients.

Add water and balsamic vinegar; season with salt and pepper.

Braise at low heat until vegetables are soft.

267 braise vegetables

1 tbsp butter

19½ oz/600 g leek, cut into slices about 2½ inches/6 cm thick

6½ oz/200 g spring onions, coarsely cut

½ cup/4 fl oz/125 ml white wine

⅔ cup/5 fl oz/150 ml vegetable stock

salt

pepper

1 tbsp parsley, minced

157 cook vegetable stock

✳ Enjoy with couscous.

199 cook couscous

30 min

5 min

Melt butter in a roasting pan, add leek and onions to the pan in a single layer, add white wine and stock. Season with salt and pepper; braise at low heat.

Take out vegetables.

Bring the sauce to a boil, then pour over the vegetables.

Sprinkle with parsley before serving.

fry and
deep-fry

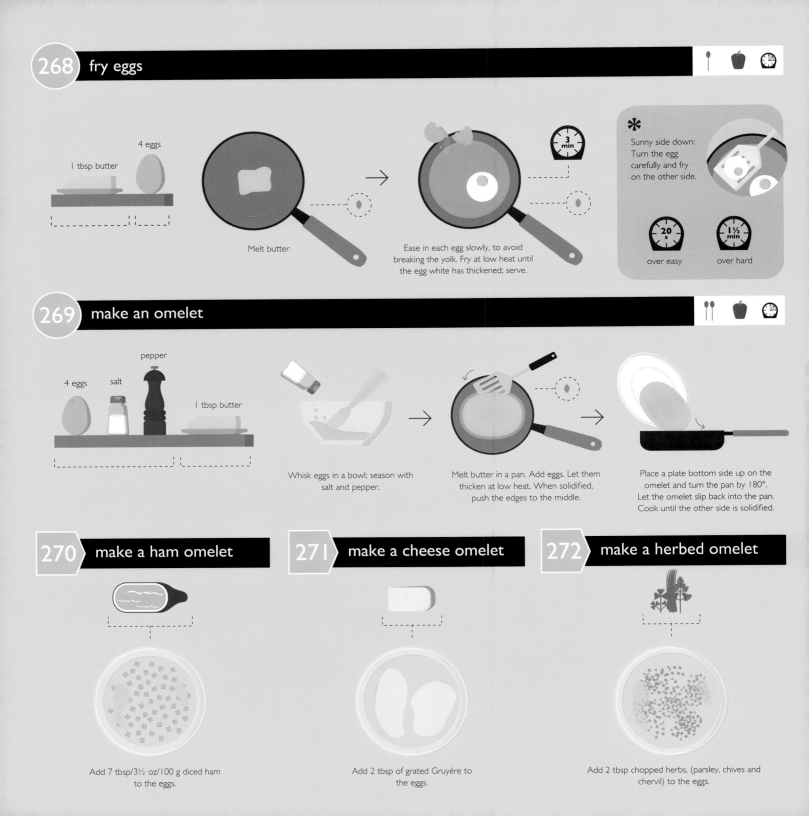

268 | fry eggs

I tbsp butter

4 eggs

Melt butter.

Ease in each egg slowly, to avoid breaking the yolk. Fry at low heat until the egg white has thickened; serve.

3 min

* Sunny side down: Turn the egg carefully and fry on the other side.

20 s — over easy

1½ min — over hard

269 | make an omelet

4 eggs

salt

pepper

I tbsp butter

Whisk eggs in a bowl; season with salt and pepper.

Melt butter in a pan. Add eggs. Let them thicken at low heat. When solidified, push the edges to the middle.

Place a plate bottom side up on the omelet and turn the pan by 180°. Let the omelet slip back into the pan. Cook until the other side is solidified.

270 | make a ham omelet

Add 7 tbsp/3½ oz/100 g diced ham to the eggs.

271 | make a cheese omelet

Add 2 tbsp of grated Gruyère to the eggs.

272 | make a herbed omelet

Add 2 tbsp chopped herbs, (parsley, chives and chervil) to the eggs.

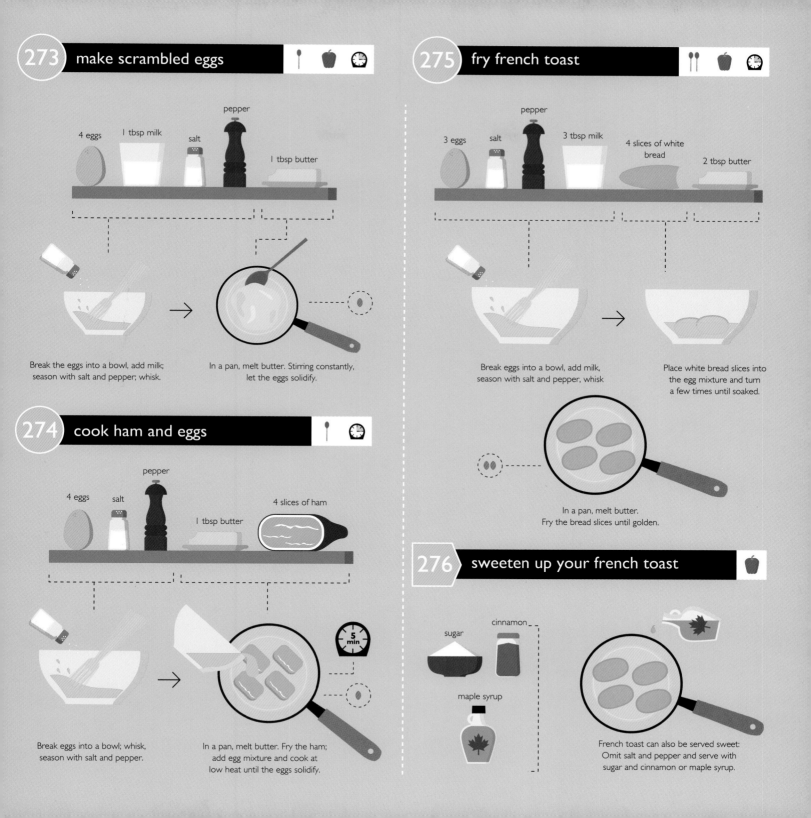

273 make scrambled eggs

4 eggs • 1 tbsp milk • salt • pepper • 1 tbsp butter

Break the eggs into a bowl, add milk; season with salt and pepper; whisk.

In a pan, melt butter. Stirring constantly, let the eggs solidify.

274 cook ham and eggs

4 eggs • salt • pepper • 1 tbsp butter • 4 slices of ham

Break eggs into a bowl; whisk, season with salt and pepper.

In a pan, melt butter. Fry the ham; add egg mixture and cook at low heat until the eggs solidify.

5 min

275 fry french toast

3 eggs • salt • pepper • 3 tbsp milk • 4 slices of white bread • 2 tbsp butter

Break eggs into a bowl, add milk, season with salt and pepper, whisk

Place white bread slices into the egg mixture and turn a few times until soaked.

In a pan, melt butter. Fry the bread slices until golden.

276 sweeten up your french toast

sugar • cinnamon • maple syrup

French toast can also be served sweet: Omit salt and pepper and serve with sugar and cinnamon or maple syrup.

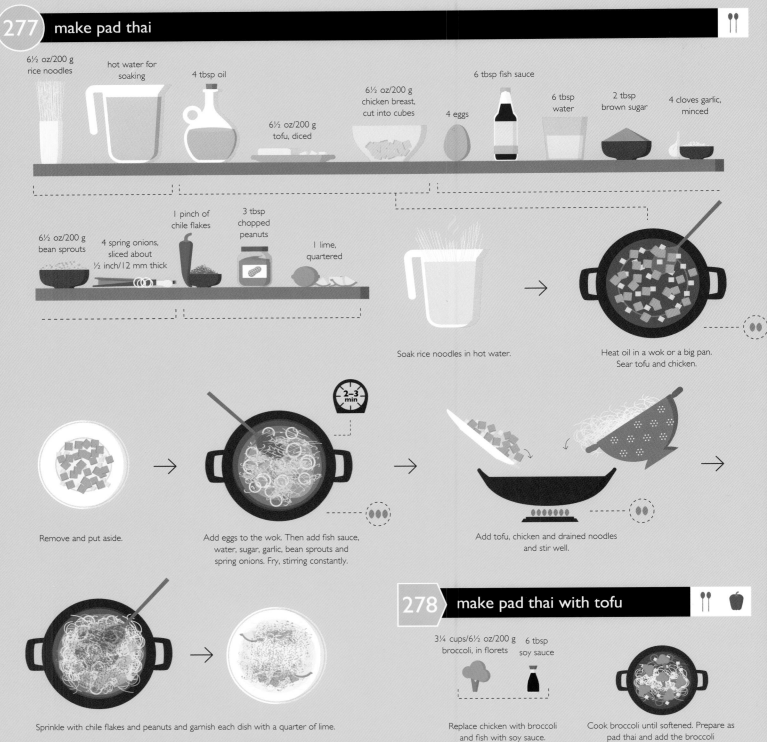

277 make pad thai

6½ oz/200 g rice noodles

hot water for soaking

4 tbsp oil

6½ oz/200 g tofu, diced

6½ oz/200 g chicken breast, cut into cubes

4 eggs

6 tbsp fish sauce

6 tbsp water

2 tbsp brown sugar

4 cloves garlic, minced

6½ oz/200 g bean sprouts

4 spring onions, sliced about ½ inch/12 mm thick

1 pinch of chile flakes

3 tbsp chopped peanuts

1 lime, quartered

Soak rice noodles in hot water.

Heat oil in a wok or a big pan. Sear tofu and chicken.

Remove and put aside.

2–3 min

Add eggs to the wok. Then add fish sauce, water, sugar, garlic, bean sprouts and spring onions. Fry, stirring constantly.

Add tofu, chicken and drained noodles and stir well.

Sprinkle with chile flakes and peanuts and garnish each dish with a quarter of lime.

278 make pad thai with tofu

3¼ cups/6½ oz/200 g broccoli, in florets

6 tbsp soy sauce

Replace chicken with broccoli and fish with soy sauce.

Cook broccoli until softened. Prepare as pad thai and add the broccoli with tofu to the wok.

4 tbsp oil

1 onion, minced

4 cloves garlic, minced

8 chicken legs

½ lb/250 g calamari, ready to cook, cut into rings

3 bell peppers, red, yellow, green, diced

2 tomatoes, peeled

½ cup/4 fl oz/ 125 ml white wine

2 cups/16 fl oz/ 500 ml chicken stock

8–10 saffron threads

159 cook chicken stock

1¼ cups/9½ oz/300 g round grain rice

salt

pepper

6½ oz/ 200 g peas

½ lb/250 g shrimp, cooked, peeled

13 oz/400 g mussels, cleaned

1 lemon, cut into wedges

Discard open or broken mussels, which don't close when giving gentle pressure. Also discard mussels that are still closed after cooking.

061 peel and devein a shrimp

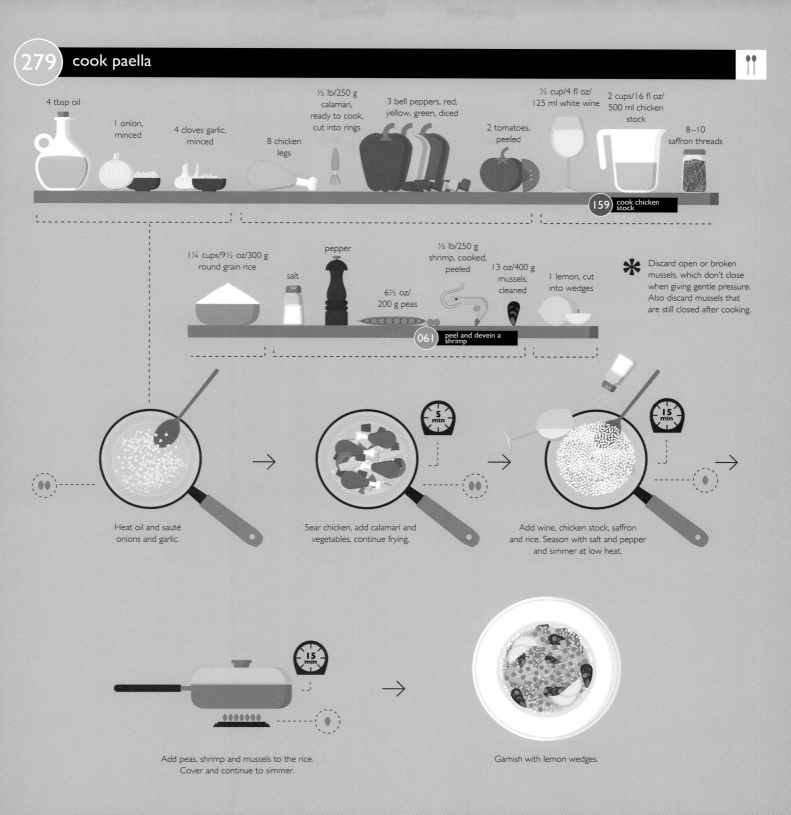

Heat oil and sauté onions and garlic.

5 min

Sear chicken, add calamari and vegetables, continue frying.

15 min

Add wine, chicken stock, saffron and rice. Season with salt and pepper and simmer at low heat.

15 min

Add peas, shrimp and mussels to the rice. Cover and continue to simmer.

Garnish with lemon wedges.

3 eggs

1 tbsp soy sauce

2 tbsp oil

6 spring onions, thinly sliced

2 onions, minced

2 cloves garlic, minced

1 small piece of ginger, minced

1 chile, minced

1½ cups/11 oz/ 350 g cooked long grain rice

177 cook rice

1 lb/500 g cooked chicken breast, cut into strips

½ lb/250 g shrimp, cooked and peeled

3 tbsp light soy sauce

2 tbsp lemon juice

1 tbsp brown sugar

salt

pepper

2 tbsp peanuts, chopped

061 peel and devein a shrimp

Whisk eggs and soy sauce.

Heat 1 tbsp of oil and add egg mixture. Cook until the egg solidifies.

Take it out; cut into strips.

Heat 1 tbsp of oil; sauté spring onions, garlic, ginger, onions and chile.

5 min

Add rice, fry; season with salt and pepper.

4 min

Sear chicken breast, shrimp, soy sauce, lemon juice and sugar at high heat, stirring constantly.

3 min

Stir in the egg strips, season with salt and pepper and garnish with peanuts.

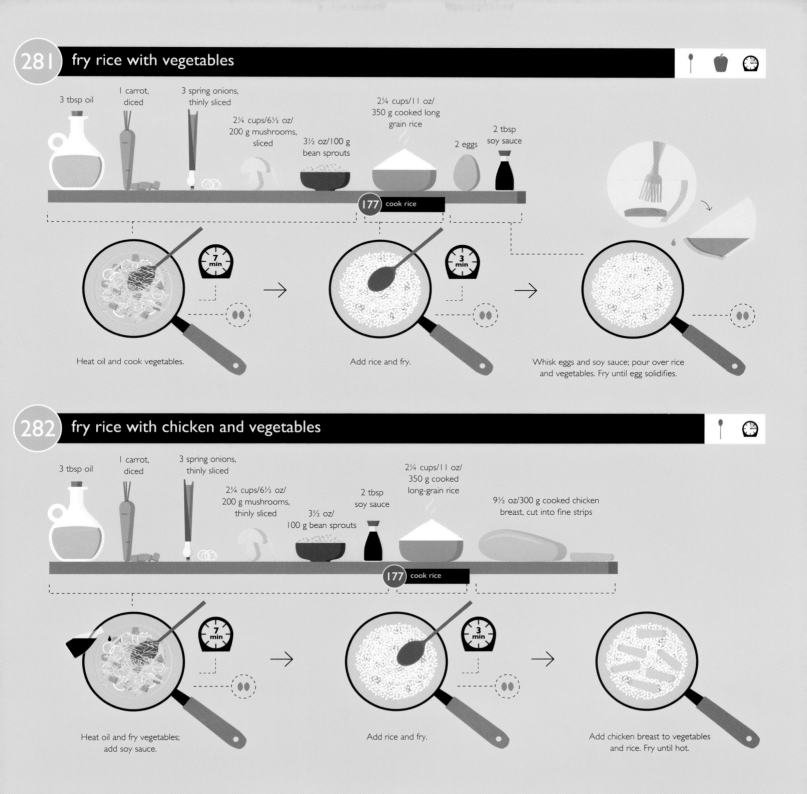

281 fry rice with vegetables

3 tbsp oil

1 carrot, diced

3 spring onions, thinly sliced

2¼ cups/6½ oz/ 200 g mushrooms, sliced

3½ oz/100 g bean sprouts

2¼ cups/11 oz/ 350 g cooked long grain rice

2 eggs

2 tbsp soy sauce

177 cook rice

7 min

3 min

Heat oil and cook vegetables.

Add rice and fry.

Whisk eggs and soy sauce; pour over rice and vegetables. Fry until egg solidifies.

282 fry rice with chicken and vegetables

3 tbsp oil

1 carrot, diced

3 spring onions, thinly sliced

2¼ cups/6½ oz/ 200 g mushrooms, thinly sliced

3½ oz/ 100 g bean sprouts

2 tbsp soy sauce

2¼ cups/11 oz/ 350 g cooked long-grain rice

9½ oz/300 g cooked chicken breast, cut into fine strips

177 cook rice

7 min

3 min

Heat oil and fry vegetables; add soy sauce.

Add rice and fry.

Add chicken breast to vegetables and rice. Fry until hot.

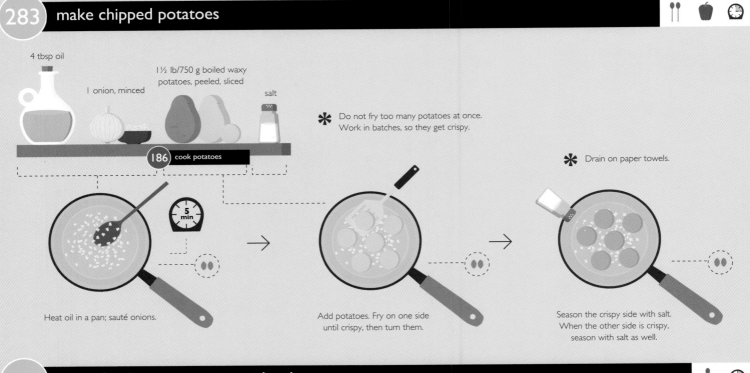

4 tbsp oil

1 onion, minced

1½ lb/750 g boiled waxy potatoes, peeled, sliced

salt

186 cook potatoes

✳ Do not fry too many potatoes at once. Work in batches, so they get crispy.

✳ Drain on paper towels.

5 min

Heat oil in a pan; sauté onions.

Add potatoes. Fry on one side until crispy, then turn them.

Season the crispy side with salt. When the other side is crispy, season with salt as well.

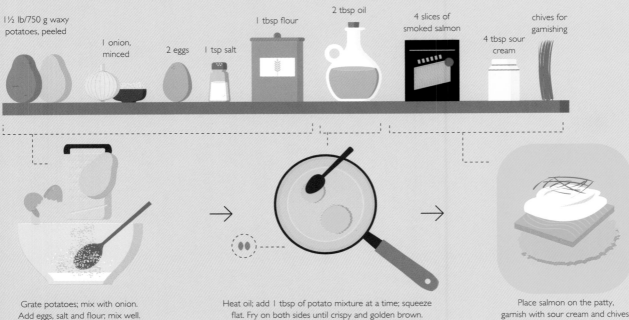

1½ lb/750 g waxy potatoes, peeled

1 onion, minced

2 eggs

1 tsp salt

1 tbsp flour

2 tbsp oil

4 slices of smoked salmon

4 tbsp sour cream

chives for garnishing

Grate potatoes; mix with onion. Add eggs, salt and flour; mix well.

Heat oil; add 1 tbsp of potato mixture at a time; squeeze flat. Fry on both sides until crispy and golden brown.

Place salmon on the patty, garnish with sour cream and chives.

8 cups/64 fl oz/
2 l oil

1½ lb/750 g waxy
potatoes, peeled

salt

✱ The oil is hot enough
when bubbles rise at a
wooden spoon handle.

**320°F/
160°C**

Cut potatoes into sticks.

Heat the oil in a pan
or a deep fryer.

Cut the potatoes into
fine sticks (size of
matches) and fry like
french fries.

**8
min**

320°F/160°C

Add potatoes to the oil and
fry until pale yellow.

Drain on paper towels. Let cool.

13 oz/400 g sweet potatoes

**3
min**

350°F/175°C

Fry a second time until the
potatoes are golden yellow.

Take them out; drain and
season with salt.

Cut sweet potatoes
into sticks and fry
like french fries.

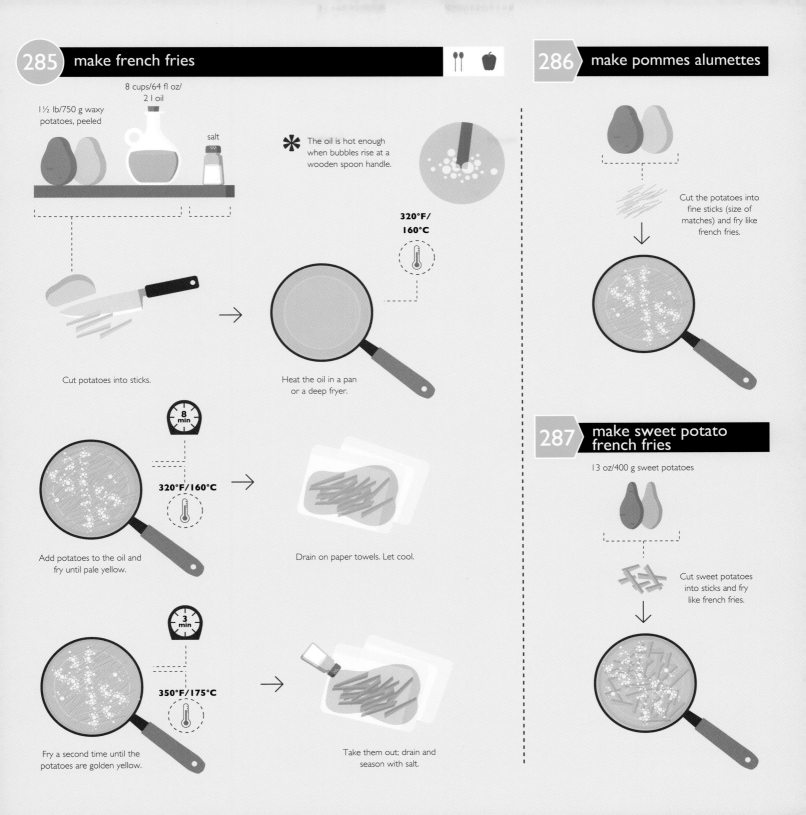

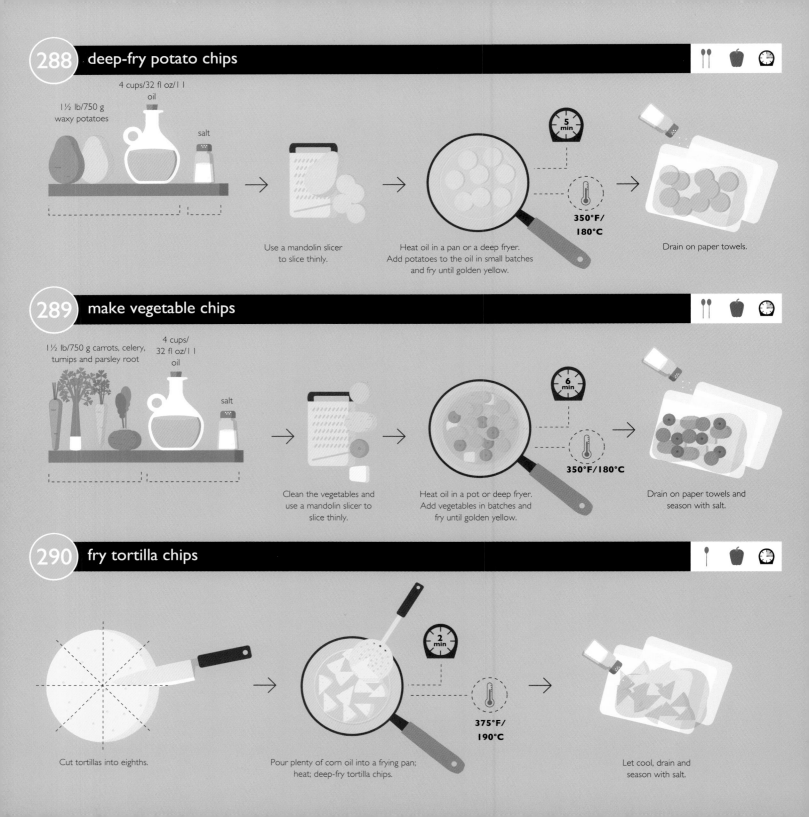

288 | deep-fry potato chips

1 ½ lb/750 g
waxy potatoes

4 cups/32 fl oz/1 l
oil

salt

5 min

350°F/
180°C

Use a mandolin slicer
to slice thinly.

Heat oil in a pan or a deep fryer.
Add potatoes to the oil in small batches
and fry until golden yellow.

Drain on paper towels.

289 | make vegetable chips

1 ½ lb/750 g carrots, celery,
turnips and parsley root

4 cups/
32 fl oz/1 l
oil

salt

6 min

350°F/180°C

Clean the vegetables and
use a mandolin slicer to
slice thinly.

Heat oil in a pot or deep fryer.
Add vegetables in batches and
fry until golden yellow.

Drain on paper towels and
season with salt.

290 | fry tortilla chips

2 min

375°F/
190°C

Cut tortillas into eighths.

Pour plenty of corn oil into a frying pan;
heat; deep-fry tortilla chips.

Let cool, drain and
season with salt.

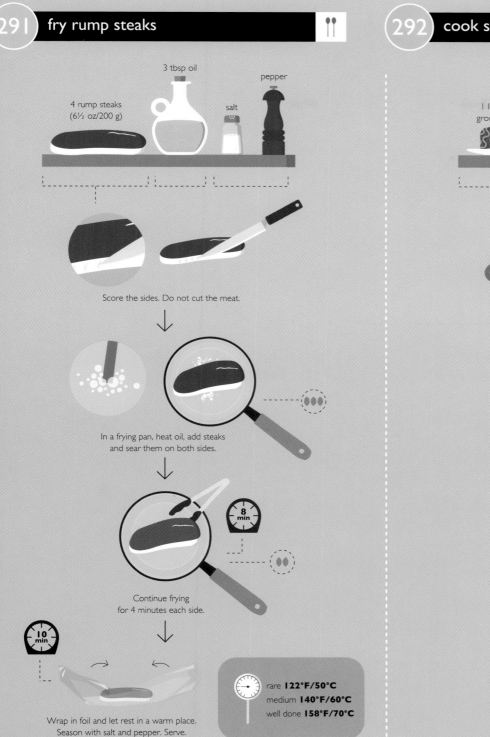

3 tbsp oil

4 rump steaks
(6½ oz/200 g)

salt

pepper

Score the sides. Do not cut the meat.

In a frying pan, heat oil, add steaks
and sear them on both sides.

8 min

Continue frying
for 4 minutes each side.

10 min

Wrap in foil and let rest in a warm place.
Season with salt and pepper. Serve.

rare **122°F/50°C**
medium **140°F/60°C**
well done **158°F/70°C**

2 tbsp oil

1 lb/500 g
ground beef

salt

pepper

Season the ground beef with salt and use
your hands to form 4 steaks.

8 min

Heat oil, put in the steaks and fry
on both sides for about 4 minutes.

Season with pepper before serving.

335 stack mean
burgers

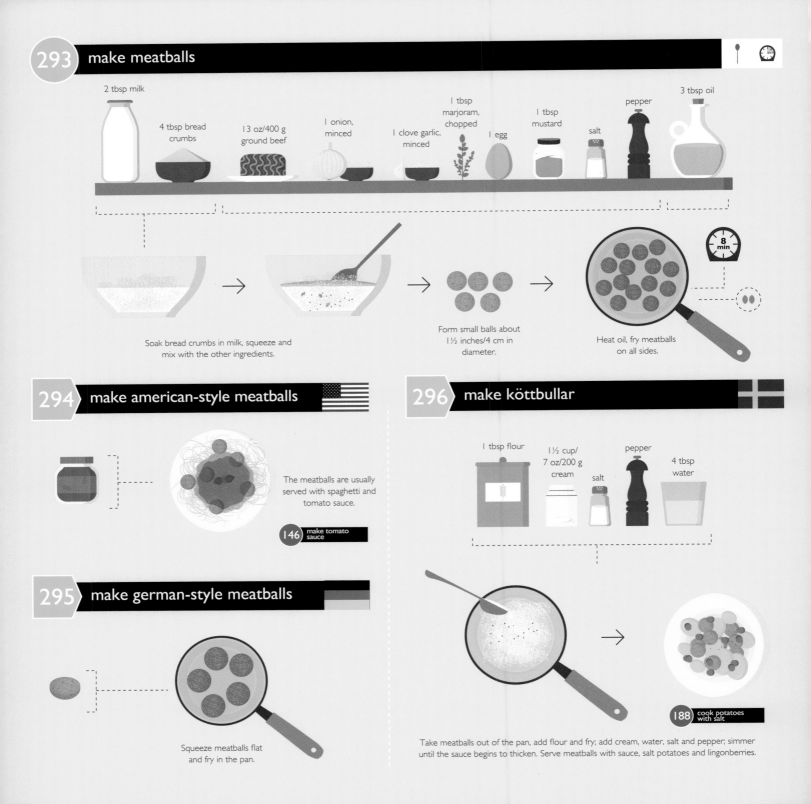

2 tbsp milk

4 tbsp bread crumbs

13 oz/400 g ground beef

1 onion, minced

1 clove garlic, minced

1 tbsp marjoram, chopped

1 egg

1 tbsp mustard

salt

pepper

3 tbsp oil

Soak bread crumbs in milk, squeeze and mix with the other ingredients.

Form small balls about 1½ inches/4 cm in diameter.

8 min

Heat oil, fry meatballs on all sides.

294 make american-style meatballs

The meatballs are usually served with spaghetti and tomato sauce.

146 make tomato sauce

295 make german-style meatballs

Squeeze meatballs flat and fry in the pan.

296 make köttbullar

1 tbsp flour

1½ cup/ 7 oz/200 g cream

salt

pepper

4 tbsp water

188 cook potatoes with salt

Take meatballs out of the pan, add flour and fry; add cream, water, salt and pepper; simmer until the sauce begins to thicken. Serve meatballs with sauce, salt potatoes and lingonberries.

297 make kofta

1 tbsp parsley, chopped
½ tsp chile powder
½ tsp ground cumin

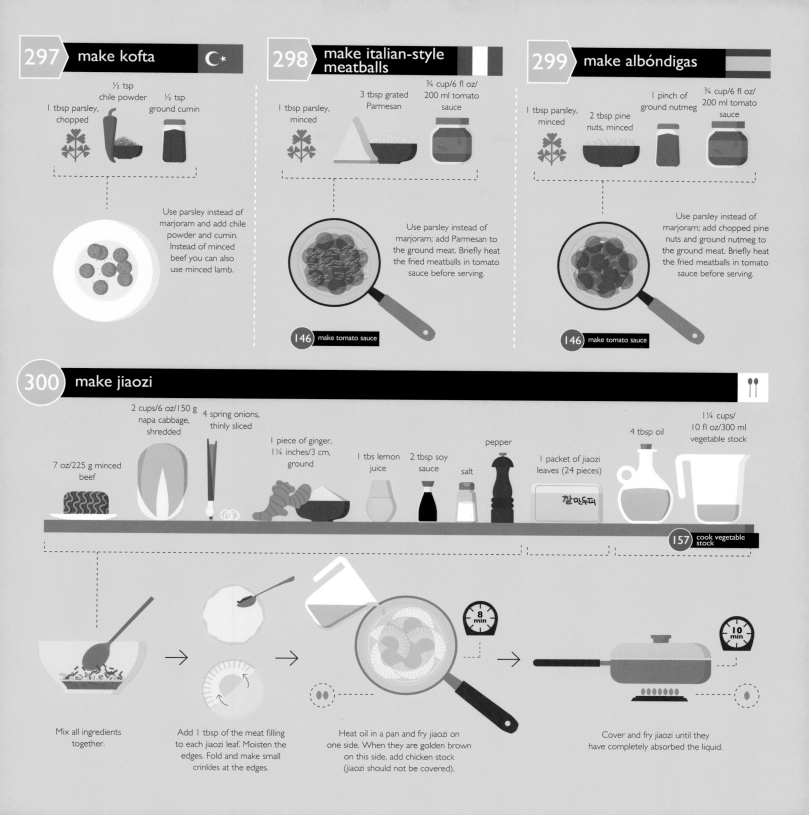

Use parsley instead of marjoram and add chile powder and cumin. Instead of minced beef you can also use minced lamb.

298 make italian-style meatballs

1 tbsp parsley, minced
3 tbsp grated Parmesan
¾ cup/6 fl oz/ 200 ml tomato sauce

Use parsley instead of marjoram; add Parmesan to the ground meat. Briefly heat the fried meatballs in tomato sauce before serving.

146 make tomato sauce

299 make albóndigas

1 tbsp parsley, minced
2 tbsp pine nuts, minced
1 pinch of ground nutmeg
¾ cup/6 fl oz/ 200 ml tomato sauce

Use parsley instead of marjoram; add chopped pine nuts and ground nutmeg to the ground meat. Briefly heat the fried meatballs in tomato sauce before serving.

146 make tomato sauce

300 make jiaozi

7 oz/225 g minced beef
2 cups/6 oz/150 g napa cabbage, shredded
4 spring onions, thinly sliced
1 piece of ginger, 1¼ inches/3 cm, ground
1 tbs lemon juice
2 tbsp soy sauce
salt
pepper
1 packet of jiaozi leaves (24 pieces)
4 tbsp oil
1¼ cups/ 10 fl oz/300 ml vegetable stock

찰만두피

157 cook vegetable stock

Mix all ingredients together.

Add 1 tbsp of the meat filling to each jiaozi leaf. Moisten the edges. Fold and make small crinkles at the edges.

8 min

Heat oil in a pan and fry jiaozi on one side. When they are golden brown on this side, add chicken stock (jiaozi should not be covered).

10 min

Cover and fry jiaozi until they have completely absorbed the liquid.

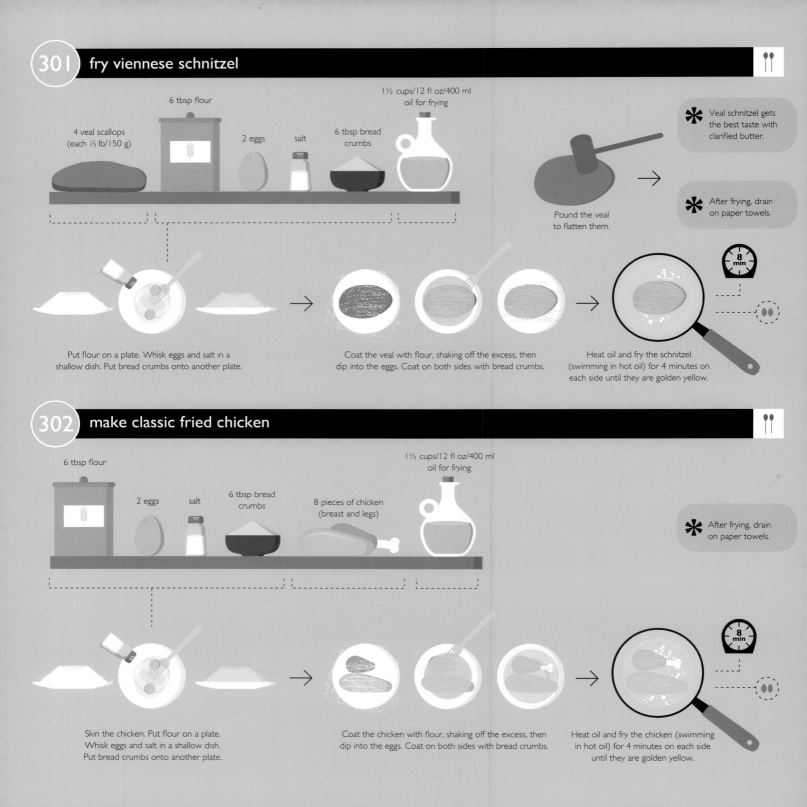

301 fry viennese schnitzel

4 veal scallops
(each ⅓ lb/150 g)

6 tbsp flour

2 eggs

salt

6 tbsp bread crumbs

1½ cups/12 fl oz/400 ml oil for frying

Pound the veal to flatten them.

Veal schnitzel gets the best taste with clarified butter.

After frying, drain on paper towels.

8 min

Put flour on a plate. Whisk eggs and salt in a shallow dish. Put bread crumbs onto another plate.

Coat the veal with flour, shaking off the excess, then dip into the eggs. Coat on both sides with bread crumbs.

Heat oil and fry the schnitzel (swimming in hot oil) for 4 minutes on each side until they are golden yellow.

302 make classic fried chicken

6 tbsp flour

2 eggs

salt

6 tbsp bread crumbs

8 pieces of chicken (breast and legs)

1½ cups/12 fl oz/400 ml oil for frying

After frying, drain on paper towels.

8 min

Skin the chicken. Put flour on a plate. Whisk eggs and salt in a shallow dish. Put bread crumbs onto another plate.

Coat the chicken with flour, shaking off the excess, then dip into the eggs. Coat on both sides with bread crumbs.

Heat oil and fry the chicken (swimming in hot oil) for 4 minutes on each side until they are golden yellow.

prepare saltimbocca

8 small veal scallops
(size of a hand, each
2½ oz/75 g)

8 slices
raw ham

8 leaves
of sage

salt

pepper

3 tbsp oil

½ cup/4 fl oz/
125 ml white wine

2 tsp cold
butter

Pound the veal
to flatten them.

Cover with raw ham and sage.
fold scallops and fasten with toothpicks.
Season with salt and pepper.

3 min

Heat oil and fry veal for
3 minutes on each side. Remove
and set aside in a warm place.

Deglaze with white wine, cook until the
liquid is reduced by half. Remove from
the heat and stir in the cold butter.

5 min

Return the veal to the sauce
and cook until warm.

learn folding techniques for galettes, pancakes and crepes

ROLL

ROLL INTO QUARTERS

FOLD A BRETON GALETTE

FOLD IN HALF

Fold edges to the middle (put filling in
the center—it stays open in the middle).

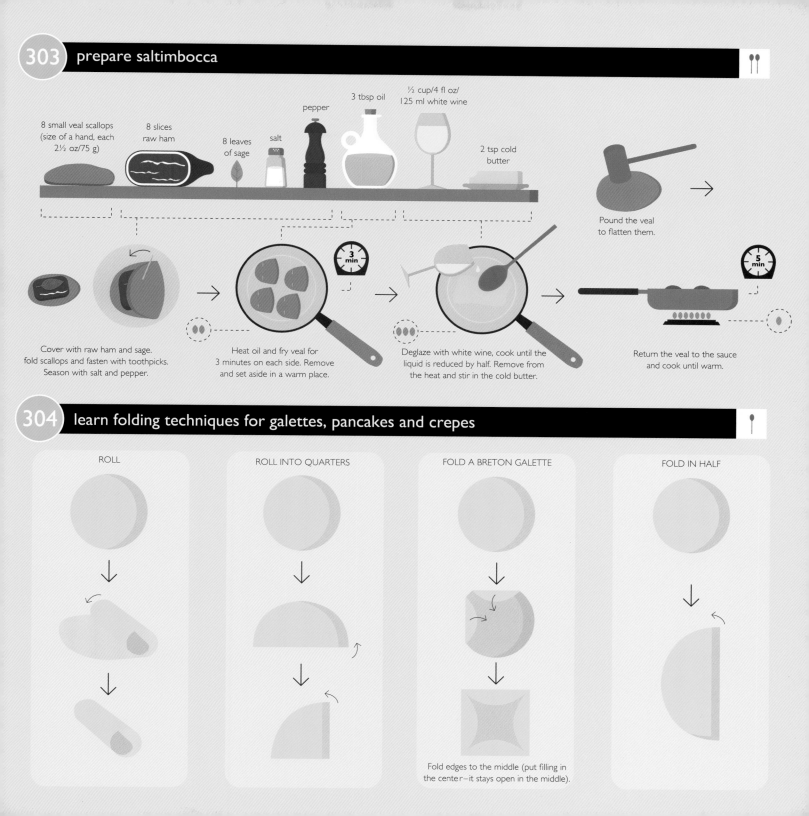

305 | make galettes

2 eggs

2 cups/8 oz/250 g buckwheat flour

1¼ cups/10 fl oz/300 ml water

3 tbsp sparkling water

salt

2 tbsp melted butter, plus butter for frying

4 h

Combine all ingredients and leave the batter to rest.

Heat pan and melt butter. Add 1 scoop of batter and turn the pan until the batter covers the base evenly. Galettes should be very thin.

Fry one side golden brown, turn with a spatula. Fry the other side golden brown.

306 | make savory pancakes

4 eggs

2 cups/8 oz/250 g flour

1½ cups/12 fl oz/400 ml milk

3 tbsp sparkling water

1 pinch of salt

butter for frying

30 min

Combine all ingredients and leave the batter to rest.

Melt 1 tsp of butter. Add 1 scoop of batter and turn the pan until the batter covers the base evenly.

Fry golden brown, turn with a spatula. Fry the other side golden brown.

307 | make herbed galettes

1½ cup/7 oz/200 g cottage cheese

2 tbsp milk

4 tbsp mixed herbs (parsley, chives, chervil, dill, rosemary, thyme), minced

1 tbsp lemon juice

salt

pepper

1 h

In a bowl, combine all ingredients and stir well. Leave to stand.

Use to stuff galettes or pancakes.

✳ Herbed cottage cheese is also great as spread for toasted brown bread or fresh baguette.

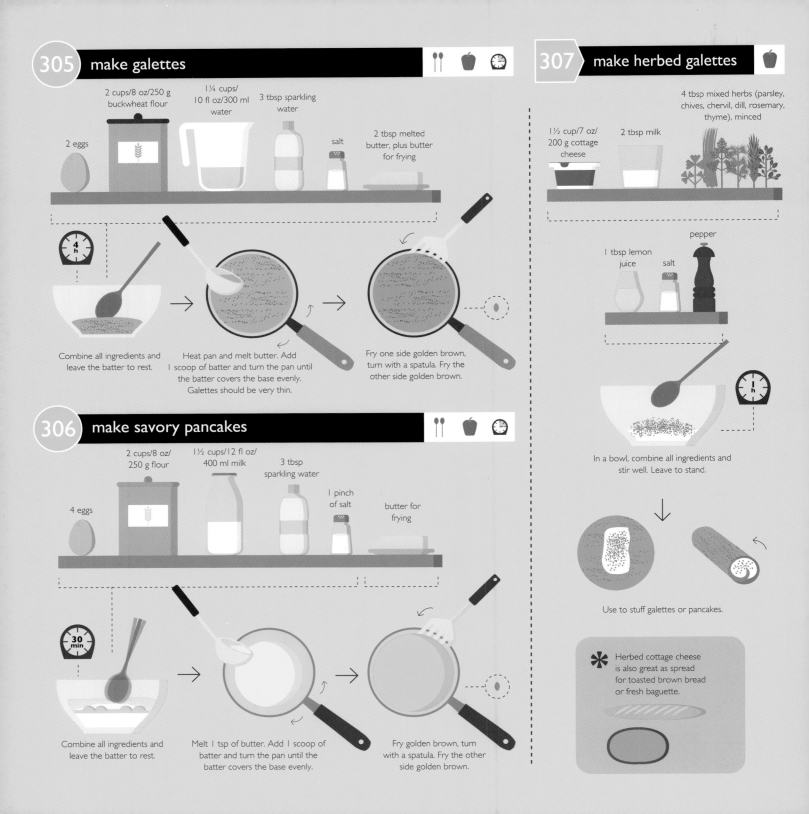

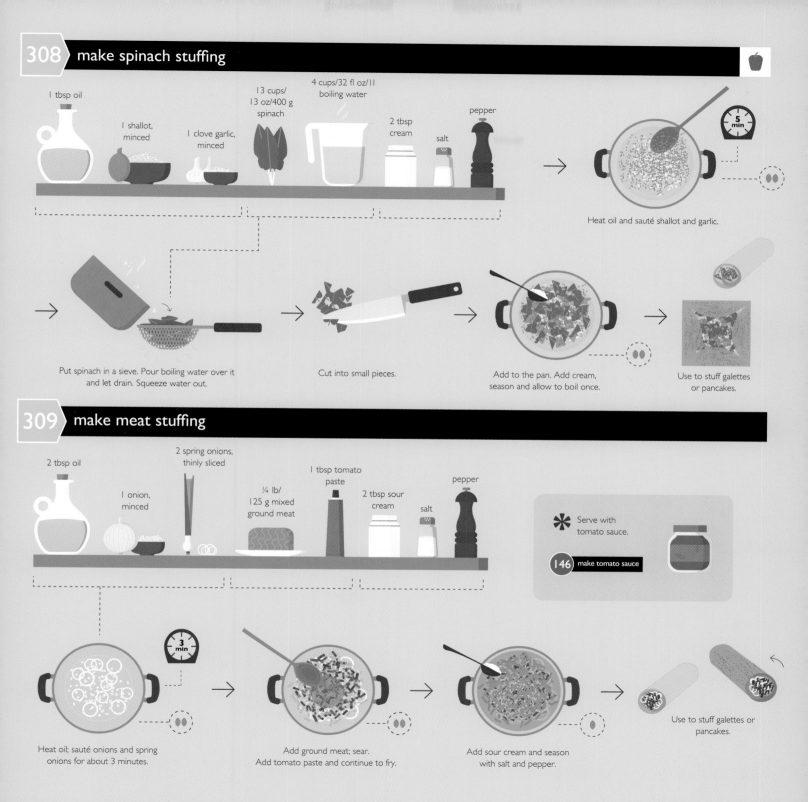

308 make spinach stuffing

1 tbsp oil

1 shallot, minced

1 clove garlic, minced

13 cups/ 13 oz/400 g spinach

4 cups/32 fl oz/1l boiling water

2 tbsp cream

salt

pepper

5 min

Heat oil and sauté shallot and garlic.

Put spinach in a sieve. Pour boiling water over it and let drain. Squeeze water out.

Cut into small pieces.

Add to the pan. Add cream, season and allow to boil once.

Use to stuff galettes or pancakes.

309 make meat stuffing

2 tbsp oil

1 onion, minced

2 spring onions, thinly sliced

¼ lb/ 125 g mixed ground meat

1 tbsp tomato paste

2 tbsp sour cream

salt

pepper

Serve with tomato sauce.

146 make tomato sauce

3 min

Heat oil; sauté onions and spring onions for about 3 minutes.

Add ground meat; sear. Add tomato paste and continue to fry.

Add sour cream and season with salt and pepper.

Use to stuff galettes or pancakes.

8 tbsp flour

8 tbsp cornstarch

8 tbsp iced water

1½ cups/12 fl oz/ 400 ml oil

salt

9½ oz/300 g mixed vegetables (carrots, celery, spring onions, mushrooms, oyster mushroom, bell pepper or asparagus), cut into bite-sized pieces

Stir together flour, cornstarch, salt and iced water.

Heat oil

Dip the vegetables into the flour mixture, working in small batches.

Let drain.

6 min

Fry swimming in oil.

Drain on paper towels.

311 prepare tempura with shrimp

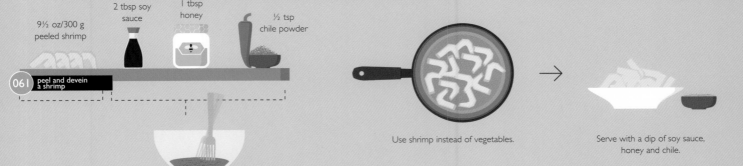

9½ oz/300 g peeled shrimp

2 tbsp soy sauce

1 tbsp honey

½ tsp chile powder

061 peel and devein a shrimp

Use shrimp instead of vegetables.

Serve with a dip of soy sauce, honey and chile.

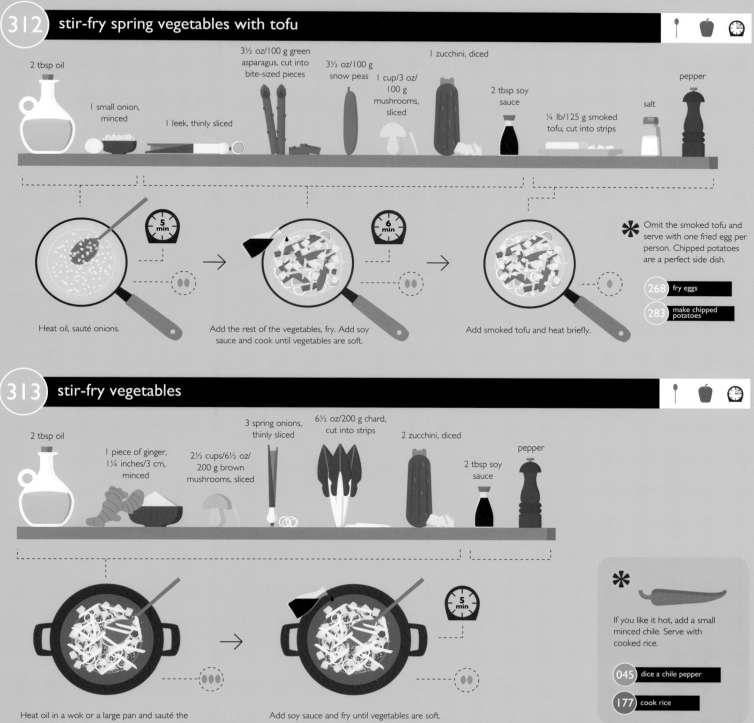

312 stir-fry spring vegetables with tofu

2 tbsp oil

1 small onion, minced

1 leek, thinly sliced

3½ oz/100 g green asparagus, cut into bite-sized pieces

3½ oz/100 g snow peas

1 cup/3 oz/100 g mushrooms, sliced

1 zucchini, diced

2 tbsp soy sauce

¼ lb/125 g smoked tofu, cut into strips

salt

pepper

5 min — Heat oil, sauté onions.

6 min — Add the rest of the vegetables, fry. Add soy sauce and cook until vegetables are soft.

Add smoked tofu and heat briefly.

* Omit the smoked tofu and serve with one fried egg per person. Chipped potatoes are a perfect side dish.

268 fry eggs

283 make chipped potatoes

313 stir-fry vegetables

2 tbsp oil

1 piece of ginger, 1¼ inches/3 cm, minced

2½ cups/6½ oz/200 g brown mushrooms, sliced

3 spring onions, thinly sliced

6½ oz/200 g chard, cut into strips

2 zucchini, diced

2 tbsp soy sauce

pepper

Heat oil in a wok or a large pan and sauté the ginger. Add vegetables and fry briefly.

5 min — Add soy sauce and fry until vegetables are soft.

* If you like it hot, add a small minced chile. Serve with cooked rice.

045 dice a chile pepper

177 cook rice

314 deep-fry artichokes

3 eggs

3 tbsp grated Parmesan

salt

pepper

6 small artichokes, trimmed and quartered

½ cup/ 2 oz/60 g bread crumbs

2 cups/16 fl oz/ 500 ml oil

053 trim an artichoke

✳ Drain on paper towels.

In a bowl, whisk eggs. Add Parmesan, season with salt and pepper, and stir well.

Dip the artichokes into the egg mixture.

Coat with bread crumbs.

Heat oil.

Fry swimming in oil until golden.

4 min

315 fry tofu with ginger

2 stalks of lemongrass, finely sliced

1 piece of ginger, ¼ inches/3 cm, minced

1 tbsp soy sauce

1 tbsp lemon juice

1 tsp sugar

3 tbsp oil

salt

pepper

1 tbsp oil

13 oz/400 g tofu, diced

1 tbsp thai basil, cut into fine strips

060 prepare lemongrass

Combine the ingredients for the marinade in a plastic bag.

Add tofu. Shake well and let marinate. Remove tofu and drain.

2 h

Heat oil and fry tofu on all sides. Remove tofu and put aside in a warm place.

7 min

Add the rest of the marinade and simmer until the liquid is reduced. Mix with tofu and garnish with thai basil.

1 min

316 prepare garlic shrimp

2 tbsp oil

5 cloves garlic, minced

1 chile, minced

13 oz/400 g shrimp, peeled

1 tbsp lemon juice

salt

1 tbsp parsley, minced

061 peel and devein a shrimp

2 min

5 min

Heat oil in a pan, add spices and sauté.

Add shrimp, fry on all sides.

Sprinkle with lemon juice, season with salt and garnish with parsley.

317 make little crab cakes

3 tbsp mayonnaise

1 tbsp mustard

½ cup/2 oz/ 60 g bread crumbs

salt

pepper

1 celery stalk, minced

2 spring onions, minced

2 cups/1 lb/500 g crab meat

½ cup/2 oz/ 60 g bread crumbs

4 tbsp oil

❋ Serve with tartar sauce.

084 make tartar sauce

080 make mayonnaise

6 min

In a bowl, stir together all ingredients. Gently fold in the crab meat.

With your hands, shape the crab mixture into 8 patties.

Put bread crumbs on a plate, place each cake in the bread crumbs and turn to coat evenly.

Heat oil and fry the crab cakes 3–4 minutes on each side until golden brown.

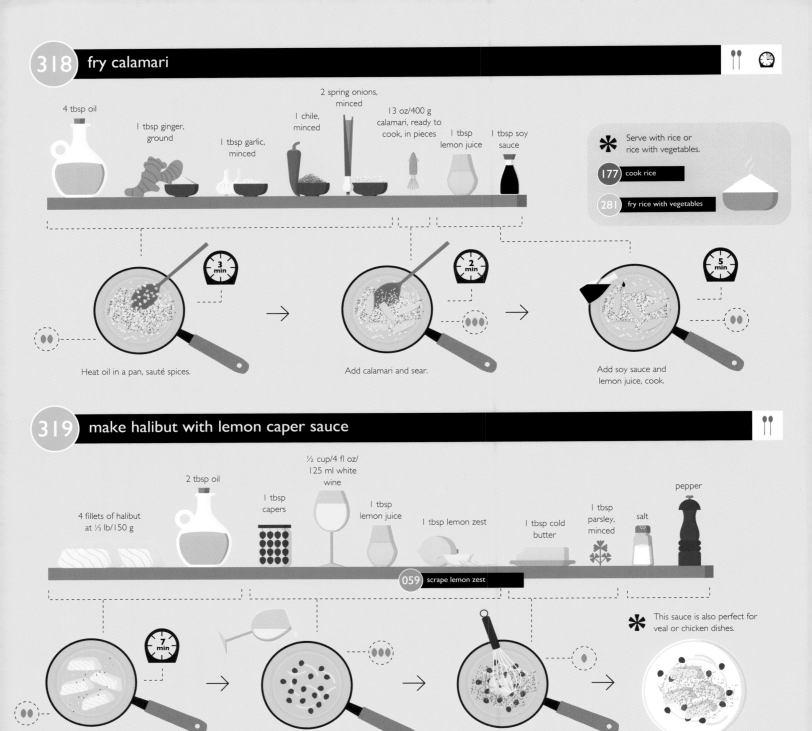

318 fry calamari

4 tbsp oil

1 tbsp ginger, ground

1 tbsp garlic, minced

1 chile, minced

2 spring onions, minced

13 oz/400 g calamari, ready to cook, in pieces

1 tbsp lemon juice

1 tbsp soy sauce

Serve with rice or rice with vegetables.

177 cook rice

281 fry rice with vegetables

3 min — Heat oil in a pan, sauté spices.

2 min — Add calamari and sear.

5 min — Add soy sauce and lemon juice, cook.

319 make halibut with lemon caper sauce

4 fillets of halibut at ⅓ lb/150 g

2 tbsp oil

1 tbsp capers

½ cup/4 fl oz/ 125 ml white wine

1 tbsp lemon juice

1 tbsp lemon zest

1 tbsp cold butter

1 tbsp parsley, minced

salt

pepper

059 scrape lemon zest

This sauce is also perfect for veal or chicken dishes.

7 min — Season fillets with salt and pepper. Heat oil and fry the fillets on both sides. Remove fillets and set aside in a warm place.

Add all ingredients for the sauce to the pan and bring to a boil.

Gradually, stir small pieces of butter into the sauce. Add parsley.

Transfer the fillets to plates and pour over the warm sauce.

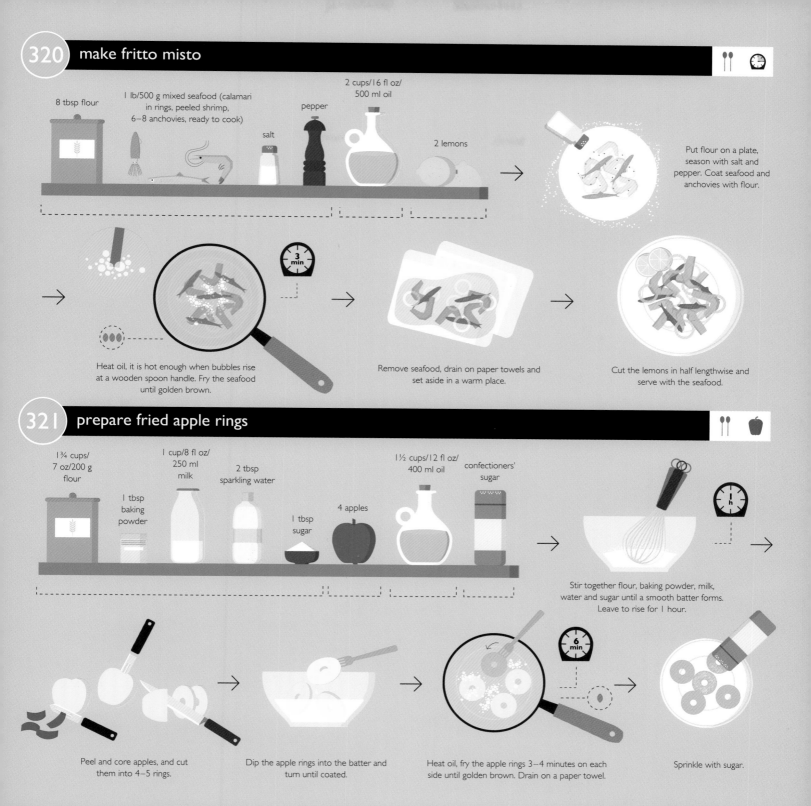

320   make fritto misto

8 tbsp flour

1 lb/500 g mixed seafood (calamari in rings, peeled shrimp, 6–8 anchovies, ready to cook)

salt

pepper

2 cups/16 fl oz/ 500 ml oil

2 lemons

Put flour on a plate, season with salt and pepper. Coat seafood and anchovies with flour.

3 min

Heat oil, it is hot enough when bubbles rise at a wooden spoon handle. Fry the seafood until golden brown.

Remove seafood, drain on paper towels and set aside in a warm place.

Cut the lemons in half lengthwise and serve with the seafood.

321   prepare fried apple rings

1 ¾ cups/ 7 oz/200 g flour

1 tbsp baking powder

1 cup/8 fl oz/ 250 ml milk

2 tbsp sparkling water

1 tbsp sugar

4 apples

1 ½ cups/12 fl oz/ 400 ml oil

confectioners' sugar

Stir together flour, baking powder, milk, water and sugar until a smooth batter forms. Leave to rise for 1 hour.

Peel and core apples, and cut them into 4–5 rings.

Dip the apple rings into the batter and turn until coated.

6 min

Heat oil, fry the apple rings 3–4 minutes on each side until golden brown. Drain on a paper towel.

Sprinkle with sugar.

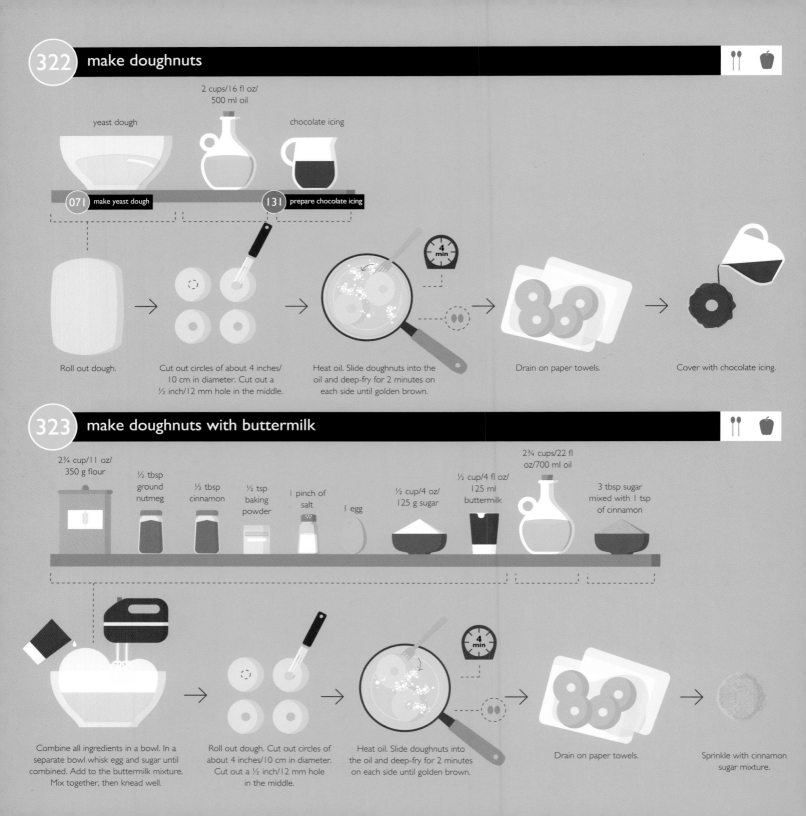

322 make doughnuts

2 cups/16 fl oz/
500 ml oil

yeast dough

chocolate icing

071 make yeast dough

131 prepare chocolate icing

4 min

Roll out dough.

Cut out circles of about 4 inches/
10 cm in diameter. Cut out a
½ inch/12 mm hole in the middle.

Heat oil. Slide doughnuts into the
oil and deep-fry for 2 minutes on
each side until golden brown.

Drain on paper towels.

Cover with chocolate icing.

323 make doughnuts with buttermilk

2¾ cup/11 oz/
350 g flour

½ tbsp
ground
nutmeg

½ tbsp
cinnamon

½ tsp
baking
powder

1 pinch of
salt

1 egg

½ cup/4 oz/
125 g sugar

½ cup/4 fl oz/
125 ml
buttermilk

2¾ cups/22 fl
oz/700 ml oil

3 tbsp sugar
mixed with 1 tsp
of cinnamon

4 min

Combine all ingredients in a bowl. In a
separate bowl whisk egg and sugar until
combined. Add to the buttermilk mixture.
Mix together, then knead well.

Roll out dough. Cut out circles of
about 4 inches/10 cm in diameter.
Cut out a ½ inch/12 mm hole
in the middle.

Heat oil. Slide doughnuts into
the oil and deep-fry for 2 minutes
on each side until golden brown.

Drain on paper towels.

Sprinkle with cinnamon
sugar mixture.

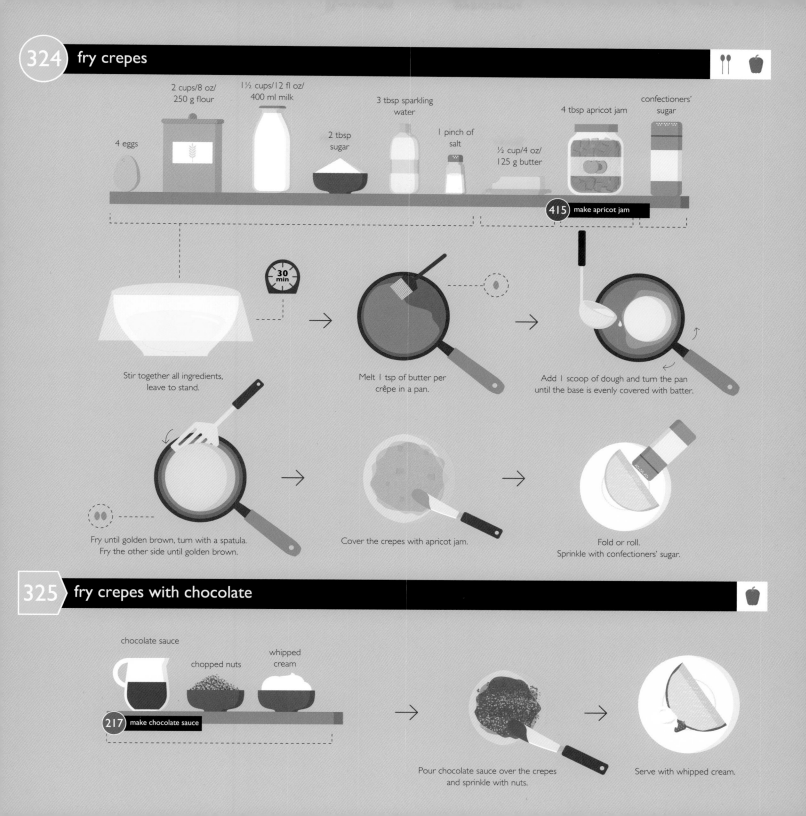

324 | fry crepes

4 eggs

2 cups/8 oz/ 250 g flour

1 ½ cups/12 fl oz/ 400 ml milk

2 tbsp sugar

3 tbsp sparkling water

1 pinch of salt

½ cup/4 oz/ 125 g butter

4 tbsp apricot jam

confectioners' sugar

415 make apricot jam

Stir together all ingredients, leave to stand.

Melt 1 tsp of butter per crêpe in a pan.

Add 1 scoop of dough and turn the pan until the base is evenly covered with batter.

Fry until golden brown, turn with a spatula. Fry the other side until golden brown.

Cover the crepes with apricot jam.

Fold or roll. Sprinkle with confectioners' sugar.

325 | fry crepes with chocolate

chocolate sauce

chopped nuts

whipped cream

217 make chocolate sauce

Pour chocolate sauce over the crepes and sprinkle with nuts.

Serve with whipped cream.

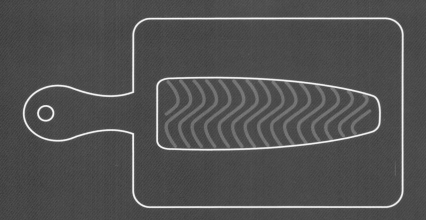

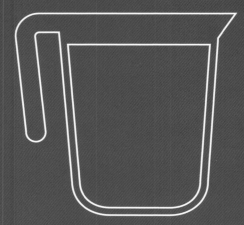

grill

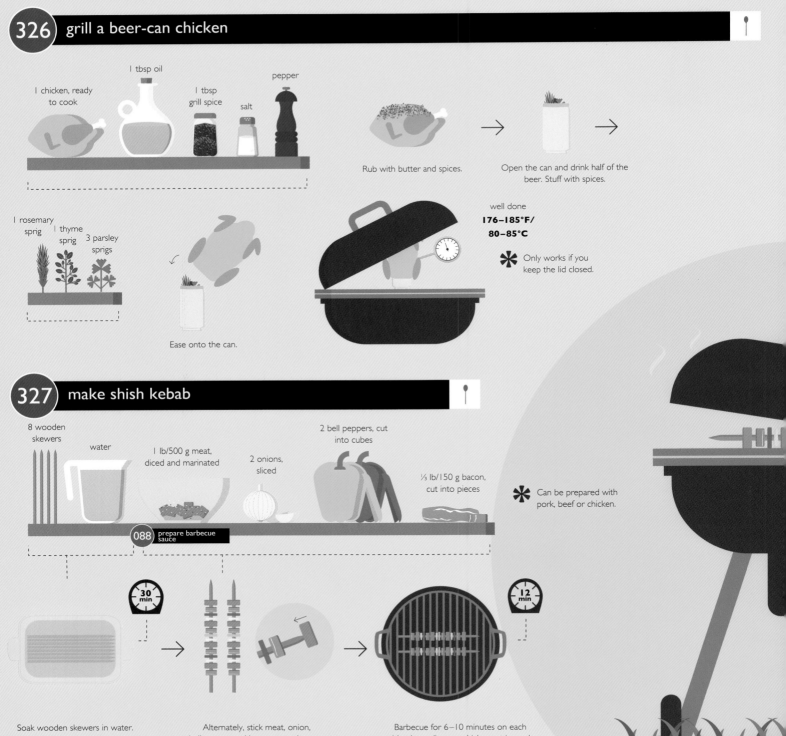

1 chicken, ready to cook

1 tbsp oil

1 tbsp grill spice

salt

pepper

Rub with butter and spices.

Open the can and drink half of the beer. Stuff with spices.

1 rosemary sprig

1 thyme sprig

3 parsley sprigs

Ease onto the can.

well done
176–185°F/ 80–85°C

✻ Only works if you keep the lid closed.

8 wooden skewers

water

1 lb/500 g meat, diced and marinated

2 onions, sliced

2 bell peppers, cut into cubes

⅓ lb/150 g bacon, cut into pieces

088 prepare barbecue sauce

✻ Can be prepared with pork, beef or chicken.

30 min

12 min

Soak wooden skewers in water.

Alternately, stick meat, onion, bell pepper and bacon onto skewers.

Barbecue for 6–10 minutes on each side, depending on which meat is used.

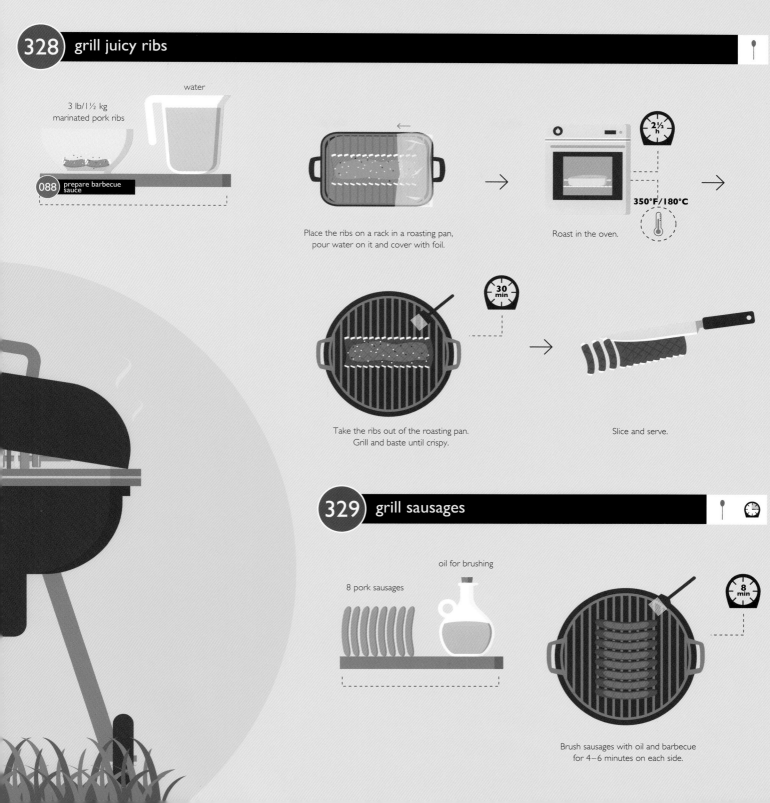

328 grill juicy ribs

3 lb/1½ kg
marinated pork ribs

water

088 prepare barbecue sauce

Place the ribs on a rack in a roasting pan,
pour water on it and cover with foil.

2½ h

350°F/180°C

Roast in the oven.

30 min

Take the ribs out of the roasting pan.
Grill and baste until crispy.

Slice and serve.

329 grill sausages

8 pork sausages

oil for brushing

8 min

Brush sausages with oil and barbecue
for 4–6 minutes on each side.

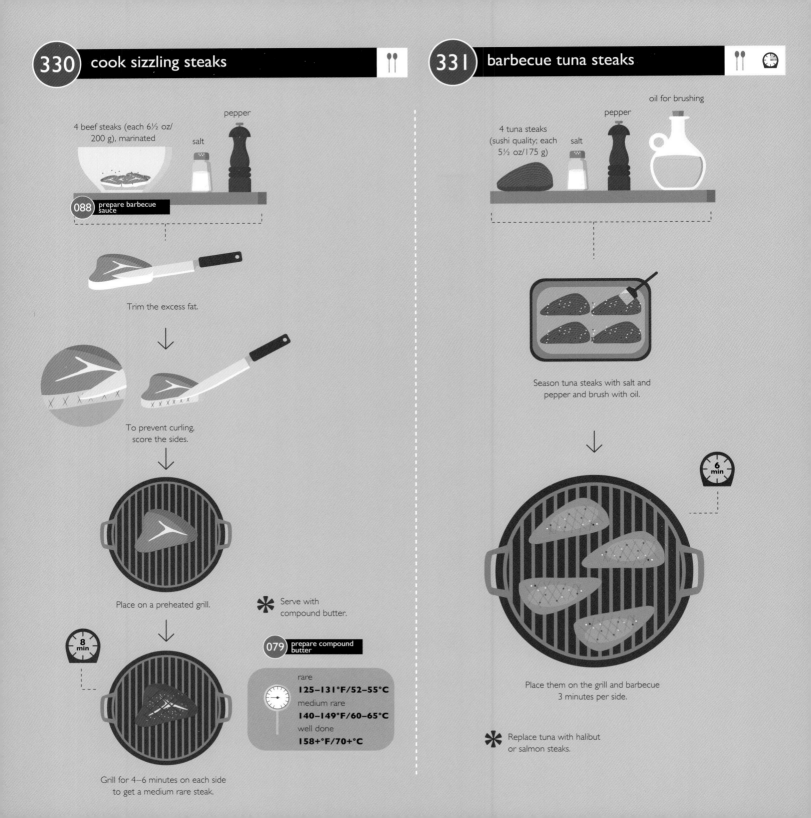

330 cook sizzling steaks

4 beef steaks (each 6½ oz/200 g), marinated

salt

pepper

088 prepare barbecue sauce

Trim the excess fat.

To prevent curling, score the sides.

Place on a preheated grill.

8 min

Grill for 4–6 minutes on each side to get a medium rare steak.

✳ Serve with compound butter.

079 prepare compound butter

rare
125–131°F/52–55°C
medium rare
140–149°F/60–65°C
well done
158+°F/70+°C

331 barbecue tuna steaks

oil for brushing

4 tuna steaks (sushi quality; each 5½ oz/175 g)

salt

pepper

Season tuna steaks with salt and pepper and brush with oil.

6 min

Place them on the grill and barbecue 3 minutes per side.

✳ Replace tuna with halibut or salmon steaks.

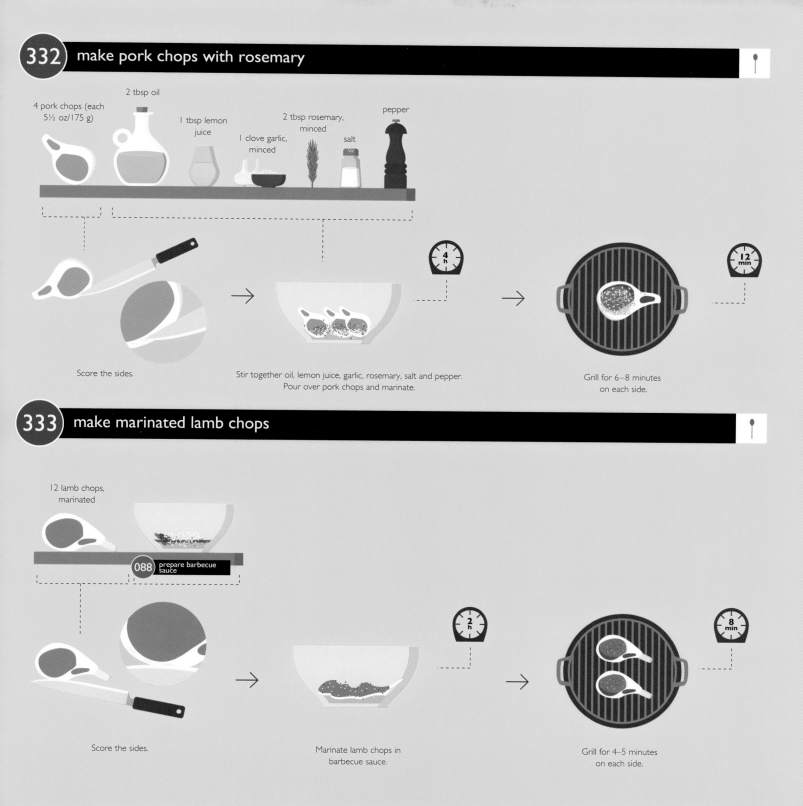

332 make pork chops with rosemary

4 pork chops (each 5½ oz/175 g)

2 tbsp oil

1 tbsp lemon juice

1 clove garlic, minced

2 tbsp rosemary, minced

salt

pepper

Score the sides.

Stir together oil, lemon juice, garlic, rosemary, salt and pepper. Pour over pork chops and marinate.

4 h

Grill for 6–8 minutes on each side.

12 min

333 make marinated lamb chops

12 lamb chops, marinated

088 prepare barbecue sauce

Score the sides.

Marinate lamb chops in barbecue sauce.

2 h

Grill for 4–5 minutes on each side.

8 min

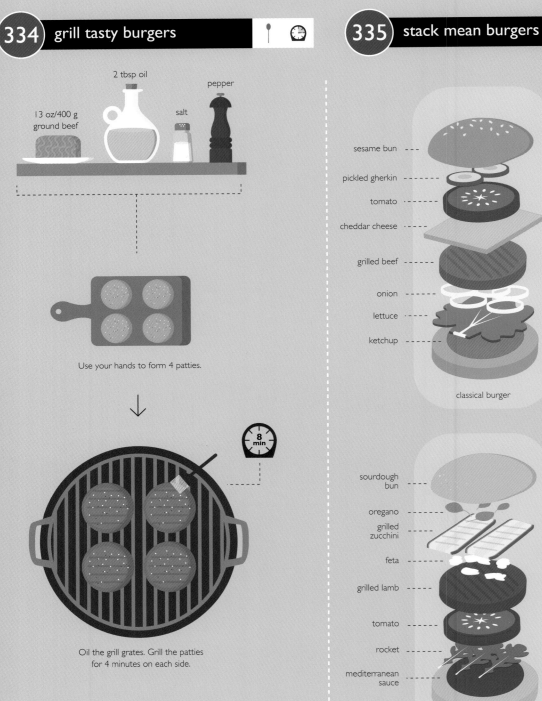

13 oz/400 g ground beef

2 tbsp oil

salt

pepper

Use your hands to form 4 patties.

8 min

Oil the grill grates. Grill the patties for 4 minutes on each side.

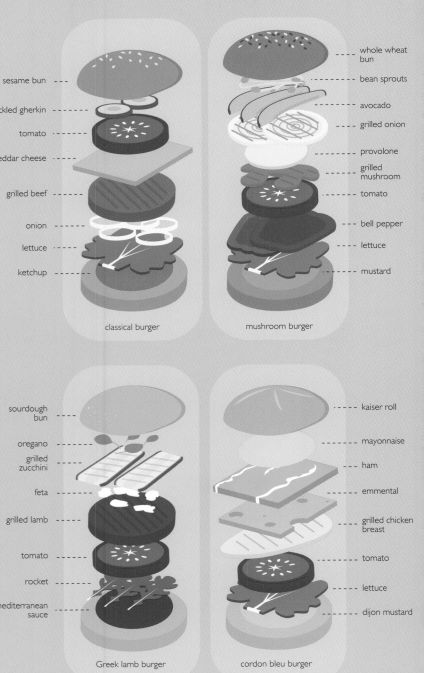

sesame bun
pickled gherkin
tomato
cheddar cheese
grilled beef
onion
lettuce
ketchup

classical burger

whole wheat bun
bean sprouts
avocado
grilled onion
provolone
grilled mushroom
tomato
bell pepper
lettuce
mustard

mushroom burger

sourdough bun
oregano
grilled zucchini
feta
grilled lamb
tomato
rocket
mediterranean sauce

Greek lamb burger

kaiser roll
mayonnaise
ham
emmental
grilled chicken breast
tomato
lettuce
dijon mustard

cordon bleu burger

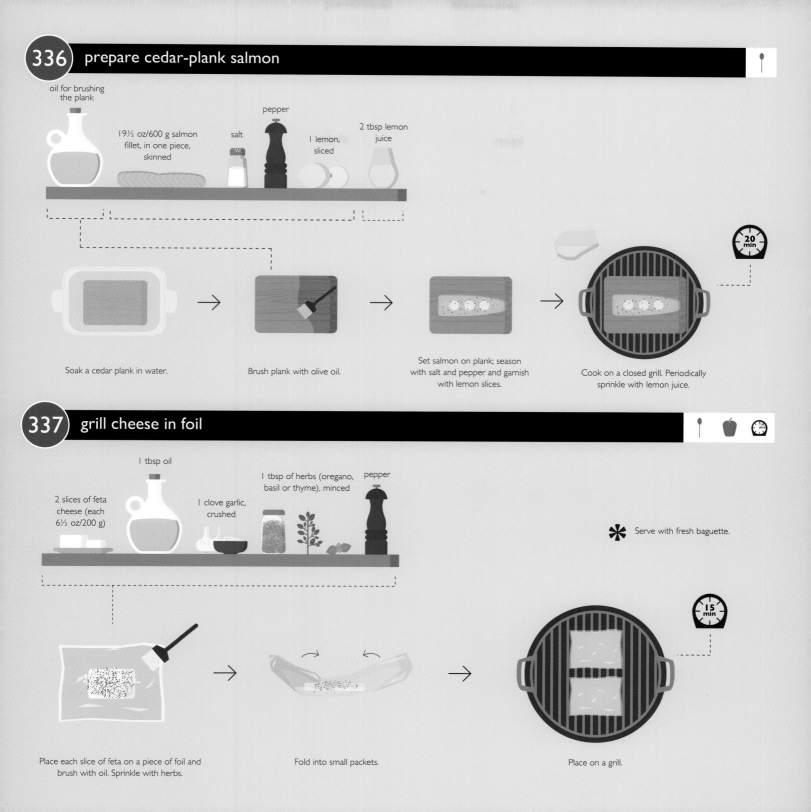

336 prepare cedar-plank salmon

oil for brushing the plank

19½ oz/600 g salmon fillet, in one piece, skinned

salt

pepper

1 lemon, sliced

2 tbsp lemon juice

20 min

Soak a cedar plank in water.

Brush plank with olive oil.

Set salmon on plank; season with salt and pepper and garnish with lemon slices.

Cook on a closed grill. Periodically sprinkle with lemon juice.

337 grill cheese in foil

2 slices of feta cheese (each 6½ oz/200 g)

1 tbsp oil

1 clove garlic, crushed

1 tbsp of herbs (oregano, basil or thyme), minced

pepper

Serve with fresh baguette.

15 min

Place each slice of feta on a piece of foil and brush with oil. Sprinkle with herbs.

Fold into small packets.

Place on a grill.

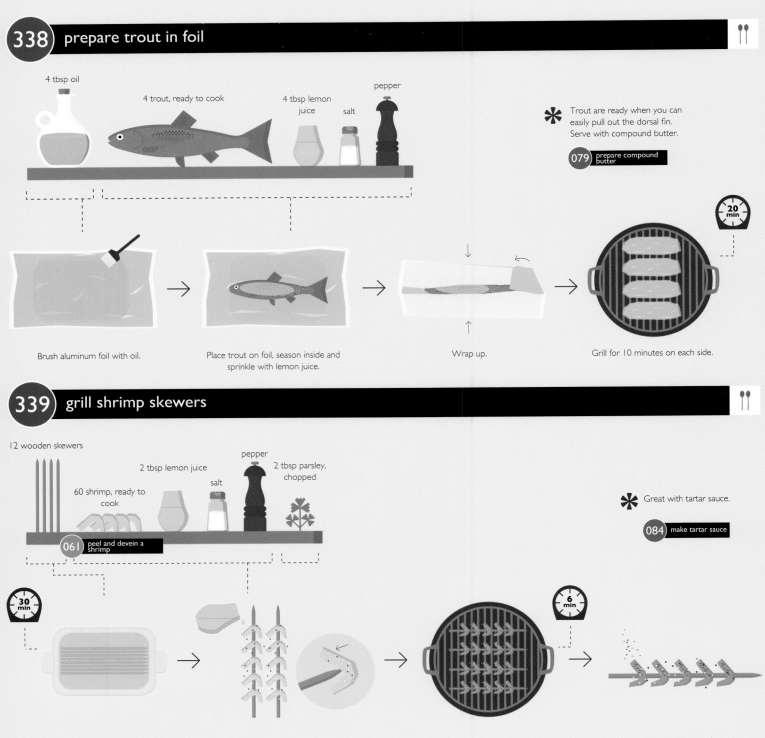

338 prepare trout in foil

4 tbsp oil

4 trout, ready to cook

4 tbsp lemon juice

salt

pepper

Trout are ready when you can easily pull out the dorsal fin. Serve with compound butter.

079 prepare compound butter

20 min

Brush aluminum foil with oil.

Place trout on foil, season inside and sprinkle with lemon juice.

Wrap up.

Grill for 10 minutes on each side.

339 grill shrimp skewers

12 wooden skewers

60 shrimp, ready to cook

2 tbsp lemon juice

salt

pepper

2 tbsp parsley, chopped

061 peel and devein a shrimp

Great with tartar sauce.

084 make tartar sauce

30 min

6 min

Soak skewers in water.

Stick 5 shrimp on each skewer. Season with lemon juice, salt and pepper.

Grill shrimp for 3 minutes on each side.

Garnish with parsley.

340 grill antipasti

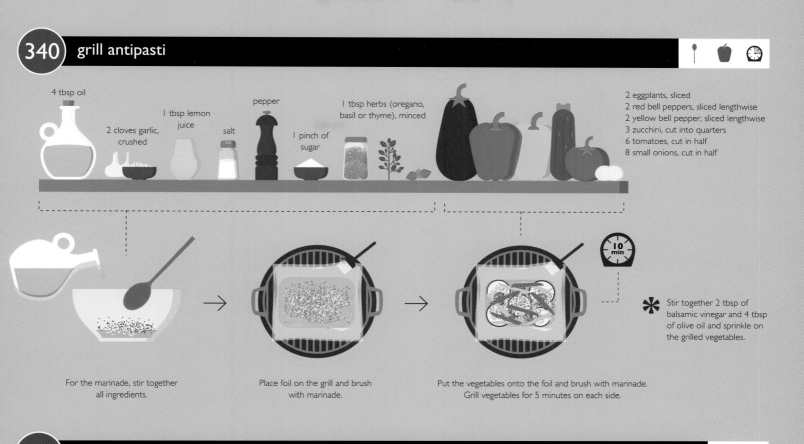

4 tbsp oil

2 cloves garlic, crushed

1 tbsp lemon juice

salt

pepper

1 pinch of sugar

1 tbsp herbs (oregano, basil or thyme), minced

2 eggplants, sliced
2 red bell peppers, sliced lengthwise
2 yellow bell pepper, sliced lengthwise
3 zucchini, cut into quarters
6 tomatoes, cut in half
8 small onions, cut in half

For the marinade, stir together all ingredients.

Place foil on the grill and brush with marinade.

Put the vegetables onto the foil and brush with marinade. Grill vegetables for 5 minutes on each side.

*Stir together 2 tbsp of balsamic vinegar and 4 tbsp of olive oil and sprinkle on the grilled vegetables.

341 grill leeks with chives and parsley

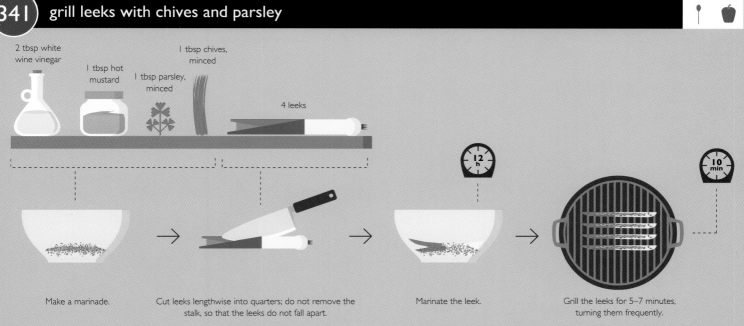

2 tbsp white wine vinegar

1 tbsp hot mustard

1 tbsp parsley, minced

1 tbsp chives, minced

4 leeks

Make a marinade.

Cut leeks lengthwise into quarters; do not remove the stalk, so that the leeks do not fall apart.

Marinate the leek.

Grill the leeks for 5–7 minutes, turning them frequently.

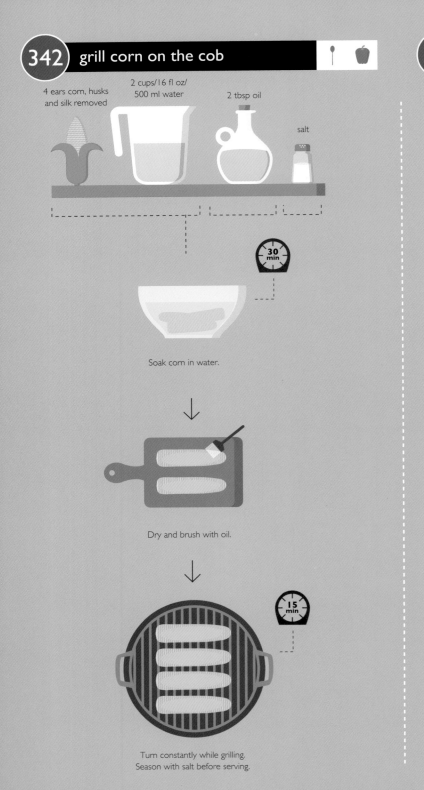

342 grill corn on the cob

4 ears corn, husks and silk removed

2 cups/16 fl oz/ 500 ml water

2 tbsp oil

salt

30 min

Soak corn in water.

↓

Dry and brush with oil.

↓

15 min

Turn constantly while grilling.
Season with salt before serving.

343 roast potatoes on the grill

3 tbsp sunflower oil

8 medium potatoes, cut into ½ inch/12 mm slices

salt

pepper

Brush potato slices with oil on both sides.

↓

Season.

↓

12 min

Grill for 6–7 minutes on each side.

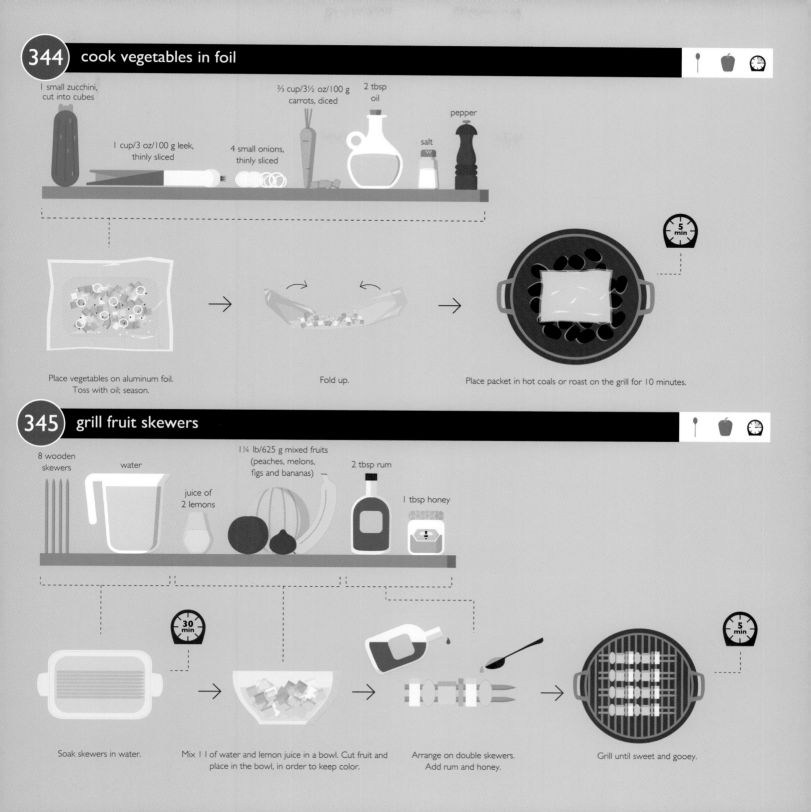

344 cook vegetables in foil

I small zucchini, cut into cubes

I cup/3 oz/100 g leek, thinly sliced

⅔ cup/3½ oz/100 g carrots, diced

4 small onions, thinly sliced

2 tbsp oil

salt

pepper

5 min

Place vegetables on aluminum foil. Toss with oil; season.

Fold up.

Place packet in hot coals or roast on the grill for 10 minutes.

345 grill fruit skewers

8 wooden skewers

water

juice of 2 lemons

1¼ lb/625 g mixed fruits (peaches, melons, figs and bananas)

2 tbsp rum

1 tbsp honey

30 min

5 min

Soak skewers in water.

Mix 1 l of water and lemon juice in a bowl. Cut fruit and place in the bowl, in order to keep color.

Arrange on double skewers. Add rum and honey.

Grill until sweet and gooey.

bake

346 make baked potatoes

4 large floury potatoes

Makes an ideal side dish for grilled foods.

Wash potatoes and wrap in foil. Place in a baking dish.

50 min

350°F/180°C

Test with a needle—the needle must pierce the potato easily. Place potatoes on a plate and open foil.

347 make baked potatoes with dip

salt

pepper

½ cup/¼ lb/125 g sour cream

2 tbsp of chives, finely snipped

Stir together and spoon into the potatoes.

348 make potatoes with scrambled eggs

2 tbsp fresh herbs, minced

scrambled eggs

273 make scrambled eggs

Prepare scrambled eggs with fresh herbs and use to fill the potatoes.

349 make baked potatoes with shrimp

3 tbsp mayonnaise

080 make mayonnaise

6½ oz/200 g cooked shrimp

Coat the shrimp with mayonnaise and use to fill the potatoes.

350 make baked potatoes with cheese sauce

¾ cup/6½ oz/200 g cheese béchamel sauce

198 make cheese béchamel sauce

Spoon warm cheese béchamel sauce into the potatoes.

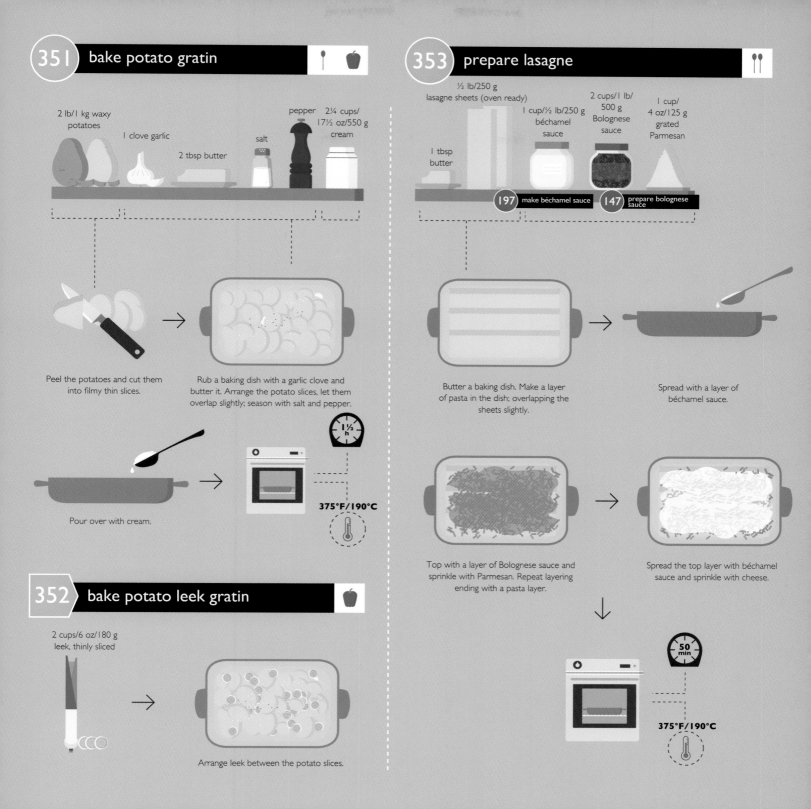

351 bake potato gratin

2 lb/1 kg waxy potatoes

1 clove garlic

2 tbsp butter

salt

pepper

2¼ cups/ 17½ oz/550 g cream

Peel the potatoes and cut them into filmy thin slices.

Rub a baking dish with a garlic clove and butter it. Arrange the potato slices, let them overlap slightly; season with salt and pepper.

Pour over with cream.

1½ h

375°F/190°C

352 bake potato leek gratin

2 cups/6 oz/180 g leek, thinly sliced

Arrange leek between the potato slices.

353 prepare lasagne

½ lb/250 g lasagne sheets (oven ready)

1 tbsp butter

1 cup/½ lb/250 g béchamel sauce

2 cups/1 lb/ 500 g Bolognese sauce

1 cup/ 4 oz/125 g grated Parmesan

197 make béchamel sauce

147 prepare bolognese sauce

Butter a baking dish. Make a layer of pasta in the dish; overlapping the sheets slightly.

Spread with a layer of béchamel sauce.

Top with a layer of Bolognese sauce and sprinkle with Parmesan. Repeat layering ending with a pasta layer.

Spread the top layer with béchamel sauce and sprinkle with cheese.

50 min

375°F/190°C

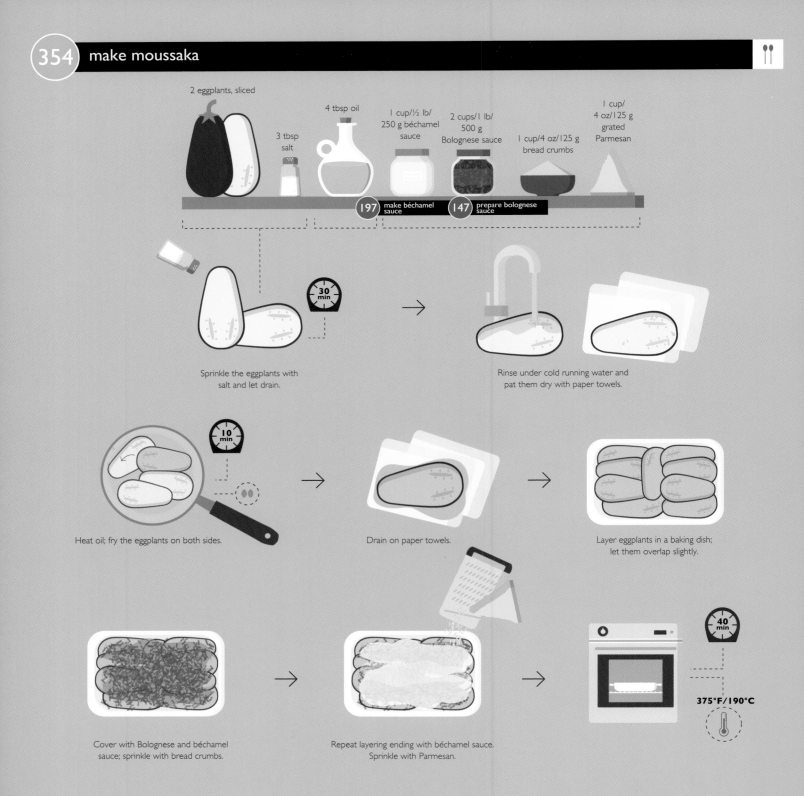

2 eggplants, sliced

3 tbsp salt

4 tbsp oil

1 cup/½ lb/ 250 g béchamel sauce

2 cups/1 lb/ 500 g Bolognese sauce

1 cup/4 oz/125 g bread crumbs

1 cup/ 4 oz/125 g grated Parmesan

197 make béchamel sauce

147 prepare bolognese sauce

Sprinkle the eggplants with salt and let drain.

30 min

Rinse under cold running water and pat them dry with paper towels.

10 min

Heat oil; fry the eggplants on both sides.

Drain on paper towels.

Layer eggplants in a baking dish; let them overlap slightly.

Cover with Bolognese and béchamel sauce; sprinkle with bread crumbs.

Repeat layering ending with béchamel sauce. Sprinkle with Parmesan.

40 min

375°F/190°C

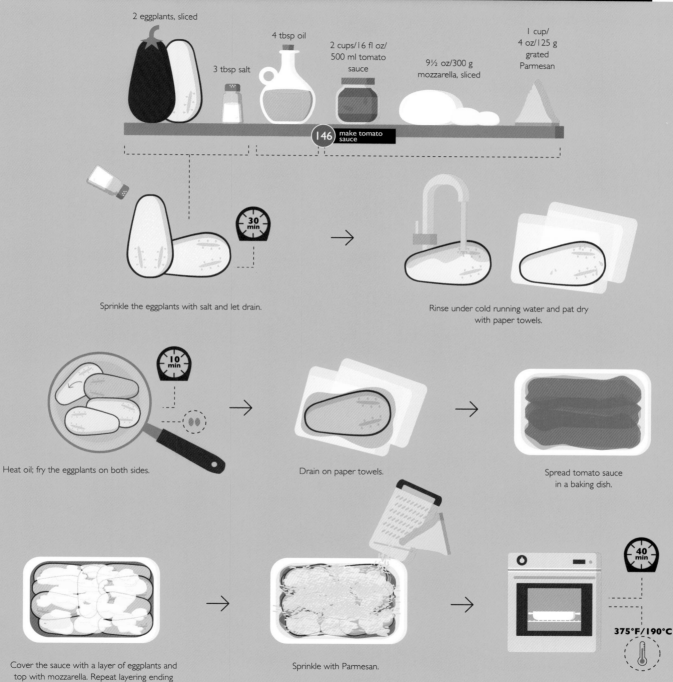

2 eggplants, sliced

3 tbsp salt

4 tbsp oil

2 cups/16 fl oz/ 500 ml tomato sauce

9½ oz/300 g mozzarella, sliced

1 cup/ 4 oz/125 g grated Parmesan

146 make tomato sauce

30 min

Sprinkle the eggplants with salt and let drain.

Rinse under cold running water and pat dry with paper towels.

10 min

Heat oil; fry the eggplants on both sides.

Drain on paper towels.

Spread tomato sauce in a baking dish.

Cover the sauce with a layer of eggplants and top with mozzarella. Repeat layering ending with tomato sauce.

Sprinkle with Parmesan.

40 min

375°F/190°C

356 | bake pizza

pizza dough

070 prepare pizza dough

Roll out a thin layer of dough.

↓

Top.

↓

20 min

400°F/200°C

357 | bake pizza napoletana

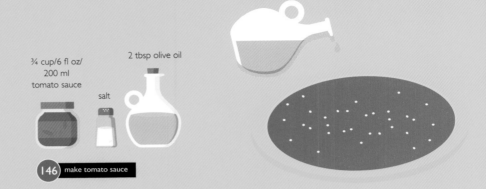

¾ cup/6 fl oz/
200 ml
tomato sauce

salt

2 tbsp olive oil

146 make tomato sauce

358 | bake pizza pomodoro e mozzarella

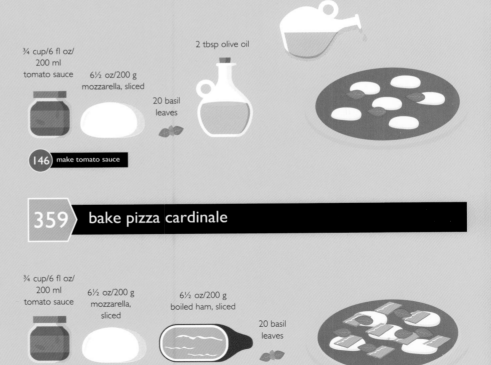

¾ cup/6 fl oz/
200 ml
tomato sauce

6½ oz/200 g
mozzarella, sliced

20 basil
leaves

2 tbsp olive oil

146 make tomato sauce

359 | bake pizza cardinale

¾ cup/6 fl oz/
200 ml
tomato sauce

6½ oz/200 g
mozzarella,
sliced

6½ oz/200 g
boiled ham, sliced

20 basil
leaves

146 make tomato sauce

360　bake pizza with onions and olives

4 tbsp oil

3 cups/10½ oz/300 g onions, thinly sliced

1⅔ cups/½ lb/250 g feta cheese, cut into cubes

16 pitted black olives

8 min

Heat oil, sauté onions until they are soft.

Spread onions, feta and olives on the pizza.

361　bake pizza bianca

13 oz/400 g mozzarella, sliced

2 tbsp fresh herbs (rosemary, thyme, oregano), minced

4 tbsp oil

362　bake pizza quattro formaggi

¾ cup/6 fl oz/200 ml tomato sauce

1½ oz/50 g Gorgonzola, in pieces
1 cup/4 oz/125 g grated Gruyère
1 cup/⅓ lb/150 g grated Gouda
⅓ lb/150 g mozzarella, sliced

146 make tomato sauce

Spread Gorgonzola and grated cheese on the pizza, top with mozzarella.

363　bake focaccia

2 tbsp olive oil

2 tbsp rosemary, minced

sea salt

Using a spoon handle make a pattern of dimples into the dough.

Sprinkle with sea salt and rosemary, then drizzle with oil.

20 min

400°F/200°C

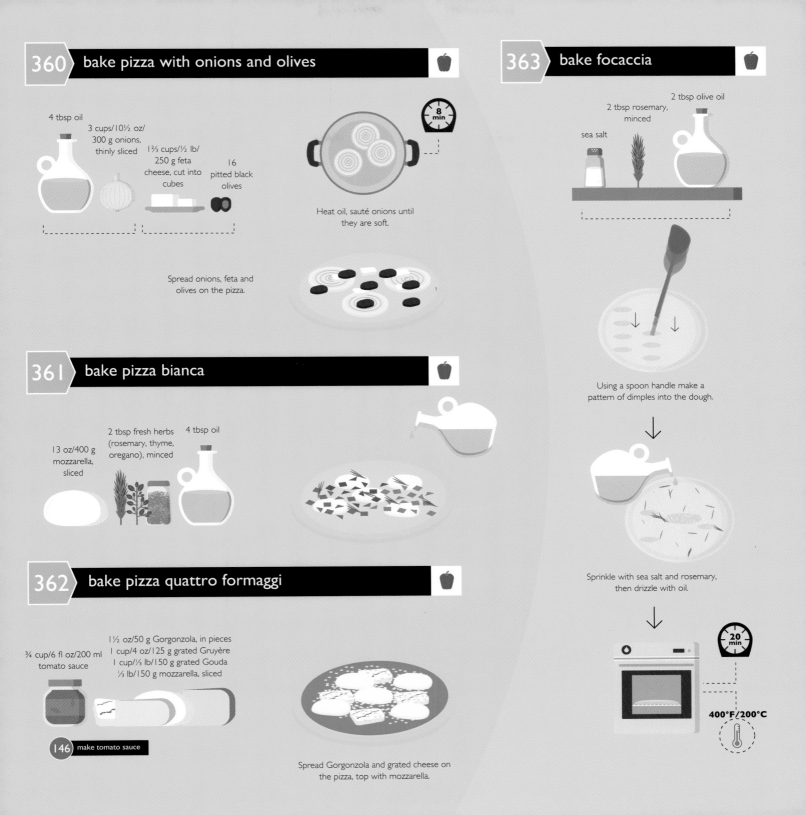

make bread

make corn bread

2 cups/
8 oz/235 g
cornstarch

½ cup/2½ oz/
75 g flour

1 tbsp
sugar

1 tbsp salt

1 tbsp baking
soda

1 tbsp baking
powder

2 eggs

3 tbsp oil, plus
oil for greasing

¾ cup/6 fl oz/
200 ml milk

bread dough

1 egg white

069 make bread dough

Whisk egg white.

+

Transfer the dough into a loaf pan,
brush with egg white.

Stir together cornstarch, flour,
sugar, salt, baking soda and
baking powder in a bowl.

+

Whisk eggs, oil and milk.

→

Add to the flour mixture and stir
with a fork—the dough
should not be too smooth.

366 **make sweet corn bread**

2 tbsp honey

2 tbsp
sugar

Transfer into a greased loaf pan.

↓

45
min

20
min

350°F/180°C

400°F/200°C

✱ You can also form small bread rolls.
Bake for just 25 minutes!

Add 2 tbsp of sugar and 2 tbsp of honey to the
cornstarch dough and bake like corn bread.

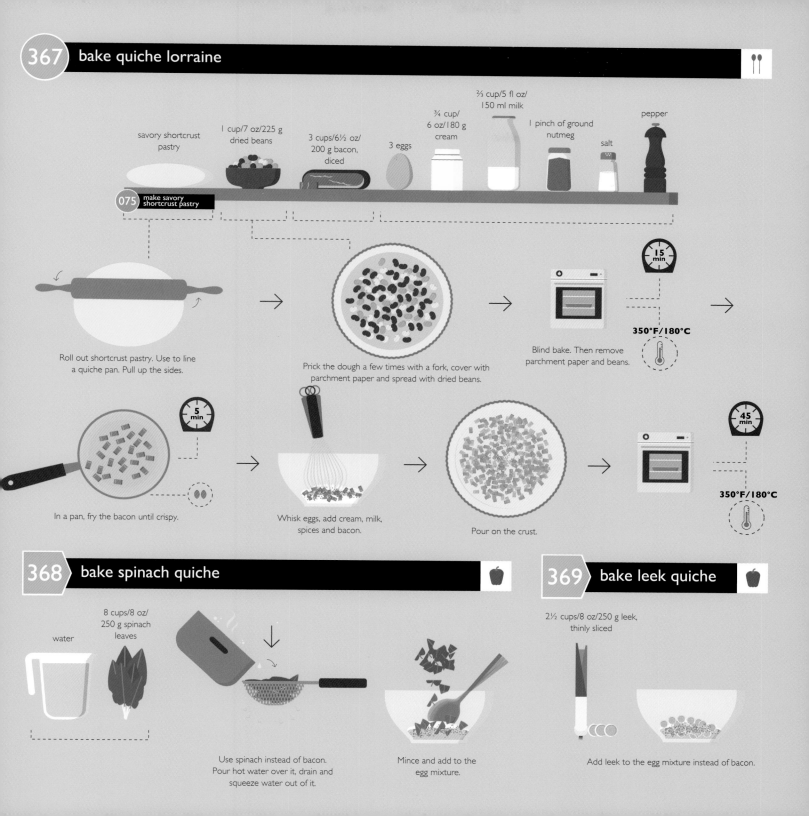

367 bake quiche lorraine

savory shortcrust pastry

1 cup/7 oz/225 g dried beans

3 cups/6½ oz/ 200 g bacon, diced

3 eggs

¾ cup/ 6 oz/180 g cream

⅔ cup/5 fl oz/ 150 ml milk

1 pinch of ground nutmeg

salt

pepper

075 make savory shortcrust pastry

Roll out shortcrust pastry. Use to line a quiche pan. Pull up the sides.

Prick the dough a few times with a fork, cover with parchment paper and spread with dried beans.

15 min
350°F/180°C

Blind bake. Then remove parchment paper and beans.

5 min

In a pan, fry the bacon until crispy.

Whisk eggs, add cream, milk, spices and bacon.

Pour on the crust.

45 min
350°F/180°C

368 bake spinach quiche

water

8 cups/8 oz/ 250 g spinach leaves

Use spinach instead of bacon. Pour hot water over it, drain and squeeze water out of it.

Mince and add to the egg mixture.

369 bake leek quiche

2½ cups/8 oz/250 g leek, thinly sliced

Add leek to the egg mixture instead of bacon.

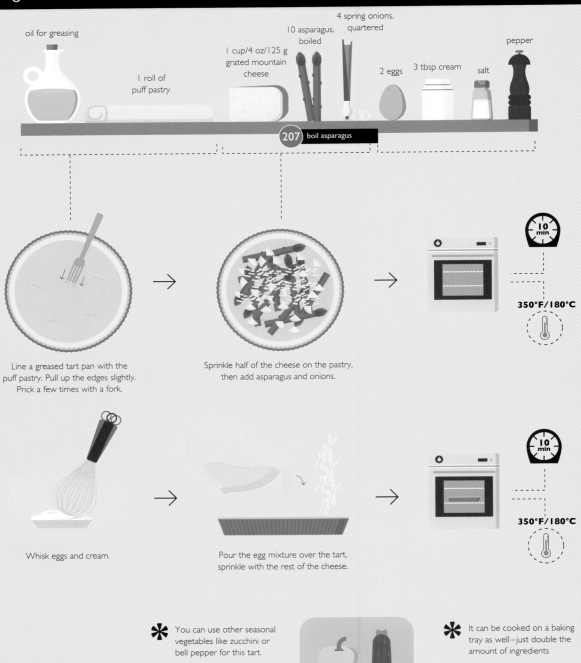

oil for greasing

1 roll of
puff pastry

1 cup/4 oz/125 g
grated mountain
cheese

10 asparagus,
boiled

4 spring onions,
quartered

2 eggs

3 tbsp cream

salt

pepper

207 boil asparagus

Line a greased tart pan with the
puff pastry. Pull up the edges slightly.
Prick a few times with a fork.

Sprinkle half of the cheese on the pastry,
then add asparagus and onions.

10 min

350°F/180°C

Whisk eggs and cream.

Pour the egg mixture over the tart,
sprinkle with the rest of the cheese.

10 min

350°F/180°C

✳ You can use other seasonal
vegetables like zucchini or
bell pepper for this tart.

✳ It can be cooked on a baking
tray as well—just double the
amount of ingredients

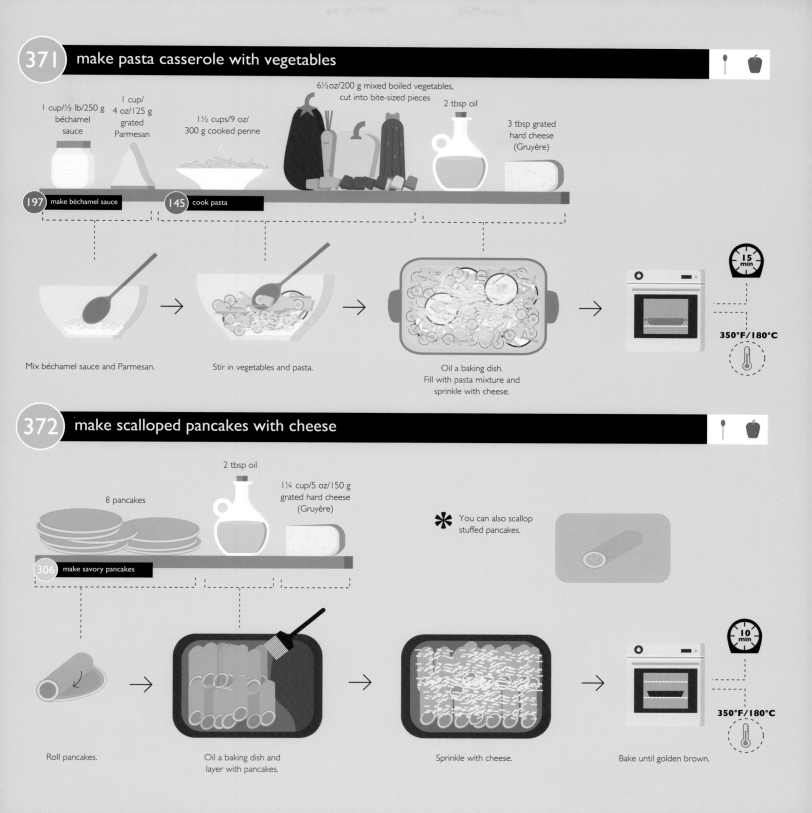

371 make pasta casserole with vegetables

1 cup/½ lb/250 g béchamel sauce

1 cup/4 oz/125 g grated Parmesan

1½ cups/9 oz/300 g cooked penne

6½oz/200 g mixed boiled vegetables, cut into bite-sized pieces

2 tbsp oil

3 tbsp grated hard cheese (Gruyère)

197 make béchamel sauce

145 cook pasta

Mix béchamel sauce and Parmesan.

Stir in vegetables and pasta.

Oil a baking dish.
Fill with pasta mixture and sprinkle with cheese.

15 min

350°F/180°C

372 make scalloped pancakes with cheese

8 pancakes

2 tbsp oil

1¼ cup/5 oz/150 g grated hard cheese (Gruyère)

306 make savory pancakes

✳ You can also scallop stuffed pancakes.

Roll pancakes.

Oil a baking dish and layer with pancakes.

Sprinkle with cheese.

Bake until golden brown.

10 min

350°F/180°C

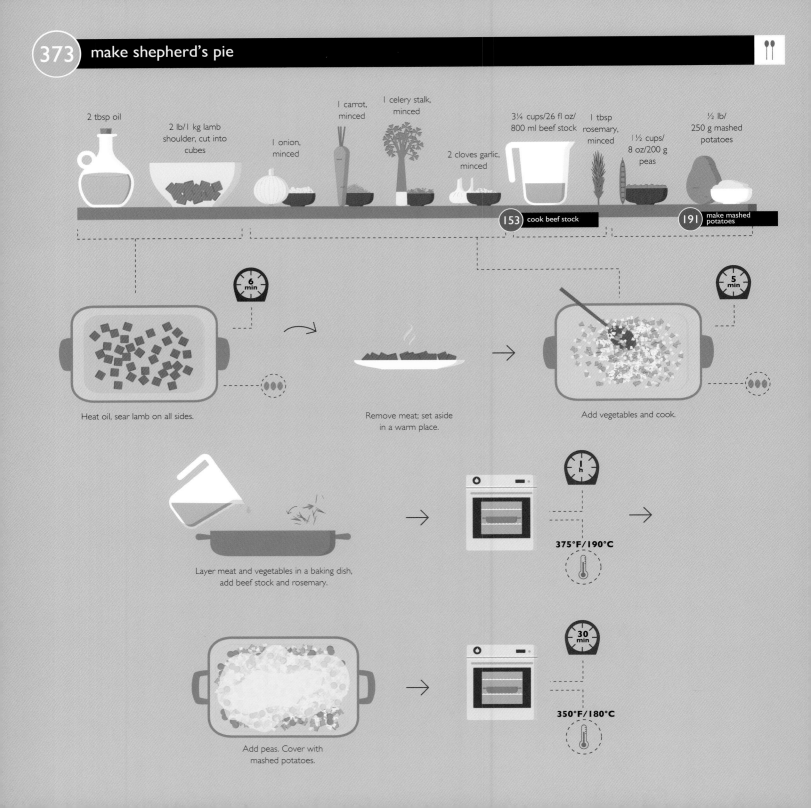

2 tbsp oil

2 lb/1 kg lamb shoulder, cut into cubes

1 onion, minced

1 carrot, minced

1 celery stalk, minced

2 cloves garlic, minced

3¼ cups/26 fl oz/ 800 ml beef stock

1 tbsp rosemary, minced

1½ cups/ 8 oz/200 g peas

½ lb/ 250 g mashed potatoes

153 cook beef stock

191 make mashed potatoes

6 min

5 min

Heat oil, sear lamb on all sides.

Remove meat; set aside in a warm place.

Add vegetables and cook.

Layer meat and vegetables in a baking dish, add beef stock and rosemary.

1 h

375°F/190°C

Add peas. Cover with mashed potatoes.

30 min

350°F/180°C

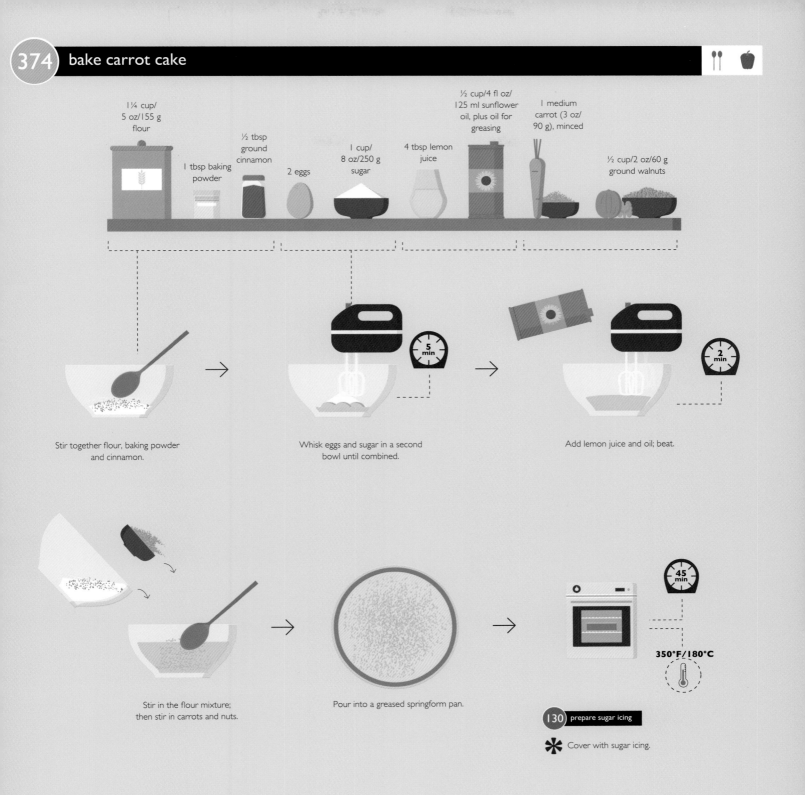

1¼ cup/
5 oz/155 g
flour

1 tbsp baking
powder

½ tbsp
ground
cinnamon

2 eggs

1 cup/
8 oz/250 g
sugar

4 tbsp lemon
juice

½ cup/4 fl oz/
125 ml sunflower
oil, plus oil for
greasing

1 medium
carrot (3 oz/
90 g), minced

½ cup/2 oz/60 g
ground walnuts

Stir together flour, baking powder
and cinnamon.

Whisk eggs and sugar in a second
bowl until combined.

5 min

Add lemon juice and oil; beat.

2 min

Stir in the flour mixture;
then stir in carrots and nuts.

Pour into a greased springform pan.

45 min

350°F/180°C

130 prepare sugar icing

✳ Cover with sugar icing.

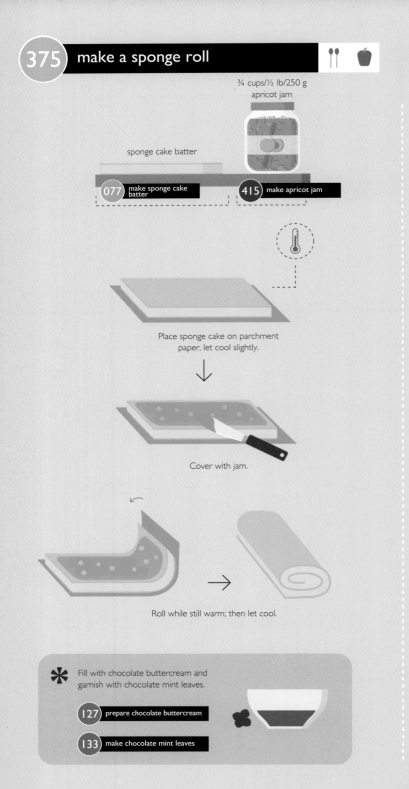

375 make a sponge roll

¾ cups/½ lb/250 g
apricot jam

sponge cake batter

077 make sponge cake batter

415 make apricot jam

Place sponge cake on parchment paper, let cool slightly.

Cover with jam.

Roll while still warm; then let cool.

Fill with chocolate buttercream and garnish with chocolate mint leaves.

127 prepare chocolate buttercream

133 make chocolate mint leaves

376 bake marble cake

1 tbsp butter

1 tbsp bread crumbs

cake batter

2 tbsp cocoa powder

076 prepare cake batter

Butter a loaf pan and cover with bread crumbs.

Separate the dough into two bowls. Mix half of the batter with cocoa powder.

Alternate light and dark batter when filling the loaf pan. Repeat the process.

30 min

350°F/180°C

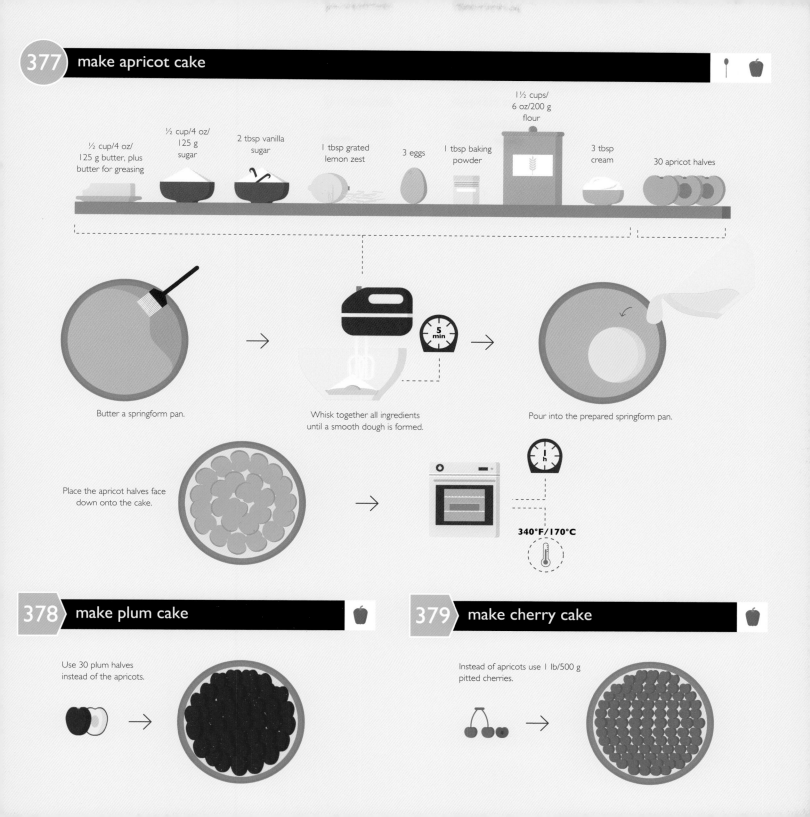

377 make apricot cake

½ cup/4 oz/ 125 g butter, plus butter for greasing

½ cup/4 oz/ 125 g sugar

2 tbsp vanilla sugar

1 tbsp grated lemon zest

3 eggs

1 tbsp baking powder

1½ cups/ 6 oz/200 g flour

3 tbsp cream

30 apricot halves

Butter a springform pan.

5 min

Whisk together all ingredients until a smooth dough is formed.

Pour into the prepared springform pan.

Place the apricot halves face down onto the cake.

1 h

340°F/170°C

378 make plum cake

Use 30 plum halves instead of the apricots.

379 make cherry cake

Instead of apricots use 1 lb/500 g pitted cherries.

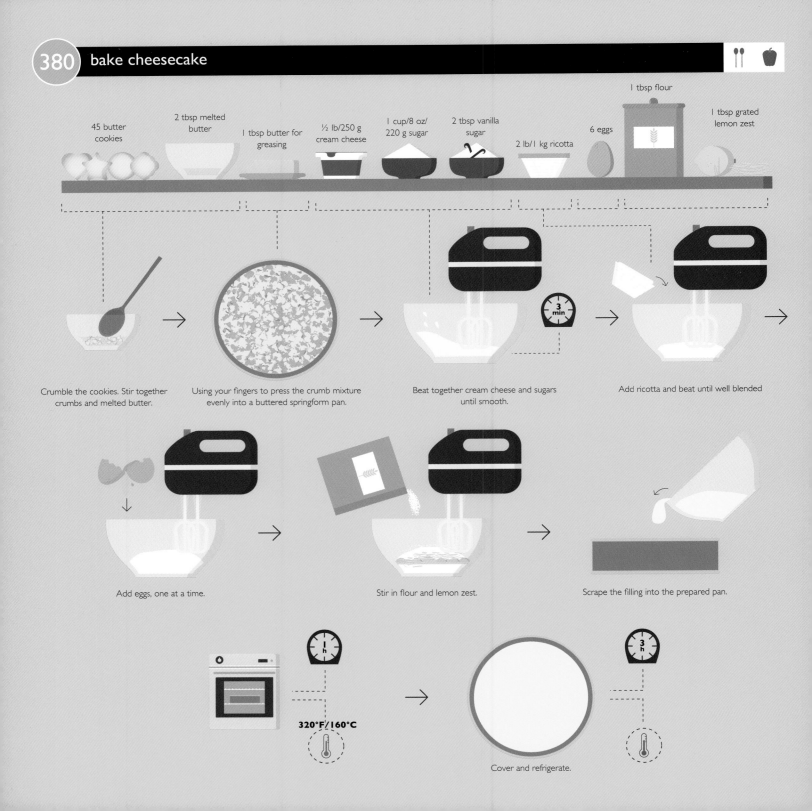

45 butter cookies

2 tbsp melted butter

1 tbsp butter for greasing

½ lb/250 g cream cheese

1 cup/8 oz/ 220 g sugar

2 tbsp vanilla sugar

2 lb/1 kg ricotta

6 eggs

1 tbsp flour

1 tbsp grated lemon zest

Crumble the cookies. Stir together crumbs and melted butter.

Using your fingers to press the crumb mixture evenly into a buttered springform pan.

Beat together cream cheese and sugars until smooth.

3 min

Add ricotta and beat until well blended

Add eggs, one at a time.

Stir in flour and lemon zest.

Scrape the filling into the prepared pan.

320°F/160°C

1 h

Cover and refrigerate.

3 h

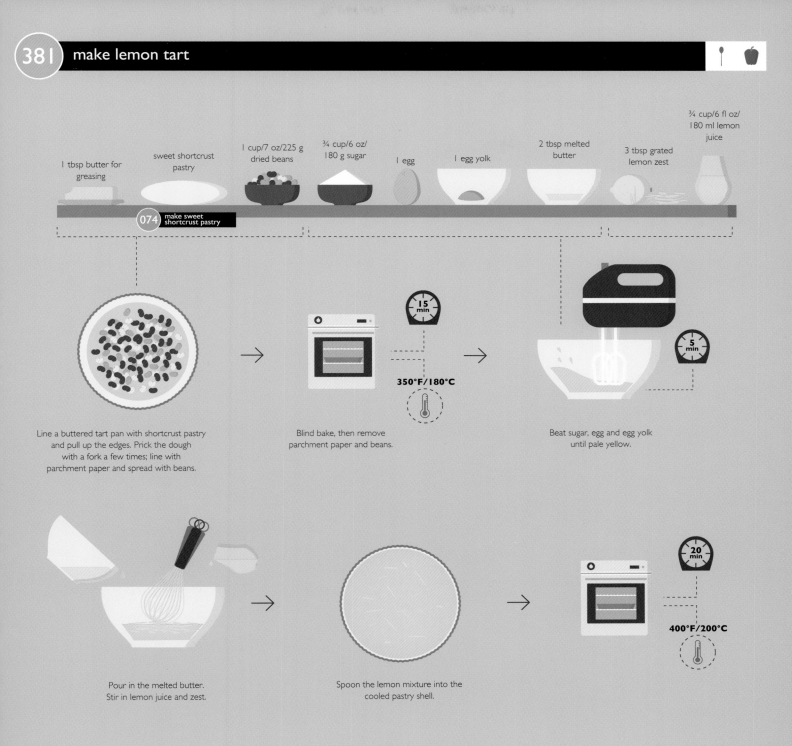

1 tbsp butter for greasing

sweet shortcrust pastry

1 cup/7 oz/225 g dried beans

¾ cup/6 oz/ 180 g sugar

1 egg

1 egg yolk

2 tbsp melted butter

3 tbsp grated lemon zest

¾ cup/6 fl oz/ 180 ml lemon juice

074 make sweet shortcrust pastry

Line a buttered tart pan with shortcrust pastry and pull up the edges. Prick the dough with a fork a few times; line with parchment paper and spread with beans.

Blind bake, then remove parchment paper and beans.

15 min

350°F/180°C

Beat sugar, egg and egg yolk until pale yellow.

5 min

Pour in the melted butter. Stir in lemon juice and zest.

Spoon the lemon mixture into the cooled pastry shell.

20 min

400°F/200°C

382 bake flourless chocolate cake

6½ oz/200 g chocolate

¾ cup/6½ oz/200 g butter, plus butter for greasing

⅔ cup/5 oz/150 g sugar

2½ cups/10 oz/300 g ground almonds

1 tbsp vanilla sugar

5 eggs

Melt the chocolate in a double boiler.

Beat butter and sugar until combined.

Add all other ingredients; stir together.

5 min

Butter a springform pan. Pour the batter into the prepared pan.

40 min

350°F/180°C

383 make brownies

6½ oz/200 g dark chocolate

½ cup/4 oz/125 g butter, plus butter for greasing

2 eggs

¾ cup/6½ oz/200 g sugar

1 tbsp vanilla sugar

1 cup/4 oz/130 g flour

1 tbsp baking powder

3 tbsp chopped walnuts

✳ Do not overbake, the brownies should be moist inside.

Melt chocolate and butter in a double boiler.

Beat eggs, sugar and vanilla sugar until combined.

5 min

Stir in the chocolate. Add flour, baking powder and nuts.

Spread the batter on a buttered baking tray and bake.

20 min

350°F/180°C

Let cool; cut the brownie into squares.

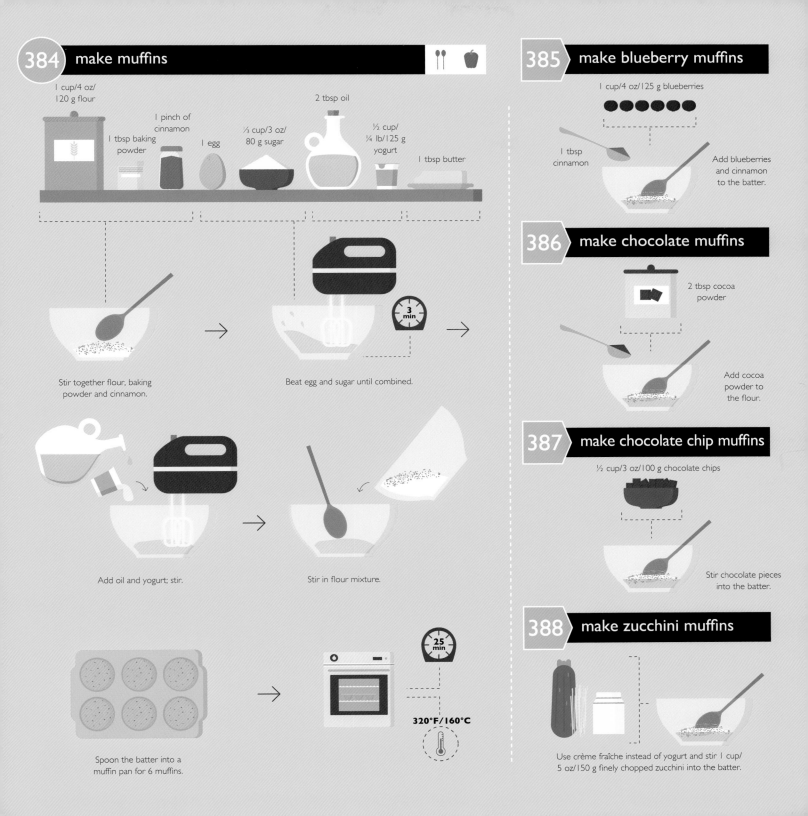

384 make muffins

1 cup/4 oz/120 g flour

1 tbsp baking powder

1 pinch of cinnamon

1 egg

⅓ cup/3 oz/80 g sugar

2 tbsp oil

½ cup/¼ lb/125 g yogurt

1 tbsp butter

Stir together flour, baking powder and cinnamon.

Beat egg and sugar until combined.

3 min

Add oil and yogurt; stir.

Stir in flour mixture.

Spoon the batter into a muffin pan for 6 muffins.

25 min

320°F/160°C

385 make blueberry muffins

1 cup/4 oz/125 g blueberries

1 tbsp cinnamon

Add blueberries and cinnamon to the batter.

386 make chocolate muffins

2 tbsp cocoa powder

Add cocoa powder to the flour.

387 make chocolate chip muffins

½ cup/3 oz/100 g chocolate chips

Stir chocolate pieces into the batter.

388 make zucchini muffins

Use crème fraîche instead of yogurt and stir 1 cup/5 oz/150 g finely chopped zucchini into the batter.

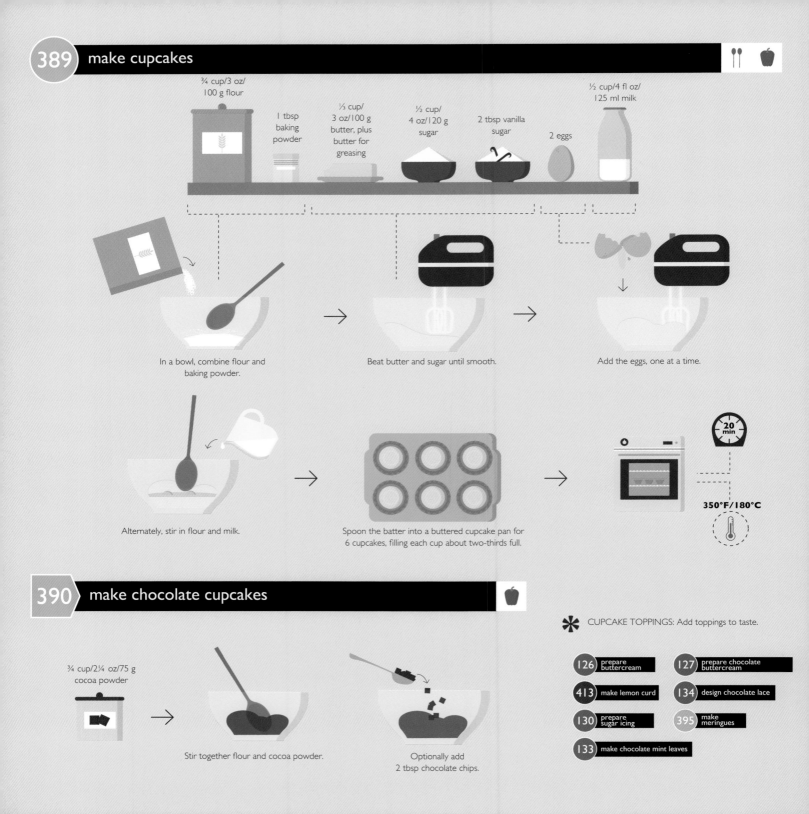

¾ cup/3 oz/ 100 g flour

1 tbsp baking powder

⅓ cup/ 3 oz/100 g butter, plus butter for greasing

½ cup/ 4 oz/120 g sugar

2 tbsp vanilla sugar

2 eggs

½ cup/4 fl oz/ 125 ml milk

In a bowl, combine flour and baking powder.

Beat butter and sugar until smooth.

Add the eggs, one at a time.

Alternately, stir in flour and milk.

Spoon the batter into a buttered cupcake pan for 6 cupcakes, filling each cup about two-thirds full.

20 min

350°F/180°C

390 | make chocolate cupcakes

¾ cup/2¼ oz/75 g cocoa powder

Stir together flour and cocoa powder.

Optionally add 2 tbsp chocolate chips.

✱ CUPCAKE TOPPINGS: Add toppings to taste.

126 prepare buttercream

127 prepare chocolate buttercream

413 make lemon curd

134 design chocolate lace

130 prepare sugar icing

395 make meringues

133 make chocolate mint leaves

391 bake scones

2 cups/
10 oz/320 g flour

¼ cup/
2 oz/60 g
sugar

1 tbsp
baking
powder

1 tbsp grated
lemon zest

6 tbsp/3 oz/90 g
butter, in small
pieces, plus butter
for greasing

3 tbsp
raisins

¾ cup/
5½ oz/180 g
cream, plus
2 tbsp cream

Stir together flour, sugar, baking powder and lemon zest.

Stir in the butter. Gradually add cream and raisins. Cover and refrigerate for about 30 minutes.

30 min

Roll out the dough on a floured surface about ¾–1¼ inches/2–3cm thick.

Use a biscuit cutter to cut out rounds of about 2½ inches/ 6 cm in diameter.

Place on a buttered baking tray and brush with cream.

10 min

430°F/220°C

392 prepare profiteroles

1¼ cups/10 fl oz/
300 ml vanilla
ice cream

choux
pastry

chocolate sauce

073 make choux pastry

217 make chocolate sauce

With a teaspoon spoon walnut sized puffs onto a baking tray.

10 min

350°F/180°C

Let profiteroles cool and cut them almost through. Fill each with a small scoop of vanilla ice cream. Top with warm chocolate sauce.

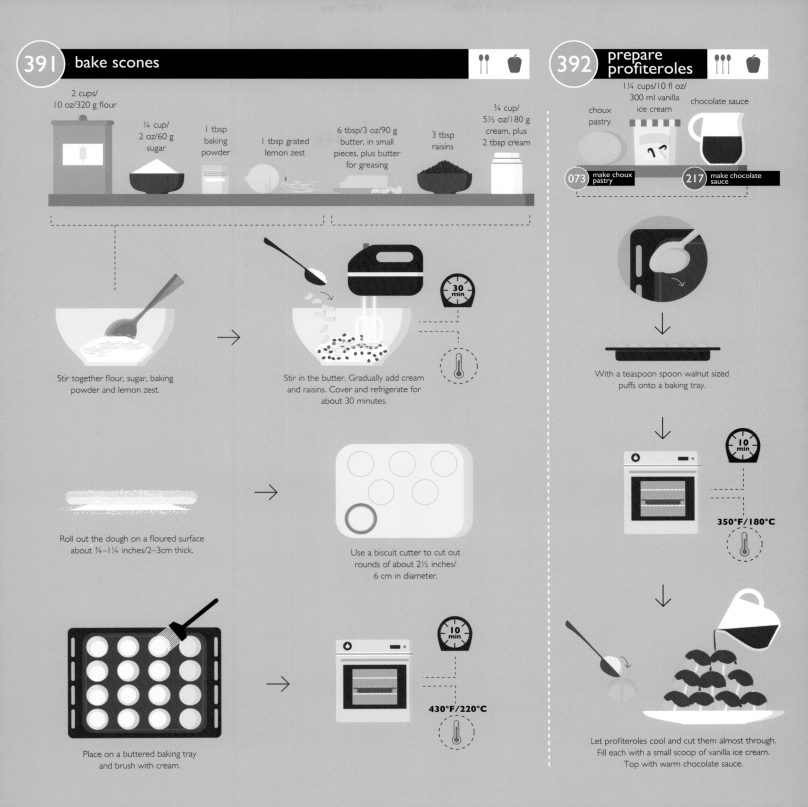

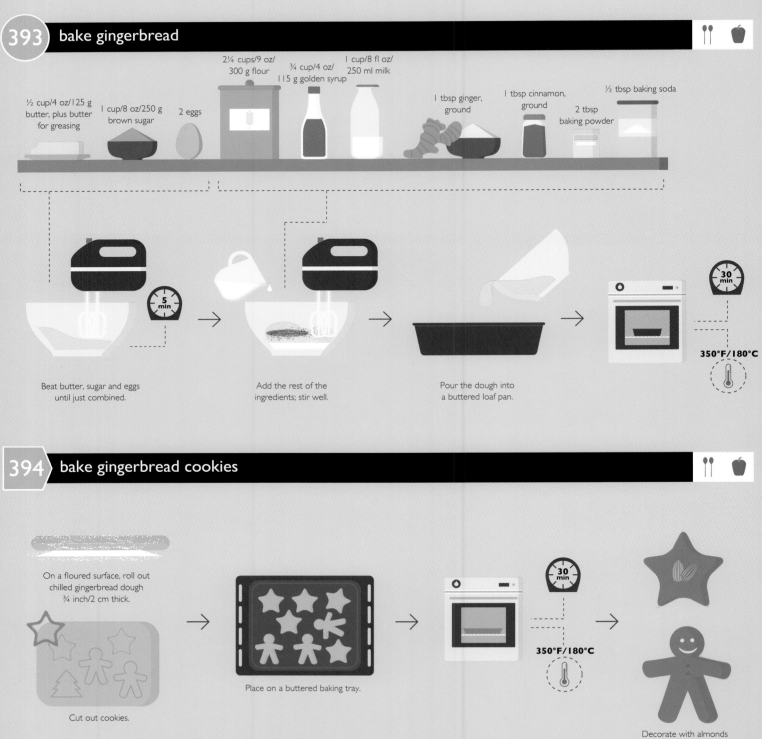

393 bake gingerbread

½ cup/4 oz/125 g butter, plus butter for greasing

1 cup/8 oz/250 g brown sugar

2 eggs

2¼ cups/9 oz/300 g flour

¾ cup/4 oz/115 g golden syrup

1 cup/8 fl oz/250 ml milk

1 tbsp ginger, ground

1 tbsp cinnamon, ground

2 tbsp baking powder

½ tbsp baking soda

5 min

30 min

350°F/180°C

Beat butter, sugar and eggs until just combined.

Add the rest of the ingredients; stir well.

Pour the dough into a buttered loaf pan.

394 bake gingerbread cookies

On a floured surface, roll out chilled gingerbread dough ¾ inch/2 cm thick.

Cut out cookies.

Place on a buttered baking tray.

30 min

350°F/180°C

Decorate with almonds or candied ginger.

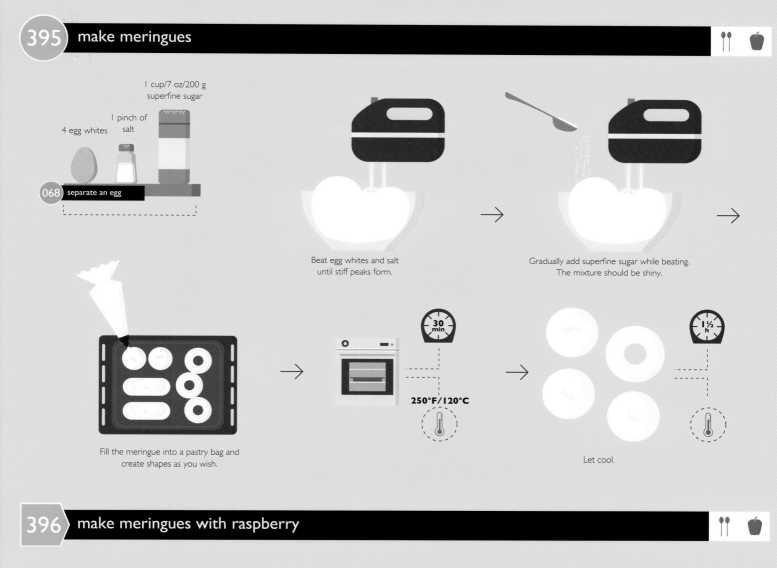

1 cup/7 oz/200 g
superfine sugar

4 egg whites

1 pinch of
salt

068 separate an egg

Beat egg whites and salt
until stiff peaks form.

Gradually add superfine sugar while beating.
The mixture should be shiny.

Fill the meringue into a pastry bag and
create shapes as you wish.

30 min

250°F/120°C

1½ h

Let cool.

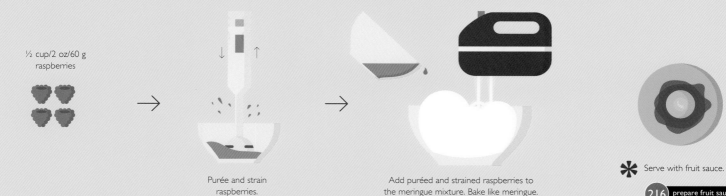

½ cup/2 oz/60 g
raspberries

Purée and strain
raspberries.

Add puréed and strained raspberries to
the meringue mixture. Bake like meringue.

Serve with fruit sauce.

216 prepare fruit sauce

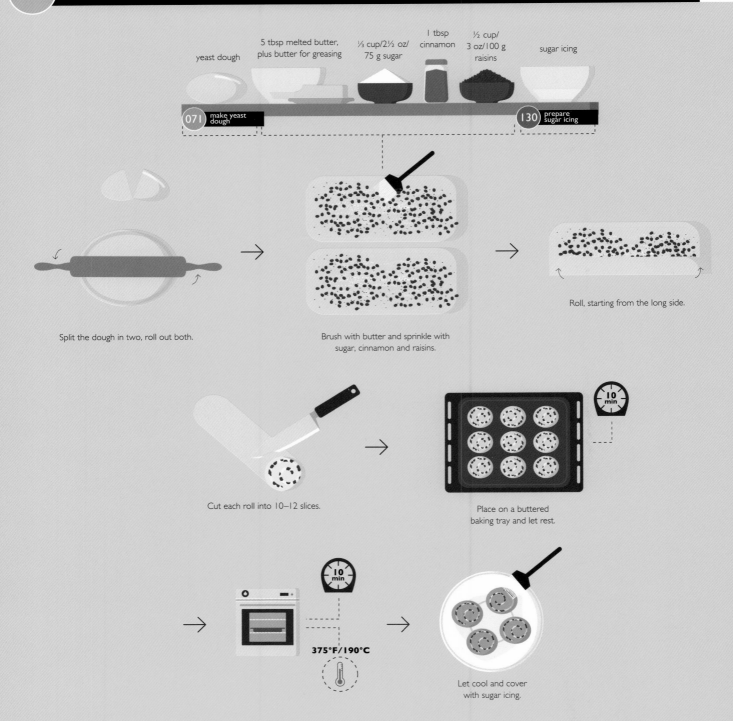

yeast dough

5 tbsp melted butter, plus butter for greasing

⅓ cup/2½ oz/ 75 g sugar

1 tbsp cinnamon

½ cup/ 3 oz/100 g raisins

sugar icing

071 make yeast dough

130 prepare sugar icing

Split the dough in two, roll out both.

Brush with butter and sprinkle with sugar, cinnamon and raisins.

Roll, starting from the long side.

Cut each roll into 10–12 slices.

Place on a buttered baking tray and let rest.

10 min

375°F/190°C

10 min

Let cool and cover with sugar icing.

398 make apple crumble

6 apples, peeled, cored and cut into wedges

3 tbsp lemon juice

⅓ cup/3 oz/100 g butter, plus butter for greasing

⅓ cup/3 oz/ 100 g sugar

1½ cups/6 oz/175 g flour

Sprinkle apple wedges with lemon juice and layer them in a buttered baking dish.

Stir together butter, sugar and flour to make a rough crumble.

Spread over the apples.

30 min

400°F/200°C

* The crumble is especially tasty when you marinate the apples in rum before baking.

399 make pear crumble

Use pears instead of apples and bake like apple crumble.

400 prepare scalloped fruit

2 lb/1 kg fresh fruit (peaches, cherries, apricots), pitted, cut in half

1 tbsp lemon juice

⅓ cup/3 oz/ 90 g sugar

half the amount of sponge cake batter

077 make sponge cake batter

Stir together fruit, lemon juice and sugar in a baking dish.

10 min

375°F/190°C

Cover with sponge cake batter.

20 min

350°F/180°C

Bake until the sponge cake batter is slightly brown.

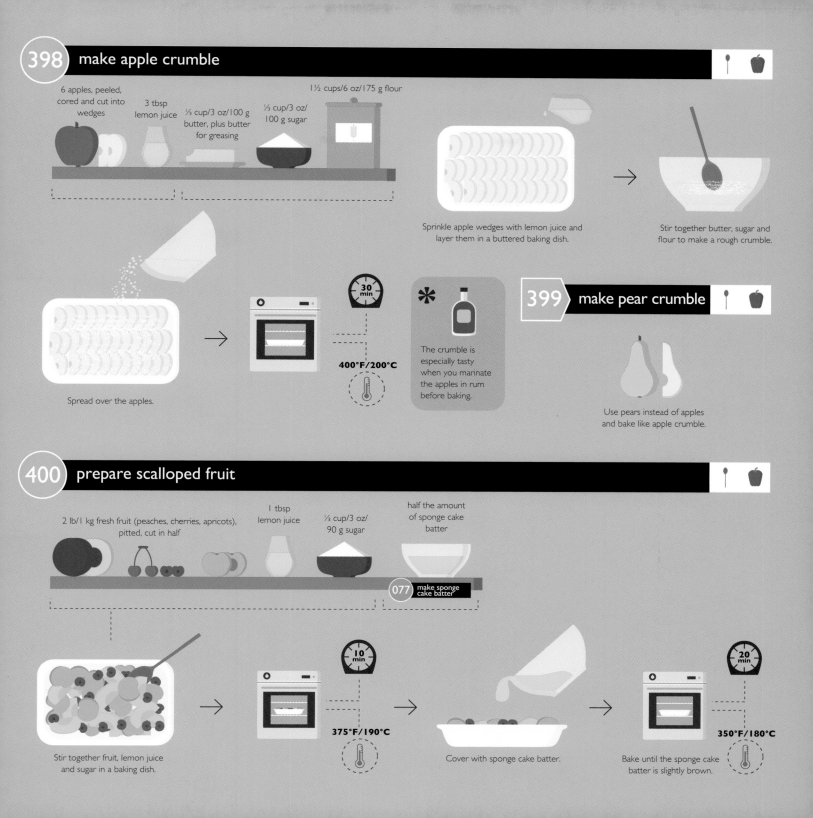

preserve

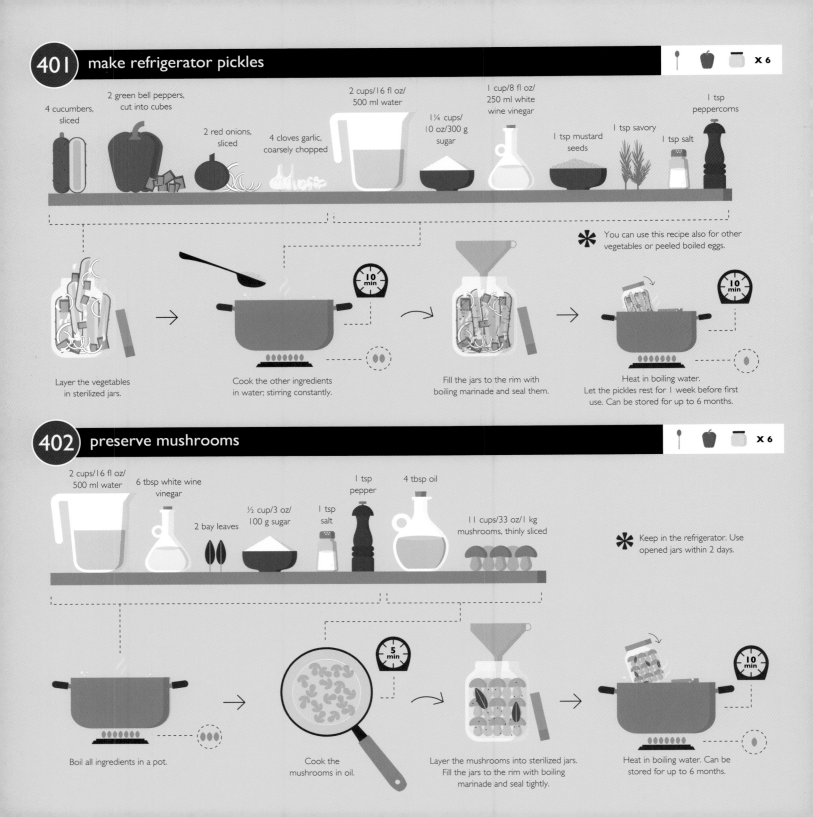

401 make refrigerator pickles

× 6

4 cucumbers, sliced

2 green bell peppers, cut into cubes

2 red onions, sliced

4 cloves garlic, coarsely chopped

2 cups/16 fl oz/ 500 ml water

1¼ cups/ 10 oz/300 g sugar

1 cup/8 fl oz/ 250 ml white wine vinegar

1 tsp mustard seeds

1 tsp savory

1 tsp salt

1 tsp peppercorns

✳ You can use this recipe also for other vegetables or peeled boiled eggs.

10 min

10 min

Layer the vegetables in sterilized jars.

Cook the other ingredients in water; stirring constantly.

Fill the jars to the rim with boiling marinade and seal them.

Heat in boiling water. Let the pickles rest for 1 week before first use. Can be stored for up to 6 months.

402 preserve mushrooms

× 6

2 cups/16 fl oz/ 500 ml water

6 tbsp white wine vinegar

2 bay leaves

½ cup/3 oz/ 100 g sugar

1 tsp salt

1 tsp pepper

4 tbsp oil

11 cups/33 oz/1 kg mushrooms, thinly sliced

✳ Keep in the refrigerator. Use opened jars within 2 days.

5 min

10 min

Boil all ingredients in a pot.

Cook the mushrooms in oil.

Layer the mushrooms into sterilized jars. Fill the jars to the rim with boiling marinade and seal tightly.

Heat in boiling water. Can be stored for up to 6 months.

403 preserve tomatoes

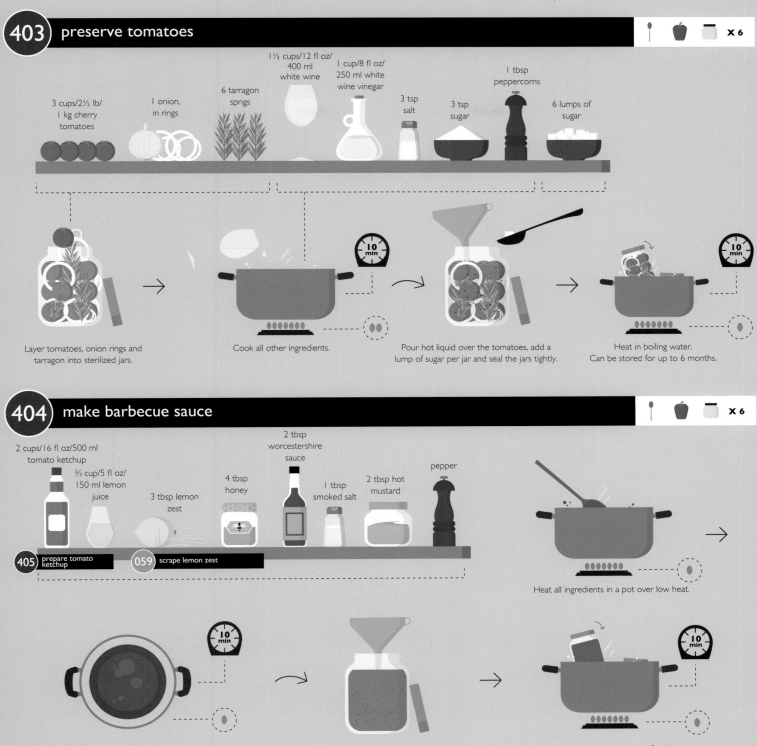

3 cups/2½ lb/ 1 kg cherry tomatoes

I onion, in rings

6 tarragon sprigs

1½ cups/12 fl oz/ 400 ml white wine

1 cup/8 fl oz/ 250 ml white wine vinegar

3 tsp salt

3 tsp sugar

1 tbsp peppercorns

6 lumps of sugar

Layer tomatoes, onion rings and tarragon into sterilized jars.

Cook all other ingredients.

Pour hot liquid over the tomatoes, add a lump of sugar per jar and seal the jars tightly.

Heat in boiling water. Can be stored for up to 6 months.

404 make barbecue sauce

2 cups/16 fl oz/500 ml tomato ketchup

⅔ cup/5 fl oz/ 150 ml lemon juice

3 tbsp lemon zest

4 tbsp honey

2 tbsp worcestershire sauce

1 tbsp smoked salt

2 tbsp hot mustard

pepper

405 prepare tomato ketchup

059 scrape lemon zest

Heat all ingredients in a pot over low heat.

Simmer until the sauce has thickened.

Pour into sterilized jars and seal tightly.

Heat in boiling water. Can be stored for up to 6 months.

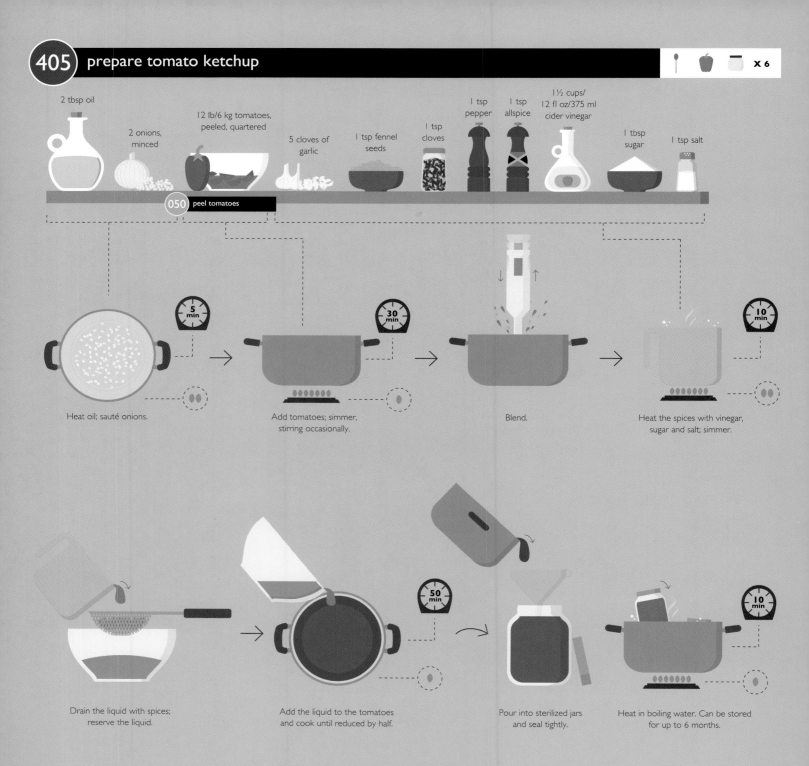

X 6

2 tbsp oil

2 onions, minced

12 lb/6 kg tomatoes, peeled, quartered

5 cloves of garlic

1 tsp fennel seeds

1 tsp cloves

1 tsp pepper

1 tsp allspice

1½ cups/ 12 fl oz/375 ml cider vinegar

1 tbsp sugar

1 tsp salt

050 peel tomatoes

5 min

30 min

10 min

Heat oil; sauté onions.

Add tomatoes; simmer, stirring occasionally.

Blend.

Heat the spices with vinegar, sugar and salt; simmer.

50 min

10 min

Drain the liquid with spices; reserve the liquid.

Add the liquid to the tomatoes and cook until reduced by half.

Pour into sterilized jars and seal tightly.

Heat in boiling water. Can be stored for up to 6 months.

1 cup/5oz/150 g pickling onions

1 cup/5 oz/150 g cucumbers, cut into strips

1 cup/5 oz/150 g bell pepper, in chunks

2½ cups/5 oz/150 g cauliflower florets

3¼ oz/100 g green beans

¾ cup/3¼ oz/100 g carrots, sliced

8 cups/64 fl oz/2 l water

3 bay leaves

2 tbsp colored pepper

1 tbsp mustard seeds

4 cups/32 fl oz/1 l white wine vinegar

3 cups/24 fl oz/750 ml water

½ cup/3 oz/100 g sugar

5 min

Heat the vegetables in cold water, then cook until they are soft.

Chill in iced water.

Use a skimmer to fill sterilized jars with vegetables.

Cook spices, vinegar, water and sugar.

Fill the jars to the rim with boiling liquid; seal them tightly.

10 min

Heat in boiling water. Can be stored for up to 6 months.

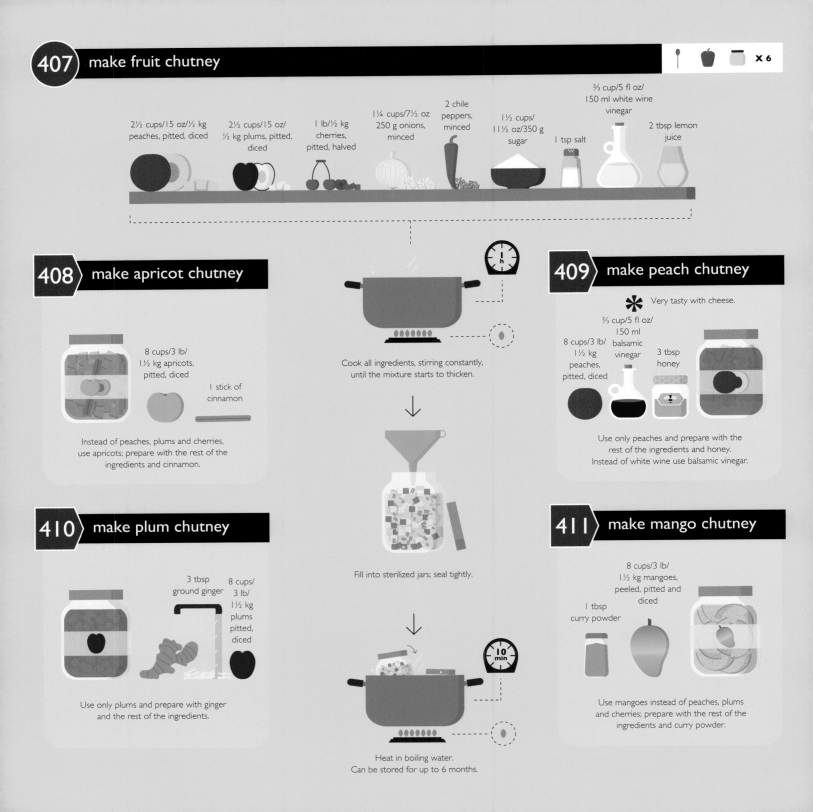

407 make fruit chutney

x 6

2½ cups/15 oz/½ kg peaches, pitted, diced

2½ cups/15 oz/½ kg plums, pitted, diced

1 lb/½ kg cherries, pitted, halved

1¼ cups/7½ oz 250 g onions, minced

2 chile peppers, minced

1½ cups/11½ oz/350 g sugar

1 tsp salt

⅔ cup/5 fl oz/150 ml white wine vinegar

2 tbsp lemon juice

Cook all ingredients, stirring constantly, until the mixture starts to thicken.

Fill into sterilized jars; seal tightly.

Heat in boiling water. Can be stored for up to 6 months.

408 make apricot chutney

8 cups/3 lb/1½ kg apricots, pitted, diced

1 stick of cinnamon

Instead of peaches, plums and cherries, use apricots; prepare with the rest of the ingredients and cinnamon.

409 make peach chutney

✳ Very tasty with cheese.

8 cups/3 lb/1½ kg peaches, pitted, diced

⅔ cup/5 fl oz/150 ml balsamic vinegar

3 tbsp honey

Use only peaches and prepare with the rest of the ingredients and honey. Instead of white wine use balsamic vinegar.

410 make plum chutney

3 tbsp ground ginger

8 cups/3 lb/1½ kg plums pitted, diced

Use only plums and prepare with ginger and the rest of the ingredients.

411 make mango chutney

8 cups/3 lb/1½ kg mangoes, peeled, pitted and diced

1 tbsp curry powder

Use mangoes instead of peaches, plums and cherries; prepare with the rest of the ingredients and curry powder.

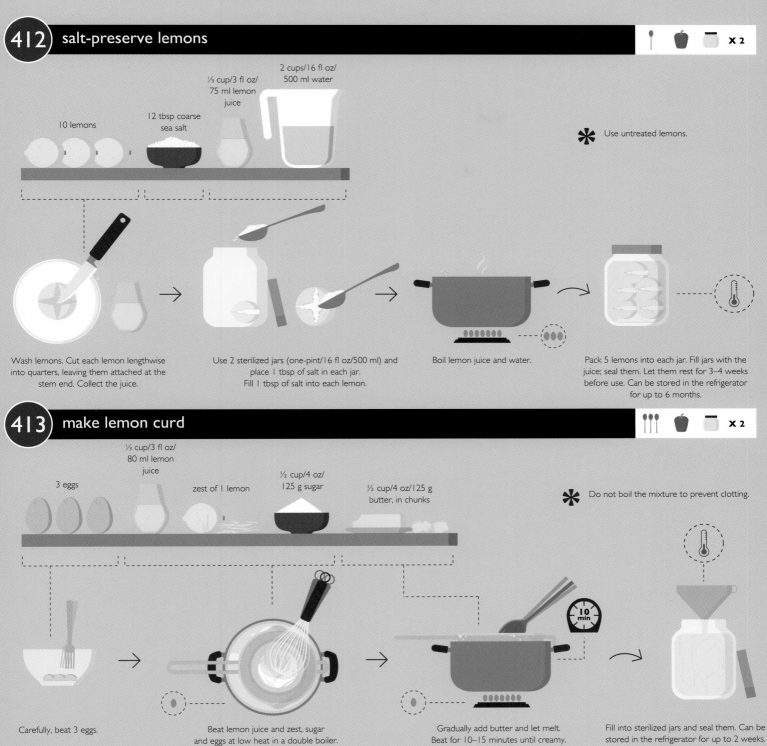

412 salt-preserve lemons

10 lemons

12 tbsp coarse sea salt

⅓ cup/3 fl oz/ 75 ml lemon juice

2 cups/16 fl oz/ 500 ml water

✳ Use untreated lemons.

Wash lemons. Cut each lemon lengthwise into quarters, leaving them attached at the stem end. Collect the juice.

Use 2 sterilized jars (one-pint/16 fl oz/500 ml) and place 1 tbsp of salt in each jar. Fill 1 tbsp of salt into each lemon.

Boil lemon juice and water.

Pack 5 lemons into each jar. Fill jars with the juice; seal them. Let them rest for 3–4 weeks before use. Can be stored in the refrigerator for up to 6 months.

413 make lemon curd

3 eggs

⅓ cup/3 fl oz/ 80 ml lemon juice

zest of 1 lemon

½ cup/4 oz/ 125 g sugar

½ cup/4 oz/125 g butter, in chunks

✳ Do not boil the mixture to prevent clotting.

Carefully, beat 3 eggs.

Beat lemon juice and zest, sugar and eggs at low heat in a double boiler.

Gradually add butter and let melt. Beat for 10–15 minutes until creamy.

Fill into sterilized jars and seal them. Can be stored in the refrigerator for up to 2 weeks.

X 4

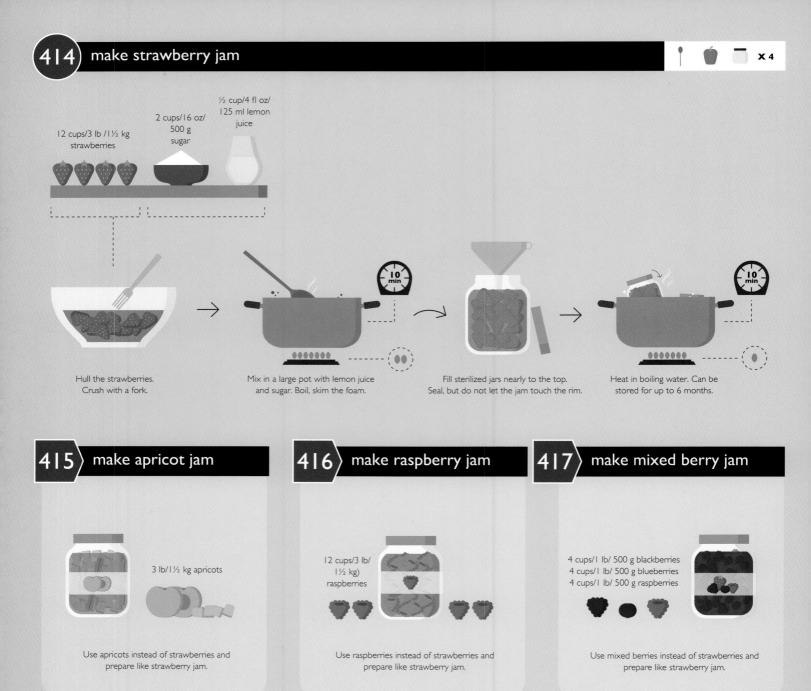

12 cups/3 lb /1½ kg
strawberries

2 cups/16 oz/
500 g
sugar

½ cup/4 fl oz/
125 ml lemon
juice

10 min

10 min

Hull the strawberries.
Crush with a fork.

Mix in a large pot with lemon juice
and sugar. Boil, skim the foam.

Fill sterilized jars nearly to the top.
Seal, but do not let the jam touch the rim.

Heat in boiling water. Can be
stored for up to 6 months.

415 > make apricot jam

3 lb/1½ kg apricots

Use apricots instead of strawberries and
prepare like strawberry jam.

416 > make raspberry jam

12 cups/3 lb/
1½ kg)
raspberries

Use raspberries instead of strawberries and
prepare like strawberry jam.

417 > make mixed berry jam

4 cups/1 lb/ 500 g blackberries
4 cups/1 lb/ 500 g blueberries
4 cups/1 lb/ 500 g raspberries

Use mixed berries instead of strawberries and
prepare like strawberry jam.

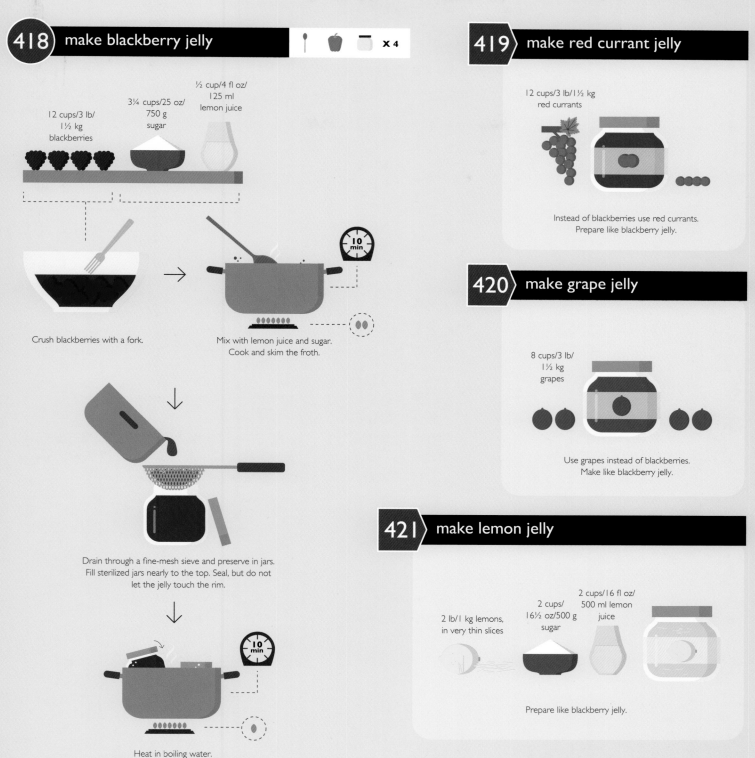

418 make blackberry jelly

X 4

12 cups/3 lb/
1½ kg
blackberries

3¼ cups/25 oz/
750 g
sugar

½ cup/4 fl oz/
125 ml
lemon juice

10 min

Crush blackberries with a fork.

Mix with lemon juice and sugar.
Cook and skim the froth.

Drain through a fine-mesh sieve and preserve in jars.
Fill sterilized jars nearly to the top. Seal, but do not
let the jelly touch the rim.

10 min

Heat in boiling water.
Can be stored for up to 6 months.

419 make red currant jelly

12 cups/3 lb/1½ kg
red currants

Instead of blackberries use red currants.
Prepare like blackberry jelly.

420 make grape jelly

8 cups/3 lb/
1½ kg
grapes

Use grapes instead of blackberries.
Make like blackberry jelly.

421 make lemon jelly

2 lb/1 kg lemons,
in very thin slices

2 cups/
16½ oz/500 g
sugar

2 cups/16 fl oz/
500 ml lemon
juice

Prepare like blackberry jelly.

422 make orange marmalade

X 6

2 lb/800 g oranges, thinly sliced

8 cups/64 fl oz/2 l water

5 cups/41 oz/ 1¼ kg sugar

1½ cups/12 fl oz/400 ml orange juice

½ cup/4 fl oz/ 125 ml lemon juice

✳ Use untreated oranges.

15 min

20 min

10 min

Bring oranges and water to a boil and cook while stirring constantly.

Add sugar, orange and lemon juice. Cook; stirring constantly, until the mixture thickens.

Pour into sterilized jars and seal tightly

Heat in boiling water. Can be stored for up to 6 months.

423 preserve apple purée

X 6

12 cups/3 lb/1½ kg apples, cored, peeled and cut into small pieces

4 cups/32 fl oz/ 1 l apple juice

3 sticks of cinnamon

3 tbsp vanilla sugar

2 tbsp lemon juice

✳ For superfine apple purée drain it through a sieve when filling the jars.

10 min

10 min

Cook the apples and the rest of the ingredients in a pot until they are soft.

Remove sticks of cinnamon. Blend.

Pour into sterilized jars and seal tightly.

Heat in boiling water. Can be stored for up to 6 months.

x 4

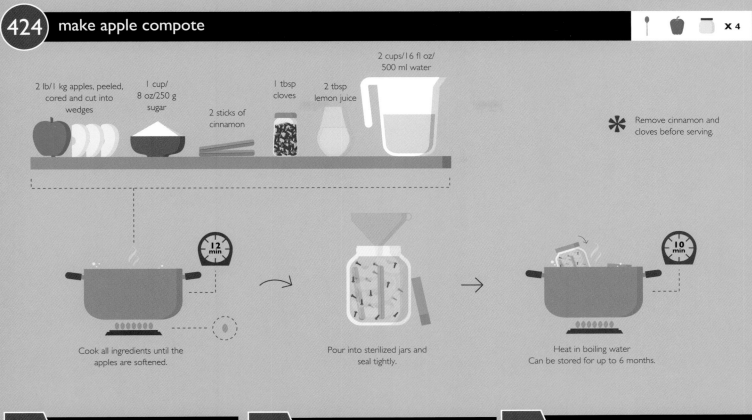

2 lb/1 kg apples, peeled, cored and cut into wedges

1 cup/ 8 oz/250 g sugar

2 sticks of cinnamon

1 tbsp cloves

2 tbsp lemon juice

2 cups/16 fl oz/ 500 ml water

* Remove cinnamon and cloves before serving.

12 min

Cook all ingredients until the apples are softened.

Pour into sterilized jars and seal tightly.

10 min

Heat in boiling water
Can be stored for up to 6 months.

425 make pear compote

2 lb/1 kg pears, pitted and peeled

Use pears instead of apples and prepare like apple compote.

426 make cherry compote

2 lb/1 kg cherries, pitted

Use cherries instead of apples and prepare like apple compote.

427 make plum compote

2 lb/1 kg plums, pitted

Use plums instead of apples and prepare like apple compote.

drink

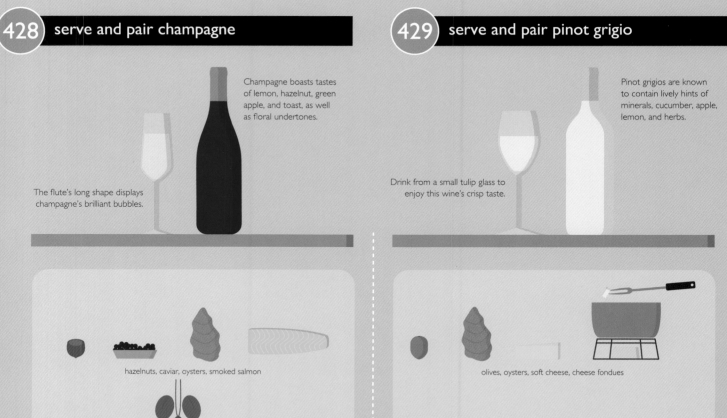

Champagne boasts tastes of lemon, hazelnut, green apple, and toast, as well as floral undertones.

The flute's long shape displays champagne's brilliant bubbles.

Pinot grigios are known to contain lively hints of minerals, cucumber, apple, lemon, and herbs.

Drink from a small tulip glass to enjoy this wine's crisp taste.

hazelnuts, caviar, oysters, smoked salmon

olives, oysters, soft cheese, cheese fondues

chicken, lobster, eggs, sushi, maki sushi

fish, chicken, sausage

corn, radish, potatoes

broccoli, legumes, asparagus, chile peppers, tomatoes

salt, hard cheese, butter, soy sauce

lemon, garlic, herbs, butter

grapefruits, strawberries, grapes

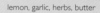

oranges, apples, pears

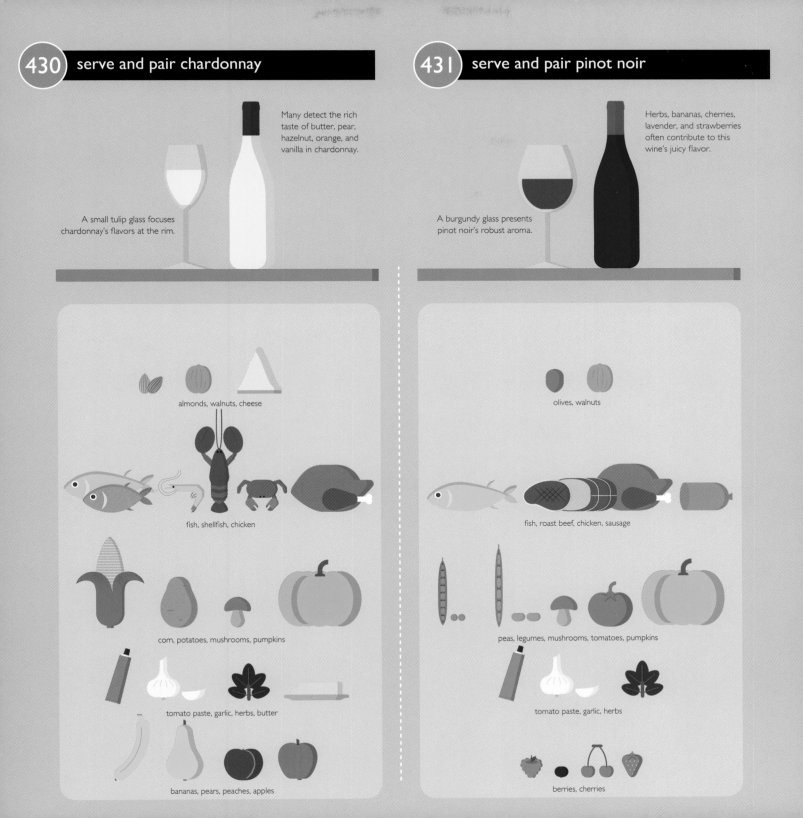

430 serve and pair chardonnay

Many detect the rich taste of butter, pear, hazelnut, orange, and vanilla in chardonnay.

A small tulip glass focuses chardonnay's flavors at the rim.

almonds, walnuts, cheese

fish, shellfish, chicken

corn, potatoes, mushrooms, pumpkins

tomato paste, garlic, herbs, butter

bananas, pears, peaches, apples

431 serve and pair pinot noir

Herbs, bananas, cherries, lavender, and strawberries often contribute to this wine's juicy flavor.

A burgundy glass presents pinot noir's robust aroma.

olives, walnuts

fish, roast beef, chicken, sausage

peas, legumes, mushrooms, tomatoes, pumpkins

tomato paste, garlic, herbs

berries, cherries

Bell peppers, mixed berries, star anise, cinnamon, and plums lend some spice to merlots.

A large tulip glass showcases merlot's earthy bouquet.

"Cabs" are enlivened by the flavors of blackberries, bell peppers, cigars, black pepper, and cloves.

The bordeaux glass's tapered shape intensifies this wine's aroma.

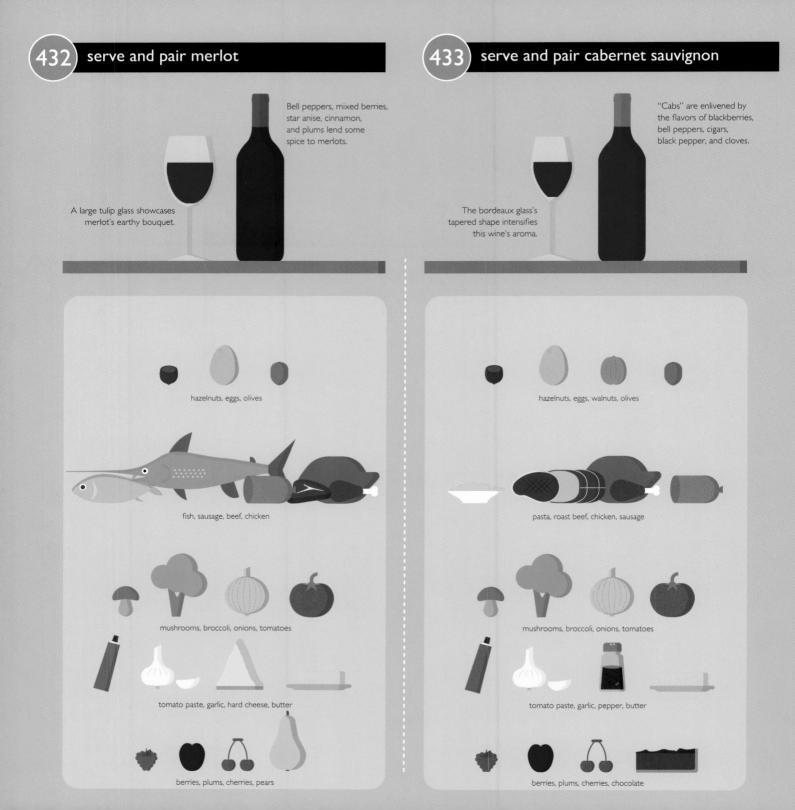

hazelnuts, eggs, olives

hazelnuts, eggs, walnuts, olives

fish, sausage, beef, chicken

pasta, roast beef, chicken, sausage

mushrooms, broccoli, onions, tomatoes

mushrooms, broccoli, onions, tomatoes

tomato paste, garlic, hard cheese, butter

tomato paste, garlic, pepper, butter

berries, plums, cherries, pears

berries, plums, cherries, chocolate

434 open a bottle of wine

To cut the foil, turn against the blade.

Twist the corkscrew worm halfway into the cork.

Pull.

Twist slightly to prevent drips.

435 remove cork bits from wine

Inspect for loose cork bits.

Place a filter over the glass.

Push the cork back; pour.

436 evaluate wine

Note the color and clarity. Swirl; observe the wine legs.

Inhale its aroma.

Fill one-third of your mouth.

Swish the wine thoroughly.

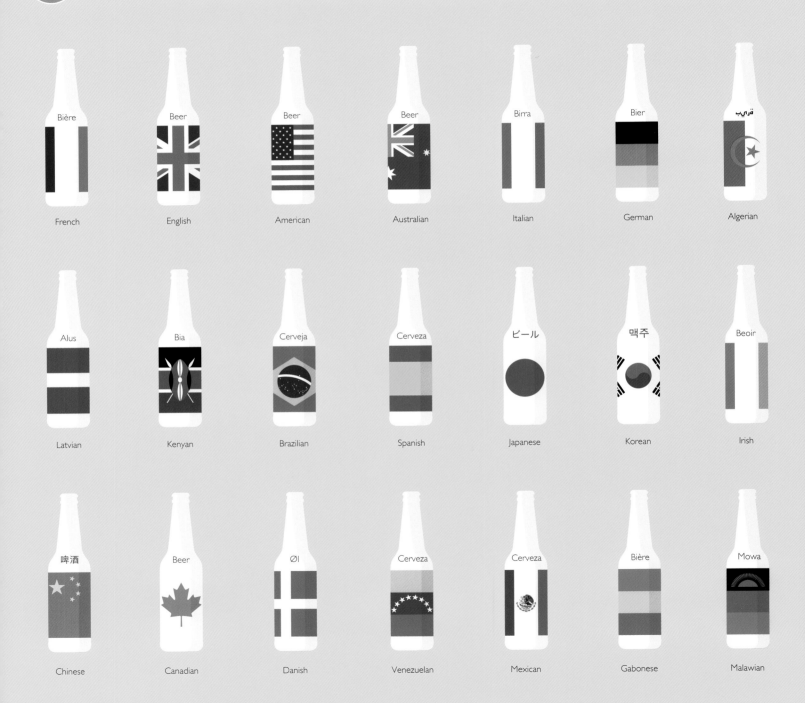

Bière — French

Beer — English

Beer — American

Beer — Australian

Birra — Italian

Bier — German

بيرة — Algerian

Alus — Latvian

Bia — Kenyan

Cerveja — Brazilian

Cerveza — Spanish

ビール — Japanese

맥주 — Korean

Beoir — Irish

啤酒 — Chinese

Beer — Canadian

Øl — Danish

Cerveza — Venezuelan

Cerveza — Mexican

Bière — Gabonese

Mowa — Malawian

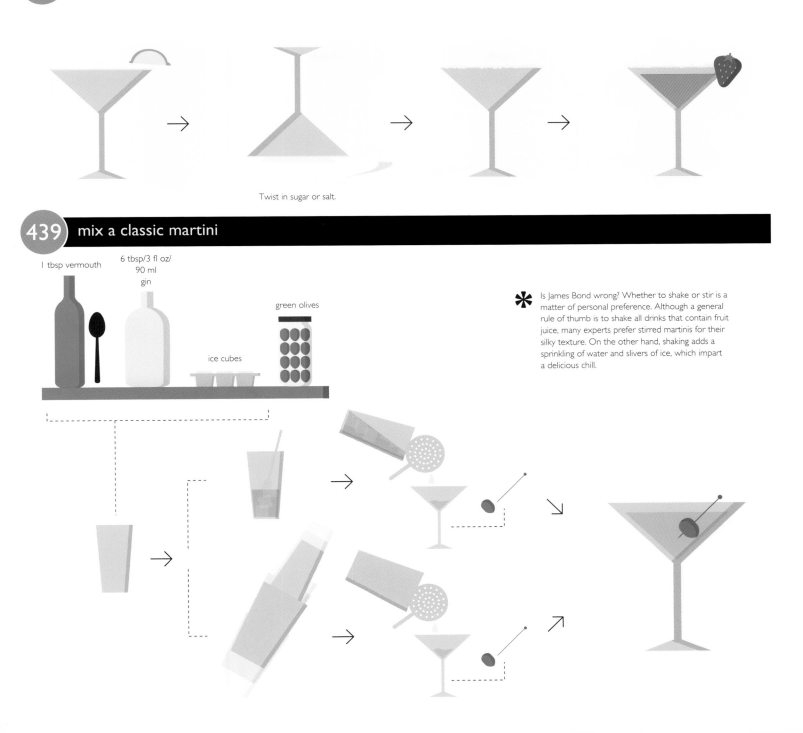

Twist in sugar or salt.

1 tbsp vermouth

6 tbsp/3 fl oz/ 90 ml gin

green olives

ice cubes

✱ Is James Bond wrong? Whether to shake or stir is a matter of personal preference. Although a general rule of thumb is to shake all drinks that contain fruit juice, many experts prefer stirred martinis for their silky texture. On the other hand, shaking adds a sprinkling of water and slivers of ice, which impart a delicious chill.

cosmo
2 fl oz/60 ml citrus vodka
1 tbsp triple sec
1 tbsp cranberry juice
1 tbsp lime juice
1 lime wedge garnish

opera
2 fl oz/60 ml gin
1 tbsp Dubonnet Rouge
1 tbsp maraschino liqueur
1 maraschino cherry garnish

cajun
2½ fl oz/75 ml pepper vodka
1 tbsp dry vermouth
1 jalapeño pepper garnish

vesper
1¼ fl oz/35 ml gin
1¼ fl oz/35 ml vodka
1 tbsp Lillet Blanc
1 lemon wedge garnish

naked
3 fl oz/90 ml gin
1 green olive garnish

bloodhound
2 fl oz/60 ml gin
1 tbsp dry vermouth
1 tbsp sweet vermouth
2 tsp strawberry purée
1 strawberry garnish

corpse reviver
1½ fl oz/45 ml triple sec
1 fl oz/30 ml dry vermouth
2 dashes absinthe
1 lemon wedge garnish

orange blossom
2½ fl oz/75 ml gin
1 fl oz/30 ml orange juice
1½ tsp simple syrup
1 orange wedge garnish

gibson
3 fl oz/90 ml gin
1 tbsp dry vermouth
1 pearl onion garnish

cooperstown
3 tbsp gin
1 tbsp sweet vermouth
1 tbsp dry vermouth
1 mint sprig garnish

tequilatini
2½ fl oz/75 ml tequila
1½ tsp sweet vermouth
1 maraschino cherry garnish

saketini
2½ fl oz/75 ml gin
1½ tsp sake
1 green olive garnish

bacontini
3 fl oz/90 ml vodka
1 dash vermouth
1 bacon strip garnish

bermuda rose
2 fl oz/60 ml gin
1 tbsp apricot brandy
1 dash grenadine
1 apricot wedge garnish

chocolate
2 fl oz/60 ml vodka
1 fl oz/30 ml crème de cacao
1 chocolate treat garnish

banana rum
2 fl oz/60 ml dark rum
1 tbsp crème de bananes
1 banana slice garnish

441 enjoy a cuba libre

roll

→ 2½ fl oz/75 ml
light rum

+ 1 fl oz/30 ml
lime juice

+ 6 fl oz/180 ml
cola

+ 1 lime wedge garnish

shake | roll | blend

442 serve a perfect piña colada

blend

→ 2 fl oz/60 ml
light rum

+ 6 fl oz/180 ml
pineapple juice

+ 2 fl oz/60 ml
coconut cream

+ 1 pineapple wedge garnish
1 maraschino cherry garnish

443 mix a strawberry margarita

blend

→ 2 fl oz/60 ml
silver tequila

+ 1 fl oz/30 ml
lime juice

+ 8 strawberries

+ salt for the rim

444 serve a manhattan

shake

→ 2 fl oz/60 ml
whiskey

+ 1 fl oz/30 ml sweet
vermouth

+ 2 dashes
bitter

+ 1 maraschino cherry garnish

445 mix a mojito

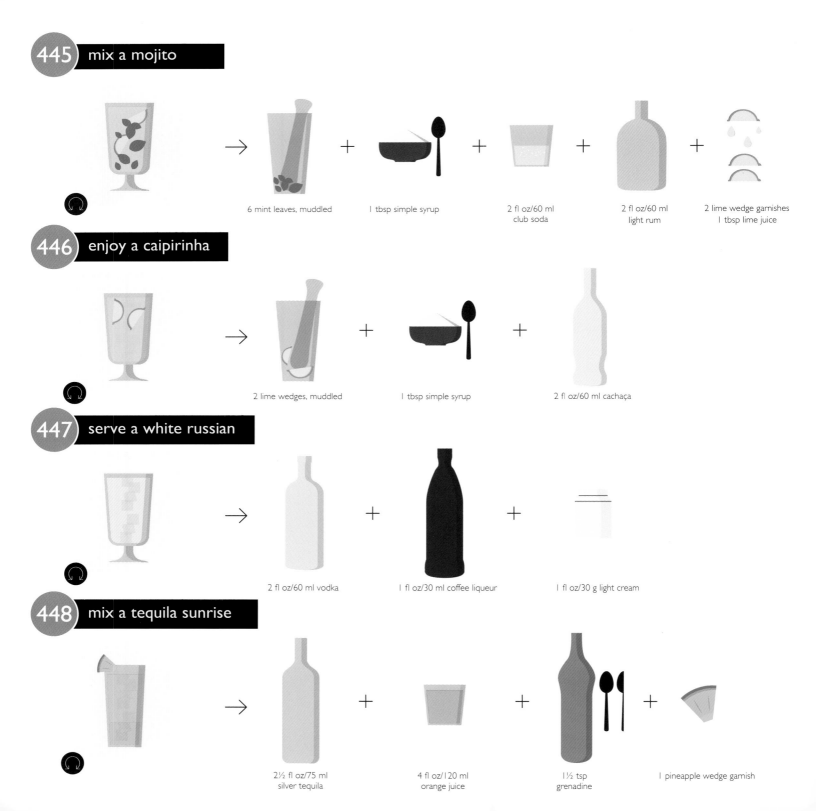

6 mint leaves, muddled + 1 tbsp simple syrup + 2 fl oz/60 ml club soda + 2 fl oz/60 ml light rum + 2 lime wedge garnishes 1 tbsp lime juice

446 enjoy a caipirinha

2 lime wedges, muddled + 1 tbsp simple syrup + 2 fl oz/60 ml cachaça

447 serve a white russian

2 fl oz/60 ml vodka + 1 fl oz/30 ml coffee liqueur + 1 fl oz/30 g light cream

448 mix a tequila sunrise

2½ fl oz/75 ml silver tequila + 4 fl oz/120 ml orange juice + 1½ tsp grenadine + 1 pineapple wedge garnish

449 serve a tom collins

2 fl oz/60 ml gin + 1 tbsp lemon juice + 1 tbsp simple syrup + 5 fl oz/150 ml club soda + 1 lemon wedge / 1 maraschino cherry garnish

450 serve a cape cod

ice cubes → 2½ fl oz/75 ml vodka + 4 fl oz/120 ml cranberry juice + 1 lime wedge garnish

451 enjoy a sidecar

1½ fl oz/30 ml brandy + 1 fl oz/30 ml triple sec + ½ fl oz/15 ml lemon juice

452 mix a negroni

1 fl oz/30 ml gin + 1 fl oz/30 ml sweet vermouth + 1 fl oz/30 ml campari + 1 orange wedge / 1 maraschino cherry garnish

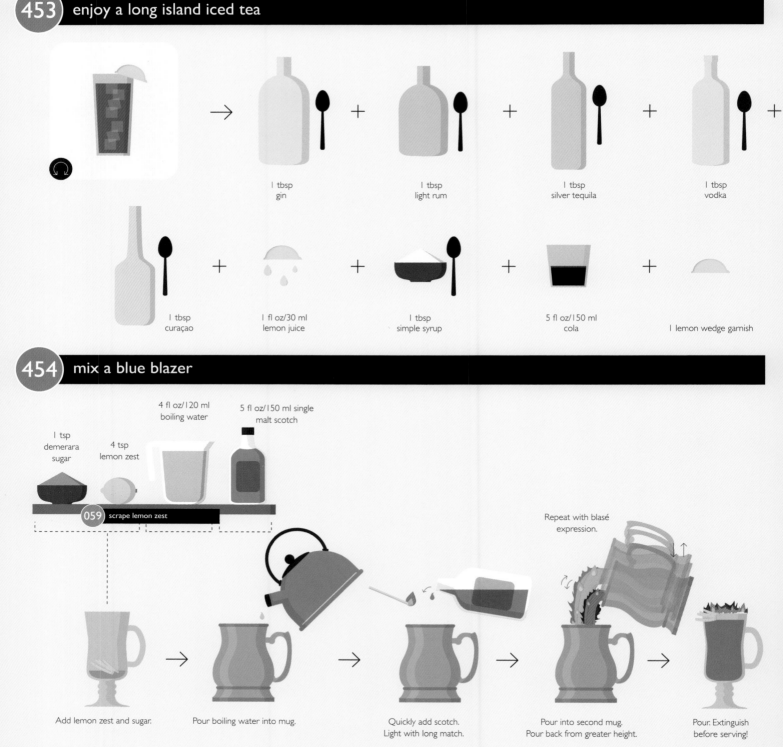

453 enjoy a long island iced tea

1 tbsp
gin

+

1 tbsp
light rum

+

1 tbsp
silver tequila

+

1 tbsp
vodka

+

1 tbsp
curaçao

+

1 fl oz/30 ml
lemon juice

+

1 tbsp
simple syrup

+

5 fl oz/150 ml
cola

+

1 lemon wedge garnish

454 mix a blue blazer

1 tsp
demerara
sugar

4 tsp
lemon zest

4 fl oz/120 ml
boiling water

5 fl oz/150 ml single
malt scotch

059 scrape lemon zest

Repeat with blasé
expression.

Add lemon zest and sugar.

Pour boiling water into mug.

Quickly add scotch.
Light with long match.

Pour into second mug.
Pour back from greater height.

Pour. Extinguish
before serving!

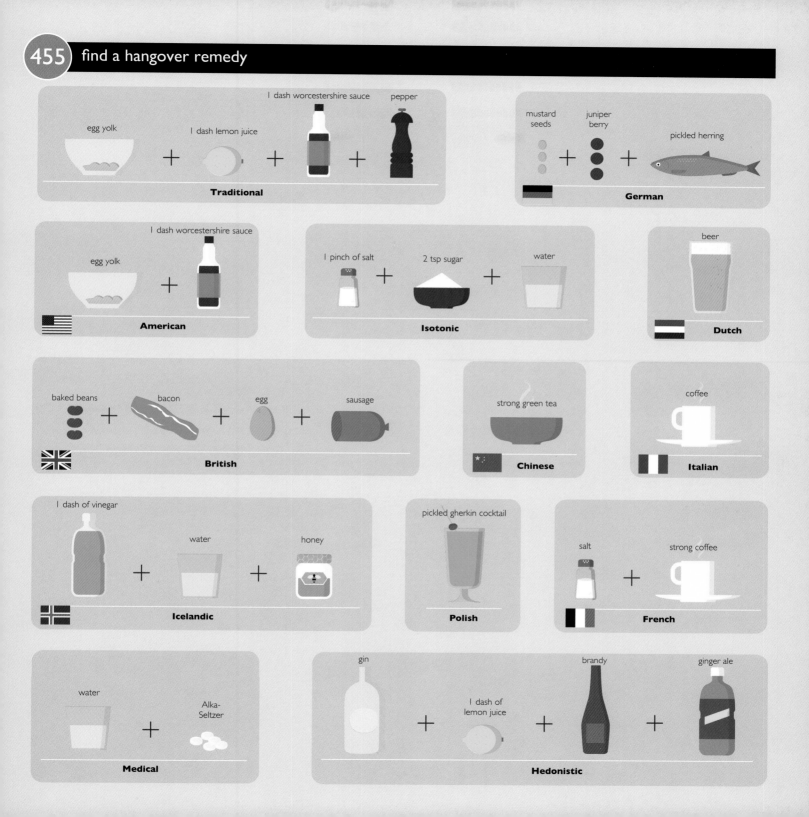

Traditional
egg yolk + 1 dash lemon juice + 1 dash worcestershire sauce + pepper

German
mustard seeds + juniper berry + pickled herring

American
egg yolk + 1 dash worcestershire sauce

Isotonic
1 pinch of salt + 2 tsp sugar + water

Dutch
beer

British
baked beans + bacon + egg + sausage

Chinese
strong green tea

Italian
coffee

Icelandic
1 dash of vinegar + water + honey

Polish
pickled gherkin cocktail

French
salt + strong coffee

Medical
water + Alka-Seltzer

Hedonistic
gin + 1 dash of lemon juice + brandy + ginger ale

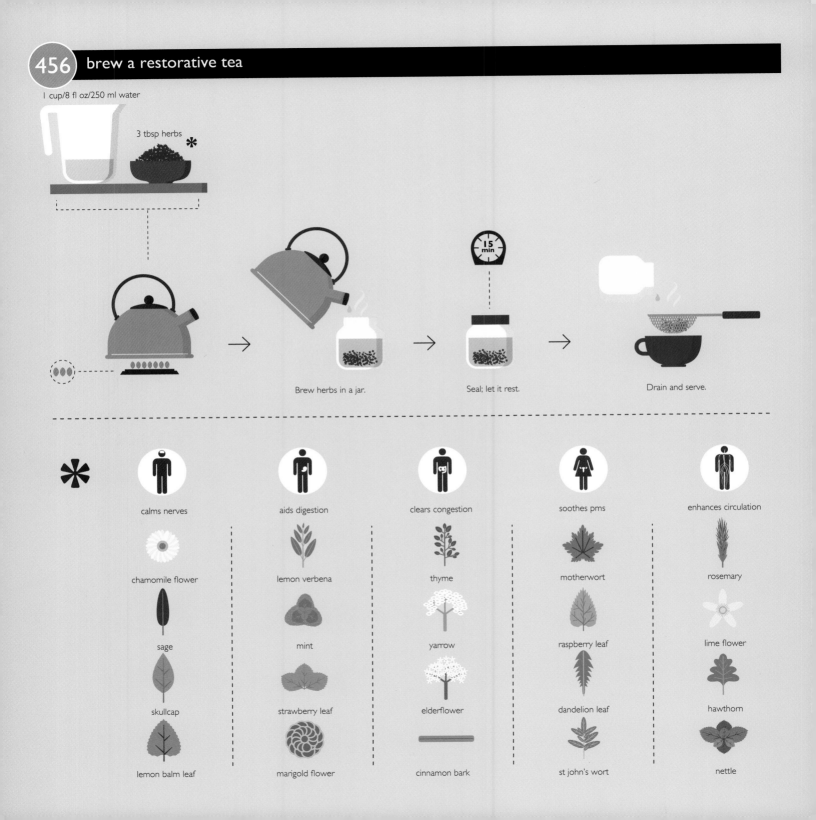

1 cup/8 fl oz/250 ml water

3 tbsp herbs ✳

15 min

Brew herbs in a jar.

Seal; let it rest.

Drain and serve.

✳

calms nerves
chamomile flower
sage
skullcap
lemon balm leaf

aids digestion
lemon verbena
mint
strawberry leaf
marigold flower

clears congestion
thyme
yarrow
elderflower
cinnamon bark

soothes pms
motherwort
raspberry leaf
dandelion leaf
st john's wort

enhances circulation
rosemary
lime flower
hawthorn
nettle

457 brew tea fit for a queen

8 fl oz/240 ml water

1 tsp black tea

milk

sugar

scones

391 bake scones

Add black tea leaves.

Let brew.

Strain.

Add milk and sugar, if desired.

458 make russian tea in a samovar

2 fl oz/60 ml water

1 tsp black tea

pinecones

lemon

Use pinecones as fuel to boil the water.
Add black indian tea leaves. Add boiling water.

Brew on top of the samovar.

Pour into the podstakannik.

serve thai iced tea

6 cups/48 fl oz/1½ l water

7 oz/225 g
thai tea leaves

¾ cup/
6½ oz/200 g
sugar

8 fl oz/240 ml
concentrated milk

ice cubes

5 min

Add spiced thai tea leaves.
Add boiling water.

Brew until bright orange.

Pour through the cloth strainer.
Add sugar and chill.

Add ice cubes and concentrated milk.

shake up a greek frappé

3 tbsp milk

1 tsp sugar

1 tsp
instant coffee

ice cubes

1 min

Combine in a shaker.

Shake hard, making a foam.

Pour foam over a glass of ice water.

Drink with a straw.

461 make a new orleans iced coffee

10 cups/80 fl oz/ 2½ l water

1 lb/500 g dark roasted coffee

1 tbsp roasted chicory

ice cubes

6 fl oz/180 ml milk

12 h

Combine; soak overnight.

Strain; pour over ice.

Add milk.

462 froth up a turkish coffee

1 cup/8 fl oz/250 ml water

1 tbsp ground coffee

2 tsp sugar

3 min

Combine in a copper pot. Continue to boil.

When foam rises, remove the pot from heat.

Boil to foam; remove the pot from heat; repeat.

Pour; let it sit before drinking.

463   pull a perfect espresso

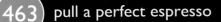

Fill with fresh grounds.   Smooth off the excess.   Tamp until tight.   Align the basket and cup.   Pull the shot.

464   pour a latte leaf

140°F/60°C

Steam milk for one cup.   Swirl; bang if bubbles arise.   Pour. Wiggle your wrist.   Complete design.

465   enjoy an irish coffee

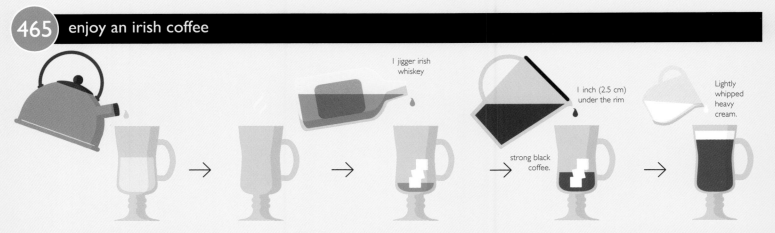

1 jigger irish whiskey

1 inch (2.5 cm) under the rim

strong black coffee.

Lightly whipped heavy cream.

Warm a glass mug with boiling water.   Add whiskey and sugar.   Fill nearly to the top with coffee   Carefully float cream on top.

466 blend a fruit smoothie

6 fl oz/200 ml
milk

2 tbsp
peanut butter

1 banana

1 lb/500 g
berries

Blend.

467 mix a vegetable smoothie

2 cups/16 fl oz/
500 ml water

3 leaves
chard

1 stalk celery

½ bunch
of parsley

juice of
1 lemon

1 avocado

pit an avocado

468 make a fruity soda pop float

2 cups/16 fl oz/
500 ml fruit syrup

2 cups/16 fl oz/
500 ml
sparkling water

juice of
1 lemon

4 scoops
ice cream

Add lemon juice to taste. Top off
with sparkling water; stir.

Add ice cream.

Garnish and serve.

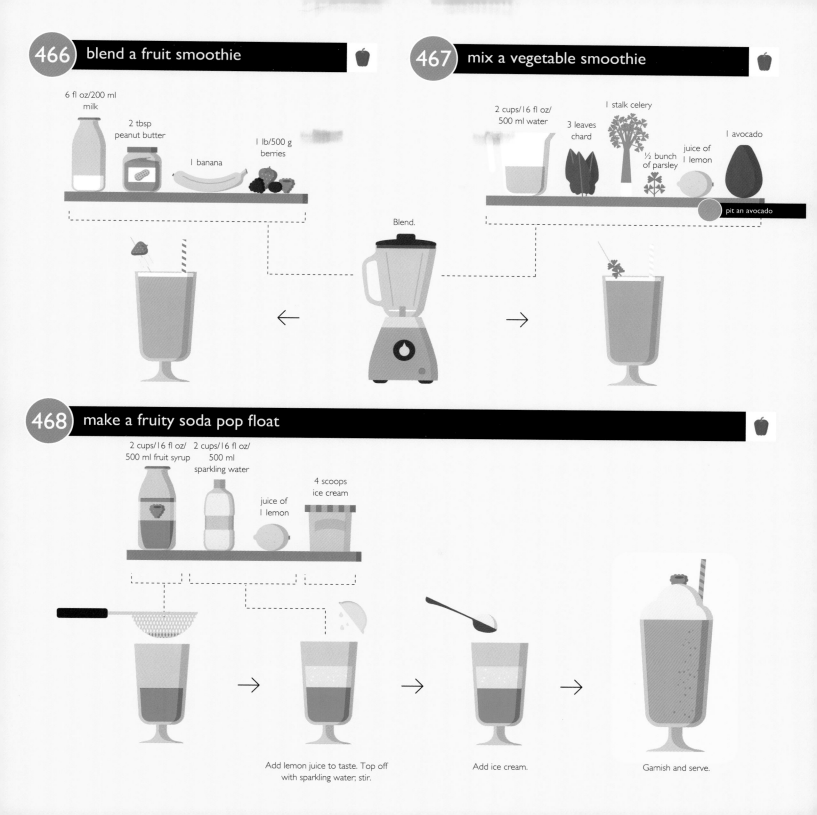

index

weldon**owen**

1045 Sansome Street, San Francisco, California, USA
www.weldonowen.com

EAT! THE QUICK-LOOK COOKBOOK

A WELDON OWEN PRODUCTION

Copyright © 2014 Weldon Owen, Inc.
Printed in China by 1010 Printing International

First printed in 2015
10 9 8 7 6 5 4 3 2 1

Library of Congress Control Number: 2014955733

ISBN 13: 978-1-61628-874-7
ISBN 10: 1-61628-874-4

Weldon Owen is a division of
BONNIER

WELDON OWEN, INC.

President & Publisher Roger Shaw
SVP, Sales & Marketing Amy Kaneko
Finance Manager Philip Paulick

Creative Director Kelly Booth
Cover Designer Debbie Berne
Senior Production Designer Rachel Lopez Metzger

Associate Publishers Mariah Bear, Jennifer Newens
Associate Editor Emma Rudolph

Production Director Chris Hemesath
Associate Production Director Michelle Duggan

Author Gabriela Scolik
Infographics no.parking, www.noparking.it
Editor Bettina Dietrich
Team Anna Hübinger, Daniela Schmid, Nathalie Soursos

A Show Me Now Book.
Show Me Now is a trademark
of Weldon Owen Inc.
www.showmenow.com